THE FIRST CAPTAIN

BOOKS BY GERALD W. JOHNSON

THE
FIRST CAPTAIN

The Story of John Paul Jones

BY

GERALD W. JOHNSON

47812

Coward-McCann, Inc.

New York

To Those Americans
led by

ERNEST JOSEPH KING

who have lately demonstrated that the
United States Navy has not lost the leg-
acy of skill and valor bequeathed it by

JOHN PAUL JONES

THE FIRST CAPTAIN

CHAPTER I.

HE WAS a gaudy fellow. He swung through the world raising so much dust and clatter that the people of his own time could rarely see what he was really like, and for a century after he was dead the most fantastic lies were still told about him and are still believed. On the other hand, the plain truth was not believed for a moment. Perhaps it is not even yet fully realized, although it is now two hundred years since his birth.

Red-faced admirals and indignant merchants in England, all the more wrathful because they were helpless to touch him, pointed out that his very name was false. He called himself Jones, but his father's name was Paul, his mother's MacDuff, and even the man whom whispering scandal charged with being his true father was named Douglas. There wasn't a Jones in the family connection; indeed, it is a Welsh name, and this fellow hailed from Kirkcudbright, Scotland. One would as soon have expected a man from Kirkcudbright to be named Li Hung-chang as Jones.

He called himself Jones, shouted the furious British, because he was wanted by the police under his true name of John Paul; and he was wanted for murder at that. This was not true. There was, in fact, a homicide charge against him, but nobody ever seriously contended that it was murder in the first degree. He had killed a man in a fight. The worst that could have been made of it was manslaughter, and those best acquainted with the facts regarded it as a plain case of self-defense. However, when he began to play hob with British shipping, to shoot up British coast towns, and to sink—or even more humiliating, to

1

capture—British warships, naturally the British were not inclined to take any lenient view of his past.

Besides, that past was pretty dubious, especially if one takes into account the way people looked at things in the latter part of the eighteenth century. Respectable gentlemen in England regarded the stage with contempt, and this man had been an actor. They regarded the best of seafaring men as pretty tough, and this one had been certainly a slaver and possibly a pirate. They regarded colonists in general as troublesome and suspicious characters, and this man had joined a group of rebellious colonists. Many of them agreed with Dr. Samuel Johnson that any Scotchman was a low fellow, and this was certainly a Scot.

He outraged the fox-hunting squires in other ways. They looked upon him as horribly un-English. He wrote poetry and courted the ladies, both with a success that Englishmen thought no honest sailor should achieve. He got along well with Frenchmen. He could be eloquent, especially on such subjects as liberty and the rights of man. He enchanted successively a duchess and an empress. He whipped successively the British and the Turks, both rated as first-class fighting men. He liked to talk, and it cannot be denied that he liked to strut a little, too. In all these ways he was the antithesis of the British ideal, and it is no wonder that they loathed him.

But before Americans laugh too loudly at the British, they will do well to consider their own attitude toward the man. Oh, it is quite correct at present. We have entombed his body—or what we think is his body—in a lordly sepulcher in a crypt under the chapel at the United States Naval Academy, and we have erected his memory into a sort of tutelary genius of the Navy. We laud him to the skies and counsel every midshipman who enters the Academy to study John Paul Jones and emulate him. He is one of our mighty heroes—now.

But it was not always so. While he lived we treated him, to our shame, more injuriously than the British. He was the great enemy of their nation, but all they could do to him was curse him. He was the great friend of our nation, and we gave him praise in plenty. Praise costs nothing. But we never paid him a penny of his salary for seven years, we never gave him his due rank, we took even his prize money from him and used it to pay a lot of job holders in government offices, and, worst of all—a thing to make us writhe even after a hundred and fifty years— some of his men, the sailors who won his greatest victory for him in the *Bon Homme Richard,* we brought back to this country chained in the hold of an American ship, chained by an officer who held a commission in the United States Navy!

No, in view of the record it doesn't lie in our mouths to speak slightingly of the British. The curious American treatment of this man did not end even with his life. Long after the fighting was over, long after John Paul Jones was laid in an unmarked grave in Paris, long after everyone who knew him was dead, American writers and historians were still taking their cue from the British and speaking of him slightingly. When he had been dead nearly a hundred years a man who was himself to be President of the United States could find no better description of him than "the daring corsair, Paul Jones." * Since "corsair" is merely a politer word for "pirate," this description is, to say the least of it, faint praise; in a British writer it might be expected, but what a word it is for an American to apply to a man regularly commissioned as a captain in the United States Navy!

The British attitude is easily understood. In addition to everything else, this man cost them a fabulous amount of money, what with losses of merchant ships and cargoes, losses of warships and their crews, expenditures of time and stores in fruitless chases, maintenance of equally fruitless blockades, and a terrific increase in marine insurance rates. Their reasons for hating him are plain enough.

But the attitude assumed by Americans—not all Americans, by any means, but a large and influential group—is something

---

* This was Theodore Roosevelt, in his life of Gouverneur Morris, published in 1888. Jones had died in 1792.

more than scandalous. It is queer. What excuse did they have for hating him, they whose battles he fought brilliantly and whose cause he served loyally?

The explanation is a long and somewhat complicated story, but it is not impossible to understand. It is not even difficult to understand, if one takes into account human nature as it was in 1747, when John Paul Jones was born, as it is in 1947, and as it presumably will be for many centuries to come.

The Captain was inconvenient. This may appear to be a trifling charge, but it isn't. It is one of the deadliest charges that can be brought against a man, especially if he appears at all in public life. He was full of ideas, and his ideas were new and usually good. If an idea is good it will be accepted, soon or late. But if it is new it will force people to abandon their old ideas, and there is nothing that men resent more bitterly than being compelled to think along new lines.

John Paul Jones had been dead for many years before his most important contribution to this country began to take real effect. Even then only a few people realized that it was his idea, and most of us continued to praise him for what were, after all, minor matters. He won naval battles that were of material help in winning the War for Independence. He laid the foundation of our prestige on the high seas. He devised strategical and tactical expedients that served us well until steam displaced sails. He designed better ships, he designed better gunnery practices, he designed better rules and regulations for the Navy.

But in addition he designed something else more important than all these things put together. He designed the modern American naval officer, who in turn has served as a model in important respects for the officers of every other great service, the British included.

It is the fact that this contribution has been so generally overlooked that justifies another book about John Paul Jones. When Jones appeared upon the scene there was no such thing as a naval officer who was just that and nothing more, with no expectation or desire of being anything more. The navy was not a career, in this or any other country; at best it was one avenue to a career. If a man were a success as a naval officer, he might expect as a reward to be raised to a position of real dignity and importance. When Rodney swept the seas, his reward—which he, like everyone else, regarded as just and fair—was to be taken out of the navy and put into the House of Peers as a baron. As great a man as Nelson was prouder of being a lord than of being an admiral.

On the continent of Europe naval officers for centuries were regarded primarily as soldiers serving afloat. Medina-Sidonia, who commanded the Spanish Armada, was given the job because he was a duke, a kinsman of the King, and had had a not too disgraceful career in the army. In France noble birth was a prerequisite for a commission; ability to sail a ship had nothing to do with it. There were sailing masters who took care of all that, and it was rather beneath the dignity of an officer to know much about it. Younger sons of noblemen served in the navy only until they could get a really good job in the army or at court.

The navy was a stepladder, useful only because it enabled a talented man to reach something better. It was this Scotch-American who first perceived clearly that the navy is, or ought to be, a career in itself, and that part of the necessary equipment of a first-class officer is a firm belief that to be a really great admiral is achievement enough for the most ambitious.

That is accepted today, not only in the American navy, but in every service that has amounted to much for the past two generations. An American admiral today may go into politics after he has retired from the service, as Admiral Hart did, but rather to round off his career than to crown it. One office only could add to the dignity of a high-ranking admiral, and that office is President of the United States, which is a thing apart from all lesser dignities. Even the Secretary of the Navy, although technically outranking all admirals, is far less considerable in the minds of his fellow citizens than is the man who has commanded a fleet successfully.

But John Paul Jones did not implant this idea in the minds

of American sailors by argument alone. He preached it incessantly and forcefully; but he lived it, too, and that is what made it irresistible. In living it, he left a startling, meteor-like trail across history that is not only spectacular in itself but casts light upon many curious events and still more curious men in the company through which he moved. Gaudy is the word for him; but his colors were those of fireworks, not tinsel, and it took stone and steel to withstand his heat.

He was born on July 6, 1747, at Arbigland, a country estate near Kirkcudbright, Scotland.

He was the son of John Paul, a gardener in the service of the laird of Arbigland, and his wife, born Jean MacDuff. John Paul was a Lowlander, but his wife's ancestors are said to have come from Argyllshire, although her family had lived near Kirkbean, not far from Kirkcudbright, for generations.

Biographers have amused themselves, if not always their readers, with intricate speculations as to the effect on the sailor of this mixture of canny Lowland blood with the mystical and romantic Highland strain. It is a fact that one son of this union was a canny businessman and yet sometimes wildly romantic, and it is not impossible that he inherited these traits from his parents; but there was another son and two daughters who were not remarkable in any way.

The dull truth seems to be that when you have said that John Paul Jones was born of poor but honest parents you have said about all there is to say. The senior John Paul was a worthy man and no doubt a competent gardener, since he held the job to the end of his life. Scotland has always produced excellent gardeners, so it could hardly have been for lack of competition that he retained his post at Arbigland; it is a fair assumption that he knew his business and attended to it faithfully. But that there was anything inspiring, or even especially noteworthy about him, is past belief, for he seems to have made little impression of any sort upon his illustrious son. When the father died the son was careful to erect a proper headstone at his grave.

Every reference to the father in the son's papers is respectful but unemotional, and there are few such references. The evidence indicates that he had nothing in the world against his father, nor very much in his favor. Paul was probably, like the father of many another famous man, simply an unobjectionable nonentity.

Jean MacDuff was a somewhat more impressive personality. She outlived her husband by many years and held her son's affectionate interest to the end. Her comfort was his first care through his most tempestuous years, and by deed as well as by word he acknowledged his debt to her many times. But it would be going beyond the record to say more of her than that she was a good mother who loved her children and did her best for them and was, in turn, loved and respected by them. This is, to be sure, high praise, perhaps the highest praise, but it throws no light on the way in which genius is produced. There were thousands of good mothers in Scotland who had no sons like this one.

In what little we know of heredity there is nothing more certain than that a union of two undistinguished persons occasionally results in extraordinary children. Yet although it has happened countless times, the world is reluctant to believe it. Whenever a man of genius comes from an obscure home, there are those who are ready to explain that he was not the son of his putative father. For example, Lincoln's paternity has been attributed to at least half a dozen distinguished men, simply because neither his father nor his mother was brilliant. Similar stories about John Paul Jones floated around after he became famous. His paternity, too, was attributed to various people, the favorite being the Earl of Selkirk, who owned an estate near by. As a matter of fact, Selkirk came into possession of the property long after the boy was born, and there is no evidence that he had ever seen Jean MacDuff before.

Some of his biographers have been embarrassed by certain indications that Jones himself half believed this story. Of course, he never said so explicitly, but he did exhibit a curious and lasting interest in the Earl, an interest hardly accounted for by the fact that he was a nobleman and a neighbor.

Yet if this half belief could be proved, it would indicate little more than that the man carried into adult life a romantic tendency almost universal among imaginative children. What boy or girl hasn't at some time had daydreams of being really a foundling of high birth, to be revealed someday as the rightful prince or princess? Yet pride of birth has diminished enormously since the first half of the eighteenth century. The tendency to indulge such fancies must have been vastly stronger two hundred years ago than it is now; so if it is still strong enough to be common, it must have been almost universal then.

It is a safe assumption that this boy, known to have been mentally alert and highly imaginative, built such air castles. He would have been abnormal had he not done so. If there is anything unusual in his case, it is merely that he continued to cherish his fancies somewhat longer than most boys do. The embarrassment of the biographers, therefore, is somewhat misplaced. If John Paul Jones half believed, even half hoped, that he was a natural son of the Earl of Selkirk, he was no doubt indulging in folly, but it was a very common and a very natural folly, considering the time and the place.

The time and the place probably counted for a great deal more in the production of this genius than heredity—or, rather, it is much easier to trace the influence of time and place. The time was forty years after the Act of Union, combining Scotland and England, had become law, and one year after the battle of Culloden had made it fact. The boy grew up, therefore, as the last waves of the last prodigious storm in Scottish history were gradually subsiding. Scotland was definitely a part of the United Kingdom when he was born; but she had been held in it by force, and by force applied with a ruthlessness that had made the very name of Cumberland, son of the King, a hissing and a byword in Scotland. After Culloden there was never again any question of a revolt; but it was many years before

Scotch opinion of the House of Hanover changed. In John Paul Jones's boyhood it was bitter and contemptuous. The Duke of Cumberland, English commander at Culloden, won a battle; but his employment of the drumhead court-martial and the gallows after the fighting was over lost the peace for a generation.

Thus when the boy had grown to be a man and found himself among a people in revolt against this same House of Hanover—for the quarrel of the American revolutionists was with the King, not with the English people, and the king of that time was a nephew of the infamous Cumberland—all his childhood memories were of a kind to make him sympathize with the revolt. The remarkable thing was not that a Scot joined the colonists, but that, even among those who were in America, some failed to do so.

The place had as obvious an effect as the time on the development of the boy. Kirkcudbright—which its inhabitants incomprehensibly pronounce "Kerr-*cood*-bree"—lies on the north shore of the Solway Firth, the wide and rather shallow estuary that divides England and Scotland along their western shore lines. Kirkcudbright itself is not directly on the Solway, but a little way up from the mouth of the river Dee and protected by St. Mary's Isle in the river. It thus had an excellent harbor for the relatively light-draft ships of two hundred years ago.

Across the Solway, on the English side, lies Whitehaven, which has more water and can accommodate larger vessels than Kirkcudbright. Today both have sunk to the level of fishing villages, for the huge, ocean-going ships of modern times can reach either only with difficulty, if at all; but in 1747 Kirkcudbright still had some foreign trade and Whitehaven was a port of considerable importance, boasting a number of mercantile firms that traded all over the world.

A few miles northeast of Kirkcudbright the last outposts of the Highlands come tumbling down to sea level, so in the shire the three conspicuous characteristics of Scotland, Highland, Lowland, and Border, are jammed closely together. Fighter, trader, and raider are inextricably mingled there, so there is nothing odd in the circumstance that the region produced a man who was all three and eminently successful in each role.

Some writers have been inclined to deny that John Paul Jones was a true Scot simply because his career was colorful and romantic, and the world is strangely reluctant to admit that that sort of thing belongs to the Caledonian character. But it does. The Scots have always been extremists, and if they have the opposite reputation it is because the sane majority have always been extremely sane. When one does go mad, however, he is the craziest thing in Bedlam. Religious fanaticism has been a specialty among them throughout their history, but other fanaticisms are no less strong. In Scottish love of liberty, for example, there is no hint of sweet reasonableness. From William Wallace and Robert the Bruce down, they have supplied martyrs to human freedom without number. Especially for the last three hundred years there has hardly been a battle fought for liberty anywhere in the world that did not spill some Scottish blood. Other fanaticisms have been scarcely less conspicuous, and frequently they have been attached to persons who were much more gay than admirable. Bonnie Prince Charlie, for example, he whose revolt against the King precipitated the disaster at Culloden, was by all accounts a charming fellow, but it was wild insanity to fight to install as head of the state a notorious drunkard.

Because Jones's acts frequently had the effect of a thunderclap, he has been denied the character of a true Scot, for the Scot is supposed to proceed cannily. But that is not always true. Perhaps the most perfect illustration of the Scottish tendency to adhere to the doctrine "everything in excess" was the forcible exit of that Lord Darnley who was briefly the husband of Mary Stuart. The entire episode of Mary, Queen of Scots, who would be better described as "Scarlet Sister Mary," could hardly have happened in any other country than Scotland, but it is all summed up, not in the fact, but in the way that Darnley departed this life.

He was a poor creature, to be sure, lying, treacherous, cowardly, and so stupid that he was a constant danger to the Queen and to the throne itself. The elimination of a husband so inconvenient is nothing unique in history. Since chronicles began to be written, queens of all nations have relieved themselves of such encumbrances in a great variety of ways, but when the Scottish nobles undertook the favor to their queen they chose a characteristic method. They touched off three barrels of gunpowder in the cellar of the house where Darnley was sleeping!

Not the eradication of the nuisance, but the manner of its doing illuminates the Scottish character. In England the eradication of Mary herself, and afterward of Charles I when he became an intolerable nuisance, was accomplished ceremoniously, with the headsman's ax. Only the Scot went out with a bang that jarred the whole city of Edinburgh; only Scots would have planned it that way; and not even John Paul Jones ever did anything louder.

Yes, the Scot is colorful, but not in pastel shades. Even his primary colors are awesome—the yellow of molten metal, the blue of brimstone set alight, the red of blood and fire. Yet the world persists in looking upon him as drab and dour, and when one appears rainbow-hued, as John Paul Jones did, he is set down as something extraordinary, not a typical Scot at all.

The typical Scot, according to prevalent fashion, was rather John Paul's employer, William Craik, laird of Arbigland. William Craik left upon history no very deep impression of any sort; but he was conspicuously a man of sense. True, his good sense could not be called excessive, for it did not prevent his becoming involved in an unauthorized love affair that resulted in a natural son, and this son achieved enough eminence to perpetuate the memory of his father's indiscretion. He studied medicine, came to America, joined the revolting colonists, and rose to be chief surgeon in Washington's army. He was the Dr. James Craik who attended Washington in his last illness—a dubious distinction, since it is the opinion of medical men today that his doctors probably did more than his disease to kill Washington. However, it is only just to note that the appalling treatment used was in accord with the best medical opinion of the time, so the blame really lies at the door of the science of medicine, not at that of the individual practitioner.

If James Craik had not achieved a niche in history for himself, this generation would have nothing whatever to register against his father, William. He had a certain celebrity as a horticulturist —more evidence that John Paul must have been a good gardener to hold a job at that place—and contemporary testimony indicates that he was regarded as an exceptionally good landlord, interested in his tenants not merely as so many labor units, but as human beings.

The strongest testimony of this sort is that of John Paul Jones himself. Once he left Arbigland, he had no claim whatever on William Craik. Yet whenever he was about to sail on a long voyage that would keep him away from Scotland for months running into years, he would write Mr. Craik, asking him to look after the comfort of his mother and sisters with the understanding that the sailor would repay whatever Craik might spend on their account when the voyage was over. Then he would sail with a quiet mind, and there is no indication that the Laird ever failed to comply with the request.

Incidentally, the term itself should not be misunderstood. A Scottish laird was by no means identical with an English lord. A laird was not necessarily a nobleman. William Craik was not. He was simply a tenant holding directly from the king, instead of from a lord who held from the king. The Craiks had held Arbigland since 1690; they belonged to the gentry, but not to the nobility, and the title of laird meant simply a particular kind of landlord.

As a matter of fact, the classes in Scotland were never divided by such a gulf as separated them in England and on the continent. Even a genuine nobleman, an earl or a duke, enjoyed more respect as head of his clan than as a peer of the king, and the position of head of the clan was patriarchal rather than political. The clan was an enlarged family, and the clansman regarded himself as the kinsman, rather than the servant, of his chief. He was capable of tremendous fealty, but not of servility. He would die for his chief—he did times without number—unhesitatingly, but he would not kowtow to him.

This characteristic should be borne in mind, for it came out strongly in John Paul Jones. It is somewhat loosely described as the democracy of Scotland, but the word should not be used in this connection without a clear understanding of its limitations. It is probably quite true to say that the Scots in 1717 did not for a moment believe that all men are created equal. At most, every Campbell held himself equal at birth to every other Campbell, every MacDonald to every other MacDonald; but that any MacDonald was born equal to any Campbell was a doctrine abhorrent to every Campbell and vice versa.

It is nevertheless true that within the clans the sense of blood relationship prevented the hardening of caste lines; and with such a start it was easier for the Scots than for some others to comprehend the doctrine of democracy when it began to be preached in earnest. To admit that a MacDonald might, perhaps, be as good as a Campbell required no such psychological upheaval as to admit that an English or French plowman might be as good as a duke. Scotland, therefore, moved into the era of democracy with an ease that gave the somewhat misleading impression that she had always been democratic. As a matter of fact, to this day Scottish democracy is perceptibly restricted to Scotland. In 1947 as in 1747 other nations have a suspicion that the Scot walks among them with a faint but palpable touch of disdain.

Some writers have been perplexed by the calm assurance with which the seaman John Paul Jones moved in any society. He had a high respect for rank and he was carefully correct in his manner of approach to nobility and royalty, but he had also a high sense of his own value. Once he appealed to the King of France over the heads of officialdom, which was a flagrant breach of protocol; but the disrespect was confined to the rules and regulations, not touching the King. Unquestionably, this was the Scot breaking out—the clansman capable of unbounded personal loyalty, but incapable of being bound by impersonal conventions. This characteristic is easily traceable to the place in which the man was born and grew up.

Of course, his whole career hinged upon the fact that the place was by the sea. Kirkcudbright was small, but no town that looks out upon salt water is altogether cut off from the world. From his birth the boy was accustomed to passing in the streets and seeing idling around the taverns and the docks men to whom the other side of the earth was as familiar as the garden at Arbigland was to him. Many of the ships trading out of Whitehaven drew their crews in part from Kirkcudbright, and the sailors brought into the familiar talk of the village strange tales and glamorous names. Probably John Paul Jones could not remember the time when he had never heard of the Horn or Java Head; to him tales of typhoons in the China Sea were as familiar as accounts of memorable hailstorms in Galloway; to him visits to the tropics or the polar seas must have seemed as normal a part of existence as visits to the market town seemed to boys of inland villages. The inhabitants of every port, even those who stay ashore, are to some extent citizens of the world, simply because the world is brought to their doorsteps.

In this boy's case, another link with the outside world was the fact that his elder brother, William, had emigrated to America while John was still a child. By all accounts William Paul had done fairly well. He settled near Fredericksburg, in Virginia, became a landowner, and prospered, not in a big way, but well enough to make his lot distinctly better than that of an apprentice gardener in Scotland. This was another influence tending to turn the boy's eyes away from the hills and toward the sea.

But with these obvious influences of the time and the place upon the making of the man our knowledge of his early life is all but finished. He never indulged in childhood reminiscences, and his family was too insignificant for any contemporary to take notice of them. After he had become notorious in England a tremendous crop of myths sprang up concerning him; but most of these tales are obvious lies, inspired by hatred, and there is no real evidence to support the rest. About his childhood activities, his companions, his schooling, we know nothing; and about more important things not much.

All that is certain is that at the age of twelve, which would have been in the year 1759, he was taken to Whitehaven and there signed as an apprentice on the *Friendship,* a vessel belonging to John Younger, a merchant engaged in the American trade, and commanded by a certain Captain Benson. We do not know even who made the arrangement, although there is some reason to believe that William Craik had a hand in it. It was, on the whole, a good arrangement. Younger was a man of some prominence, a member of the Board of Trustees of the Town and Harbor of Whitehaven, not at all the sort of man with whom a gardener could be expected to have much influence, but probably one whom a neighboring laird might approach easily. A word from William Craik in behalf of one of his tenants would certainly have been listened to, and might have had material influence. In later years the sailor acknowledged that he was accustomed to look to Craik for advice on various matters, assured him, indeed, that he would take no step without the Laird's approbation; which is the sort of thing a young man might be expected to write to an older one to whom he was indebted for his first job.

As for John Paul, if he did not make the arrangement himself, he approved it. By modern standards, it was rugged; but in 1759 a boy of twelve who could sign on a good ship owned by a prominent merchant was regarded as doing reasonably well for himself. John Paul, Jr., as he called himself then, certainly never looked upon himself as a victim of cruel circumstance; his was a normal, indeed rather an auspicious beginning, and as the *Friendship* stood out past St. Bees Head and into the Irish Sea, he may have been afflicted with normal homesickness, but certainly not with any feeling of frustration or defeat. He was doing what he wanted to do, entering a career that was open to talent as few others were in those days, and there is every reason to assume that he was as proud and excited as any normal youth would be under similar circumstances.

The *Friendship* made for the Rappahannock River, in Virginia, with the usual cargo of manufactured articles, which she was to exchange for tobacco and other colonial products. It was an unexciting business, but important, and it involved the ship's company much more then than cargo-carrying does now. The captain, especially, had to be more than merely a good seaman when there were no cables or wireless by which the home office could keep in touch and control deals. The captain had supreme authority over the cargo as well as the vessel. Frequently it was the only authority. In the Virginia trade, indeed, much of the outgoing load was consigned to individuals, and all the captain had to do was to deliver; but sometimes part of the load consisted of trade goods left to his discretion to dispose of as he saw fit, and even more frequently he was at liberty to pick up a return cargo on terms to be fixed by him.

Thus the financial success of a voyage depended as often upon the captain's business sense as upon his ability as navigator, seaman, and commander. Versatility was essential to a successful master. The sailors of the eighteenth century were a tough lot, but they had to be commanded; merchants were a shrewd lot, and their shrewdness had to be matched; port authorities and colonial governors were not infrequently a highhanded, highborn lot, and their arrogance had to be resisted, yet with a suavity that would prevent their taking umbrage. Then there were always the perils of the sea.

The voyage of the *Friendship* was described in the records as "uneventful," which it was, relatively speaking. Most writers have assumed that no inference is to be drawn from it respecting the later life of John Paul Jones except that he found his brother William in fairly prosperous circumstances and from him obtained a good impression of the country. This is true enough, but in addition he must have begun to form, on this voyage, that conception of the human dignity and worth of a master mariner that was to remain part of him, constantly growing stronger, all his days.

How could he have escaped it? He was intelligent, and no intelligent boy could have failed to see what was laid so plainly before him. England was already the world's greatest trading nation, and even in England first-class sailing masters were not to be found under every bush; yet sailing masters who could take a ship into any port in the world were common by comparison with captains of the first order of ability. A thoroughly competent captain was the ablest kind of sailing master, merely as an incidental. In addition to that, he had to be bold and forceful enough to dominate turbulent crews, a businessman able enough to deal with some of the ablest in the world, and with it all a man of the world, diplomatic enough to meet on fairly even terms the sort of nobleman who was assigned to colonial governorships—all too often a man qualified by family influence, not by native ability. The superfine captain, in short, had to be tough, smart, and smooth, and men of that type are so uncommon that when one is found he is well worth high pay and all respect.

There is nothing in the record to indicate that Captain Benson was extraordinary, but he was probably good enough to give the new ship's boy a pretty fair idea of what a merchant captain ought to be. Naturally, one voyage did not complete his education. As will be seen later, the young John Paul still had much to learn about his chosen profession; but undoubtedly he began to learn at this point, and the beginning was vastly more important than his meeting with William, or even than his impressions of Virginia. For what he learned about the country died with him; but what he learned about the sea and seafaring men is still influencing strongly the United States Navy, and all the other navies of the world.

Therefore to describe the voyage of the *Friendship* as uneventful is the reverse of true. There is no record of shipwreck, hurricane, or mutiny in connection with it. Nothing happened

to startle the seasoned mariners aboard or to make them remember this voyage as different from many others. But it was
the occasion on which one of the world's greatest seamen began
to learn about the sea, and that is an event indeed, although it
is hard for biographers and historians to make much of it.

CHAPTER II.

THE CAREER of the sailor John Paul for the next sixteen years can be traced, but only sketchily. One reason for this is that the man himself didn't want it traced in detail, and he left accounts that are deliberately vague, with one period of some twenty months completely blacked out.

The cynical instantly assume that it must have been discreditable, and it is certain that there were some episodes that he was not anxious to advertise, but that assuredly does not apply to the larger part of the time. We know, for example, that he made a number of voyages to America, and at least one in an East Indiaman. There is passing reference, too, to a short period of service on a British warship. In none of this is there anything discreditable, but to the man himself, after he had found his true career, it seemed trivial and without interest.

Nevertheless, it played an important part in making him what he was, and through him it affected the navy. It was far from trivial and historians would willingly swap a great deal of the meticulous detail with which he recounted his naval operations for a little more information on his career in the merchant marine.

All we know is that he served out his time, or the greater part of it, in the service of Younger, and almost, probably quite, exclusively in the American trade. Apparently his apprenticeship was cut short by the dissolution of the firm in 1766. Details are lacking, but there is reason to believe that Younger went bankrupt, or at least became himself embarrassed financially, for he resigned his office as trustee of the port when he closed out his business. Young John Paul's indentures were returned to him and he found himself a free man again, but now with nearly seven years' experience of the sea behind him.

More than that was behind him. Loading and unloading cargo was a leisurely process in those days, and ships lay in port for long periods between voyages. Thanks to Brother William's presence, John Paul had something better to do than to loaf around the water front during these periods. It is possible, too, that at some time during these years he obtained leave; certain it is that he spent a great many months in Virginia and possibly in North Carolina; that he made acquaintances that were to prove valuable in later life; that he learned much about the country; and that somewhere he came across books, for long afterward he mentioned intense study by which he strove to make good the deficiencies of his early education.

But it is all vague and uncertain. It is by no means impossible that it was at this time the seed was sown that grew up into a legend, still devoutly believed in eastern North Carolina and never wholly disproved, regarding the change of his name. Edenton, in North Carolina, was still a port of some importance where many trading vessels touched. It is not improbable that some of Younger's were among them, quite possible that one of these was John Paul's ship. Certain it is that ten years later he knew some Edenton people, notably the partners in the house of Hewes & Smith, merchants. It has been generally assumed that he met them later, but that is purely an assumption. There is no reason why a bright young apprentice learning the business of a merchant captain should not have come into contact with the principal merchants of every port at which his ship touched, if only as the captain's errand boy.

If he did spend any considerable length of time at Edenton, it is highly improbable that he did not hear of, and quite possible that he met, the most spectacular character in the region, a gay young blood named Willie (for some incomprehensible reason pronounced to rhyme with "highly") Jones, for he was the sort of person that nobody, not even casual visitors, could overlook. His home was not at Edenton, but at Halifax, a good fifty miles away; but Edenton knew him, all right, as did every other village and hamlet in that part of the colony.

Willie Jones was heir to what was, at the time and in the place, a princely estate. He had been educated in England and had there acquired tastes that were exotic indeed in the eyes of the inhabitants of the humdrum colony of North Carolina; for although it was a populous colony—in the census of 1790 it ranked as the third state, exceeded only by Virginia and Pennsylvania—it had already acquired that character of a sturdy and sensible but utterly unromantic region which it has retained to this day.

Against such a background any genuinely colorful personality must stand out conspicuously indeed, and Willie Jones was unquestionably colorful. Nearly two hundred years later there are still traditions of the speed of his race horses, the valor of his fighting cocks, and the vast number of his personal attendants. There are stories of how he customarily traveled down the river to Edenton in a barge lined with crimson velvet and rowed by twelve—or, as some will have it, sixteen—Negro slaves in liveries that would make the doorman of a New York night club look as modest as a Quaker maid. All this is doubtless exaggerated, but it is incontestable that he made a splash, and the records of his prodigious hospitality are authenticated by contemporary documents as well as by tradition.

If the lad from Kirkcudbright, accustomed to the sober establishment of William Craik, or at most, and from afar, to the strictly limited grandeur of John Douglas, Earl of Selkirk, encountered this fabulous creature, we may be sure that he noted and remembered it. All his days he had a taste for the sparkle and glitter of life. In addition to that, there was in Willie Jones a great deal more than mere foppishness. He liked to cut a dash mentally, as well as physically. Other men of his class, grave, substantial citizens with much to lose if order were disturbed, were repelled by any idea that had a touch of the bizarre; but Willie Jones welcomed it. A few years later he was to emerge as a leader of the extreme radicals in both politics and religion, and he ended as the mortal foe of both the Constitution and the Church.

The legend is that at some time the young John Paul paid a visit to North Carolina and was attacked by a severe illness, whereupon Willie Jones took him into his house and kept him for weeks, and the women of the household nursed him back to health. So later, when for good and sufficient reasons, as will appear, it became inconvenient to continue to use the name Paul, out of gratitude to his benefactors he took that of Jones.

The legend is not supported by a single line in John Paul Jones's hand, and since he was fervent in his expressions of gratitude to every other benefactor, some of his biographers have dismissed this story as pure moonshine. Yet it is curious that such a tale should have taken root and flourished for generations without any reason whatever. Many of Willie Jones's papers have been lost and it is not certain that he preserved much of his correspondence, so the evidence there is negative.

As for his selection of the name Jones, some writers* have pointed out that at the time he was seeking anonymity, and to call himself Jones is the closest approach thereto, except perhaps to call himself Smith, that a man may achieve and still have any name at all.

This may be true today, but was it true in 1776? Was it true, specifically, in the mind of a man from Kirkcudbright, where the Cymric infiltration was of the slightest? As a matter of fact, this man was not seeking true anonymity; emphatically, he was not seeking a complete break with the past, for he kept in touch with certain associates and through them managed considerable property interests. He was wanted on a technical charge of homicide, and it was his intention at the proper time to appear before the court; but war intervened. The assumption of a new name seems, therefore, to have been less a measure of real concealment than a conventional gesture, deceiving nobody but perhaps sparing his friends some embarrassment

* For example, Phillips Russell in his admirable biography.

by permitting them to deny knowledge of anyone named John Paul.

But if this were the explanation, why Jones? Why not some name with a dash of glamour to it, something a bit scintillant? Such a choice would have been in character, for the man had always a romantic delight in glitter.

If the legendary visit to North Carolina actually took place, but some years earlier than is traditional—that is to say, not immediately prior to the Revolution but during one of John Paul's voyages as an apprentice—the rest is not beyond credibility. Suppose the young man had been succored by Willie Jones as the stories have it and as is consistent with his hospitable character; suppose the patient after his recovery had expressed his gratitude in suitable terms in letters that were lost; would there have been any particular need to revert to it ten or fifteen years later, unless he had chanced to encounter his benefactor or someone close to him? We have no evidence that he did encounter any of the Jones family; so his silence is certainly no proof of ingratitude.

But the incident would not have passed from his memory. On the contrary, his boyish enthusiasm would probably have associated the name of Jones with certain qualities—opulence, generosity, spacious living and spacious thinking, courage of body and of mind. In short, it would have been a gorgeous name, very attractive indeed when he had to choose a new one for himself.

It is in the cards that had the moment found him in New England, he might have called himself John Paul Standish, but by no means John Paul Mather; in France he might have chosen Montmorency, or in England, Raleigh. In the country between Edenton and Norfolk Willie Jones had given his name the same sort of glitter, which would have been a good reason for John Paul's choosing it when he had to choose something.

But this, be it repeated, is speculation as to the origin of a legend, not history attested by documentary evidence. Far less open to dispute is the assumption that in these years young John Paul was amassing valuable stores of information about men and business.

William Paul's interests were not extensive, but he was a landowner and a planter, which means that he had to maintain business relations, certainly with the merchants of Fredericksburg and possibly with ship captains who came there. There is a tradition that his brother John assisted him for a while in conducting this business, and in this there is nothing improbable. Certain it is that from William and William's neighbors he acquired some knowledge of how to judge land in that region, for in later years we find him writing about prospective purchases in a way that shows him as by no means the typical Jack Ashore in that sort of dealing. It was unquestionably at this time that he began to acquire that familiarity with the products of Virginia and how to deal in them that was to serve him well in later life.

From his own standpoint nothing worthy of special emphasis happened in these years, so he paid scant attention to them; which proves only that he was somewhat deficient in his power of self-analysis. For a great deal was happening. The boy's intellect and character were taking their final, permanent shape. He was learning his trade as a seaman, but he was also learning much else. He was becoming a good businessman. Through constant reading—for the private libraries in colonial Virginia, especially in the Tidewater region, were much more respectable both in size and in quality than the bilious Henry Adams would have us believe, and the apprentice sailor had access to more than one—he was improving his acquaintance with the world of letters. Through contact with merchants and officials he was acquiring poise and readiness in dealing with affairs.*

* In Lincoln Lorenz's carefully documented life there is a facsimile of a receipt for twenty-three pounds and a "caske," payment in full for sixteen barrels of flour, and dated 1762. The signature is "Jno. Paul." This paper shows that at fifteen he was already handling some of the ship's business and becoming acquainted with business forms.

Through study of the interrelated fortunes of planters in America and merchants and shipowners in England he was acquiring a rudimentary understanding of economic theory. He was acquiring, doubtless unconsciously, a definite Americanism.

Later he was to refer to America as "my favorite country from the age of thirteen," and it is not hard to understand why. The pay of a ship's boy was far from opulent; his liking for the country was not due to the money he made here. But these six years were a peaceful interlude in a stormy career. As a seaman engaged in the transatlantic trade he had a definite place in the American scheme of things, and he was accepted on a friendly basis wherever he went in Virginia. His intelligence was respected, and apparently the Virginians saw nothing incongruous in the fact that a ship's boy should be an avid reader of books. In the colonial atmosphere the boy felt that everyone was very much interested in what he was and very little interested in his origin. He liked it. He liked it even better than he knew at the time. Insensibly he took root in this country, and when the crisis came he had not a flicker of doubt as to which was his side.

Many years afterward, in a burst of revolutionary enthusiasm, he was to declare that he was a citizen of no country but of the world. There was a certain amount of truth in this, but he was carried on the roster of the United States Navy as Lieutenant, and later Captain Jones of North Carolina, and he was apparently content to have it so, for he never made any effort to change it. If this really was his country, the six years during which he was constantly visiting it, studying it, and enjoying it played a large part in making it so. In spite of his own opinion to the contrary, much happened in this period; for it was then that John Paul Jones began to be an American.

But the closing of Younger's business abruptly ended this phase of his career and opened another phase about which he had more reason to be extremely modest in later years. By the return of his indentures in 1766 John Paul found himself a free man and a qualified ship's officer, but without a job. Freedom is gratifying, and to have the way open to a career is even more gratifying, but for a seafaring man without money the first necessity is a job.

It was probably at this time that John Paul had his brief experience in the British navy. Biographers have reached that conclusion by a process of elimination, not by direct evidence. There is a brief reference, made years later, to service on British warships and acquaintance with British naval officers, but no details are given, not even an approximate date. The records carefully pieced together make it improbable that he could have seen service at any other time, and there is a period of a few months in 1766 not otherwise accounted for. By such unsatisfactory means have historians arrived at the belief that the young man first turned to the British navy when he found himself free of his indentures.

But that service must have been brief indeed, for before the year was out he had turned in another direction. On what ship he served and what happened to fetch him out of it so soon we are left to guess. One may suspect, though, that he quit in disgust, if, indeed, he was not ejected for insubordination, for it was soon after this period that he began to exhibit that violent distaste for the naval caste system which remained with him to the end of his life.

Here, though, a careful distinction must be made. It was not the social but the professional aspect of the British caste system that he hated. He was willing to grant that a naval officer must be a gentleman; indeed, he stated it in so many words in an official report to the United States naval authorities. But he insisted as the requirement of prime importance that the gentleman must be an officer, which was a point to which the British in those days paid scant heed.

As a matter of fact, the British service at this time was close to the lowest level it has reached. The notorious "Jemmy Twitcher" had already had his paralyzing hand upon it some years earlier, and five years later he was to begin that long term as First Lord of the Admiralty which set a record for corruption and incompetence at the highest level. Lord Sandwich—called Jemmy Twitcher from a line in *The Beggar's Opera* that obviously satirized him—was unquestionably a handicap to the British navy; but he was just as unquestionably a product of the system that John Paul Jones was to fight all his life.

In the final analysis this was the system of looking upon public office as a private graft, which permeated and infected all politics in the eighteenth century, not in England only, but everywhere. The sailor from Kirkcudbright, however, did not pursue it so far. He was interested in it only as it manifested itself in the navy; and it was his effort to extirpate it from the American service that constitutes his strongest claim upon the admiration and gratitude of the nation.

It is hardly to be assumed that young John Paul at nineteen was philosopher enough to think out all the implications of what he found. All he knew through his own experience, and probably all that interested him at the time, was that advancement in the British navy depended far more upon family and political influence than upon smart seamanship and expert gunnery. It took him, as it would have taken any intelligent man, a very short time to realize that, without some all but miraculous stroke of good fortune, he might be the best sailor afloat and yet remain all his life in a subordinate position, since he had neither money nor family to back him.

This was the aspect of the caste system that infuriated him. He was opposed, strongly opposed, to giving any important command to a man whose manners were boorish and offensive; but he was even more strongly opposed to entrusting command to a fop merely because his father was a noble lord or an influential politician. He believed in making promotion difficult. He believed in making it impossibly difficult for the ignorant or the stupid. But he raged against closing it to talent unsupported by birth.

Why not? The Scotch gardener's son had no interest in guarding the hereditary rights of the nobility, and the skillful seaman had a very strong interest in seeing that good ships were not committed to the hands of incompetent captains. This man's violent antagonism to the caste system had no necessary relation to democratic theory. Plain common sense is enough to account for it.

However, it was years later that his contempt for Jemmy Twitcher's system of promotion became conspicuous. It seems to be a sufficient reason for his leaving the navy, but all we know is that he did leave, and that within a few months.

Then came the episode that he had real reason for suppressing when he had become eminent in his profession. He joined a slaver.

This is not to say that he became a criminal. On the contrary, the slave trade was perfectly legitimate in Great Britain and was to remain so for forty-one years. In 1776, ten years after John Paul shipped as third mate on the slave ship *King George,* there were 192 British vessels registered as slavers, and the traffic had reached its peak.

Nevertheless, the young man must have been very much in need of a job when he took one of that kind, for even in 1766 the business stank. Five years earlier the Quakers had resolved to expel from their fellowship anyone engaged in it; and it was to be only ten years before David Hartley introduced into the House of Commons his motion that "the slave trade was contrary to the laws of God and the rights of man."

But it was profitable, so no matter how the more enlightened elements in society might hold their noses, many ships engaged in it, which meant that it offered well-paid jobs to many seamen. It was not a service that added to any man's reputation, but it was a job and it was not illegal, so the fact that a man engaged in it at this time proves only that he was a hardheaded realist with a reasonably strong stomach, not that he was a degenerate or a criminal.

It must not be forgotten that as the slave trade came into more and more disfavor the character of the men engaged in it deteriorated. By 1807, when it was at last outlawed, the business had already acquired such an infamous look that only the most ruffianly type of seafaring man would touch it; but forty-one years earlier it had attained nothing like that foul eminence. As a matter of fact, slaving was not made an offense punishable by imprisonment under the criminal law until 1811, long after John Paul Jones was dead.

Nevertheless, it is not to be denied that to step from the British navy, even when it was approaching its worst, to the deck of a slave ship was a rather shocking descent, even in 1766. John Paul was not proud of it. But he did it, and not only that, but he made at least two voyages in slavers, first in the *King George* and afterward in the *Two Friends*, a brigantine out of Kingston in Jamaica, in which he held the rank of chief mate.

He was not fastidious at this period of his life. The fact is there and to try to argue around it or to argue it away is futile. But if it is foolish, in the face of this evidence, to try to portray him as lily-fingered, it would be equally foolish, on the authority of this evidence, to denounce him as monstrous.

Our modern conception of the slave trade as regards its physical conditions is highly colored by two factors. For one thing, we usually think of it as it existed in its last days, when it was outlawed and capture meant for the slaver imprisonment or the gallows. For another thing, most people's notion of ocean travel in those days is decidedly rosy.

The word "slaver" today conjures up in most minds the picture of a desperate ship manned by savage and lawless men, dodging the cruisers of all civilized nations and ready to hurl its living cargo to the sharks if capture seemed imminent. But the infamy of the Middle Passage—the name of the run from Africa to the West Indies as distinguished from the run up to North Atlantic ports, and the run thence to the African coast—was acquired in large part after the slave trade was outlawed. It was not the Middle Passage against which enlightened Englishmen of all factions, from Samuel Johnson to William Wilberforce, raged. It was the traffic as a whole; and if efforts were concentrated against the slaver on the Middle Passage it was not because men regarded that as the worst feature of the business, but because that was its most vulnerable point. There was where the thing could be broken up; so there all the opposing forces were brought to bear.

It is hard for us to believe, but the figures support the belief that the Middle Passage, for sheer physical torment, was not very much worse than the North Atlantic passage made by respectable merchantmen bringing free immigrants to the American colonies. Statistics show that the slavers on the average landed seven eighths of their cargo alive. Countless immigrant ships had a higher mortality rate, sometimes far higher, among passengers who had paid their fare.

The reason is not far to seek. It was economic. A dead slave was a dead loss to the captain of a slaver. A dead passenger was no loss to the captain of an immigrant ship. Indeed, he might represent a gain if he had already paid his fare and consumed no more of the ship's stores. As long as the traffic was legal, therefore, the officers of a slave ship were very definitely limited, as far as brutality was concerned. They had to stop short of risking the destruction of valuable property. On an ordinary ship there was no such limit. In theory the killing of a seaman was murder, but in practice it was difficult to convict an officer for anything that took place at sea, while it was easy to discharge a slave-ship officer who brought in his cargo largely dead or crippled. The assumption, therefore, that service on such a ship was far more brutalizing than any other service rests upon questionable bases. Once the service was outlawed, of course, it became hellish; but in 1766, while it was still legal, it may have been less, rather than more brutalizing than service on an ordinary merchantman.

All the same, it was a dirty trade when John Paul entered it, and at the first opportunity he quit it. It is interesting to note, however, that apparently what revolted him was nothing that occurred on the ship, but witnessing the slave auctions at Kingston. The inference is that it was not what he had done to these unfortunates that made him ashamed of himself, but the fate to which he had delivered them.

As a matter of fact, to say that he quit the slave trade at the first opportunity does him less than justice. He made an opportunity. There would have been small credit in signing on as an officer of a better ship than the *Two Friends*, but no such chance presented itself. In order to get out the man changed his trade; and no one goes to that extreme unless the impulse to move is very strong indeed.

There was in the West Indies at the time a strolling company of actors under the leadership of James Moody, who had some reputation as a Shakespearean. Moody took John Paul into his company. So much is known. But how and why this extraordinary venture was brought about we do not know, for the sailor always touched upon this phase of his career with great delicacy. So reticent was he on the subject that one is fairly driven to the inference that he was more ashamed of having been an actor than of having been a slaver.

This silence is maddening to a biographer, for it is easy to believe that his theatrical experience accounts for much in the later career of John Paul Jones. For one thing, the quarterdeck, although it is a great school, is not commonly regarded as a preeminently good place to learn the niceties of social intercourse. John Paul went from the gardener's cottage at Arbigland to become first a ship's boy and eventually an officer; yet somewhere in his career he acquired poise and an easy and certain familiarity with good manners.

In his later life it happened not once but repeatedly that people who had known him only by reputation on first encountering him in person were astonished to find the redoubtable sea fighter a gentleman whose bearing was composed and correct in any company, who could offer a graceful compliment to a pretty woman or a suavely flattering greeting to a distinguished man as competently as if he had been trained to the diplomatic service instead of to the sea. Nor was this astonishment confined to persons whose experience of the world was limited. As shrewd an observer as Benjamin Franklin noted it. As great a lady as the Duchesse d'Orléans noted it. Franklin had seen too many men of too many types in his long life to be deceived by any shoddy make-believe. Louise of Orléans had spent her life among people who made a career of being witty and charming; so when she described a man as charming, her dictum may be accepted as expert testimony.

For the most part, this may be attributed to the man's native intelligence sharpened by as much reading and study as he could contrive and by observation of people of good breeding encountered in his travels. Solid sense and a sincere wish to be considerate of others are the basic materials of that courtesy which makes a man acceptable anywhere. But this one was not merely acceptable; he made a memorable impression, which indicates that he had not only the essentials of good breeding, but had also picked up somewhere the trifling details of word and gesture that made him not only correct but easy in social intercourse.

Perhaps James Moody and his colleagues had much to do with that. No one knows, but the stage, especially under the direction of a Shakespearean actor, teaches a man about voice, gesture, bearing, and movement with a thoroughness and speed rivaled by no other school. John Paul Jones was somewhat theatrical—not enough so to be offensive, for his good sense corrected that, and not nearly as much so as Buell, his uninhibited biographer, would have us believe. But he was well aware of the effectiveness of the dramatic gesture in appropriate circumstances, and he knew how to make it. Since we can discover in his career no other that seems to be a fit place for the acquisition of this knowledge, it is not unreasonable to give James Moody credit.

The strangest thing about this strange episode, however, is that the sailor turned actor seems to have been a success. No doubt the audiences to which Moody's company played in the West Indies were not highly critical. Perhaps if Mr. Paul had undertaken to play Bevil in Richard Steele's *Conscious Lovers* before a London audience the effect might have been calamitous; but in the West Indies he got away with it at least passably well.

As a matter of fact, it is probable that his performance was not too bad, judged even by professional standards. He was the type that a good stage director can whip into shape rapidly. Standing five feet seven, just a shade under average height, he was compactly but not heavily built, agile and naturally graceful in his movements. His face was not too handsome, yet far from ugly—exactly the sort of face with which a good make-up artist can do wonders. The forehead was fine—high and broad, but not bulging. The blue eyes, set well apart, were good, and under stress of emotion could become extraordinary. The nose was a trifle too short to meet the highest aesthetic standard, but it was well shaped. The mouth was somewhat too thin and somewhat too wide for perfect beauty, but it could project a line to the back of the house—or a command through the roar of battle. The chin and jaw were admirably shaped, but decidedly too heavy for the rest of the face. This was the feature that prevented John Paul from being a really handsome man. The rest of his face was that of an intelligent, alert, and amiable but not particularly forceful personality. It was when one's eyes strayed to the jaw and chin that the jolt came. There was war in that chin. But the stage has a thousand tricks for disguising such a feature, and it is altogether credible that behind the footlights, with the aid of skillful make-up, he may have made a striking, if not dazzling, figure.

There is no reason to suppose that he was or could have become a great actor; but he was young, presentable, highly intelligent, and agile in mind as well as in body. With such a man any competent stage director can do wonders; it is therefore not surprising that this one served James Moody's purpose well enough, at least for a season or two.

But he was never under any illusions about it. The stage was not his business. As an avenue of escape from the slave trade it served, but that was all he really wanted of it. He seems to have remained with the company barely long enough to accumulate the money to pay for passage back to Scotland. In 1768 he found a Kirkcudbright ship, the *John*, ready to sail for her home port; and when she stood out to sea she carried John Paul as a passenger.

But when the ship—to be exact, the brigantine—came up the Solway, she carried this same John Paul as her captain. The incident is indicative both of the informality and of the hazards of ocean travel a hundred and eighty years ago. A few days out Captain MacAdam and his first mate both died of a tropical fever, and the vessel was left without any other navigator as competent as the passenger. According to the custom of the sea at the time, it would have been foolish to put back to port as long as there was a good navigator aboard, regardless of his status as a passenger. So by common consent, John Paul brought her in.

The *John* belonged to the Kirkcudbright mercantile house of Currie, Beck & Co., a concern, as it proved, then on its last legs. The skill of the late passenger so pleased the owners that they promptly gave him command of the ship and outfitted him for a return voyage, which, although Captain Paul did not know it at the time, was to be next to the last under the house flag.

Here, at last, was the open road to success, and John Paul set out upon it promptly and jauntily. He was a smart seaman and he drove the *John* smartly. His first voyage to the West Indies was made with precision and dispatch, and the business affairs connected with it seem to have been transacted with an efficiency that at least equaled the seamanship. The unreliable Buell says that Paul had accumulated a thousand guineas by the time he brought the *John* in after the death of Captain MacAdam. It is not inherently impossible, for he was clearly entitled to what was known as "summary salvage," and it is certain that he had some capital. Without doubt his first voyage as captain added to it, and may have added to it considerably. That he was no pauper is sufficiently attested by the fact that he went to the expense of erecting a headstone at the grave of his father, who had died in 1767 while the son was on the other side of the Atlantic. Lorenz presents the inscription, with the notation that the spelling is probably the stonecutter's:

In Memory
of
John Paul Senior who died at
Arbigland the 24 October 1767
Universealy Esteemed

Erected by John Paul Juneor

Lorenz regards this as evidence that the son had no doubt as to his paternity, but it would seem rather more probable that it proves only that the son was beginning to regard himself as a man of substance and dignity. It was not fitting for such a man to leave unmarked the grave even of a putative father. It was on starting again for the West Indies that he commended his mother and sister to the care of William Craik, and that worthy no doubt accepted the commission the more cheerfully since it was evident that "John Paul Juneor" was a coming man.

So he was, but he was also young, terribly young. He took command of the ship at twenty-one, and from the technical viewpoint, rightfully, for he was certainly the best mariner aboard and probably one of the best to be found anywhere on the Solway. On his first voyage in command he was to prove himself as able a businessman as he was a sailor. Currie, Beck & Co. had reason to congratulate themselves on having acquired one of the smartest young captains in the West Indian trade.

But the sea submits the master of a ship to many tests not provided for in the rulebooks. This is true today, but in the eighteenth century it was much more conspicuously true. It is a strain upon the imagination of the modern generation to comprehend the situation, because conditions have altered so radically that we nearly always overlook something essential.

To begin with, we have no adequate realization of the hazards of the sea in those days. On the transatlantic steamship lanes to cross three thousand miles of open sea today is materially less perilous than to drive as many miles in an automobile on American streets and highways; but in 1768 the chances of coming alive to the end of such a journey were far fewer. "Being in a ship is being in a jail with the chance of being drowned," Samuel Johnson's famous remark, was not one of his extravagances. A jail, said the Doctor, is preferable—"there is better air, better company, better conveniences of all kinds," as well as greater safety.

It was literally true. Even the stoutest ship of 1768 was a fabric so fragile that it might appall a modern seaman to think of crossing an ocean in one. Entirely dependent upon the wind for motive power, it had to be handled with high skill and, especially, with the utmost precision in order to survive at all, not to mention making a swift and comfortable passage.

Today precision is attained by the response of machinery, largely automatic. The human element figures principally in seeing that the machinery is kept in proper order so that it may operate as it was intended to operate. As long as his steam pressure is adequate and his engines and steering gear functioning properly, a modern captain has no need to guess; he knows beyond peradventure exactly what will happen when he issues a command.

But sails were manipulated by men, not by machines. All the rigging might be in perfect order, yet let some one fool out of a crew perhaps numbering hundreds fail to haul on his particular rope at the word of command, and it was possible for disaster to follow so swiftly that the ablest captain could not avert it. In other words, the crew, although it was composed of men, had to operate with the precision of machinery to ensure the safety of the ship, the cargo, and the lives of all on board. But men will not operate with the precision of machinery unless they are under the strictest discipline. Discipline at sea was not a matter of smartness and efficiency only; it was a matter of life and death.

The law, recognizing this, gave to the captain absolute authority. It was not merely his right, it was his duty to sacrifice the life of one man if that seemed necessary to save the ship. He was answerable to the courts of admiralty for abuse of his authority, but he possessed it. To landsmen the law of the sea in the eighteenth century sometimes seems brutal to the point of savagery; but it was really humane in that it preferred the death of one man to the loss of hundreds, and the moment that discipline failed at sea the whole ship was imperiled.

Nor was this mere theorizing. It was given point and emphasis with appalling frequency by catastrophes directly attributable to failure of discipline. The loss of some ship by a failure of the crew to obey orders promptly was an event so common that it may reasonably be described as almost a daily occurrence. The law was not more severe than the circumstances justified; for severity in such a case is the only true humanitarianism.

But it is characteristic of youth to be overlogical, and this is a defect that cannot be corrected by textbooks. Nothing but time and experience can teach a man to discern the subtle difference between right and ruthlessness. Not even time and experience can teach all men, for some remain fanatics until they descend to the grave; and the best must learn this lesson by slow degrees.

When he sailed as captain at twenty-one John Paul had not learned it, and because he had not learned it he was not quite fit for command. In all that the books taught and the law required he qualified handsomely. He was a grand seaman. He was an astute businessman. He was honest, he was brave, and he meant to be fair. Far from being an abysmal brute, he was in some respects a rank sentimentalist, an admirer of the arts, a poetaster, and a gallant. He was a highly civilized man.

Nevertheless, by the time the *John* arrived at Kirkcudbright on her return trip he was fast getting the reputation of a bucko captain. Foremast hands said among themselves that the *John* was a good ship, but a hard one. They admired her skipper as a captain, but they hated him as a man. He maintained discipline, but he had not yet acquired the art of inspiring loyalty. Perhaps as yet he did not realize the value of loyalty; so his discipline was rigid rather than firm.

But this was the situation as seen from the sailor's angle. From that of the young captain it bore a different aspect. The voyage had been a success. There is no evidence that the *John* was a startlingly good ship, but he was getting as much out of her as any man could, and his employers were amply satisfied. There was no question of his holding his command, and he had every reason to hope for a better one when a better ship became available. It was probably in a pretty self-satisfied mood that he settled with William Craik for any expenses the laird had incurred for the Paul family, and doubtless he received the congratulations of his patron; for he had justified whatever efforts Craik may have made to get him a job.

It must have been a pretty satisfactory world that Captain John Paul looked upon as the *John* reached the Indies again and dropped anchor in Rockley Bay, port of Tobago, one of the Windward Isles. He was twenty-two, he commanded not only a ship but the confidence of his employers and the respect of the old family friend who had known his father and had watched over his entire career. He had money in his pocket and seemed in a fair way to acquire a great deal more. The world was his oyster, and if he looked upon the grumblings of discontented sailors—and when were sailors ever so contented as to grumble not at all?—with a rather too lordly contempt, it was certainly a pardonable weakness.

A very satisfactory world indeed—and then, as is only too often the way in this mismanaged scheme of things, everything went to pot at once.

To begin with, he evidently picked up malaria—"several very severe fevers," he described his malady in a letter to William Craik—and malaria does not contribute notably either to optimism or to sound judgment. Perhaps the irascibility induced by illness may have made him take too stern a view of an unpleasant incident on shipboard. He had shipped as carpenter a resident of Kirkcudbright named Maxwell. and the fellow had proved unsatisfactory, being, in the Captain's eyes, both lazy and insubordinate. As the ship lay at anchor in May 1770, this Mungo Maxwell did something or said something—the details of the incident are lost—to explode the Captain's uncertain temper, and he promptly had the man flogged.

It was an error that an older man, or this man himself ten years later, would never have made. But John Paul was young and legally within his rights as master of the ship. To an older man it would have been plain that even though he had the law on his side, there were considerations that made it inadvisable to make use of the full rigor of the law. In the first place, the ship was in port, so a carpenter, even a mutinous one, could not do much to endanger it. In the second place, the port was in the tropics, where the combination of malaria and heat tended to reduce the efficiency and fray the tempers of sailors, especially those born and bred in the cool north. In the third place, this particular man came from the Captain's own home town, and any grievance he took back would be thoroughly aired and probably greatly magnified in Kirkcudbright. In the fourth place, Tobago was tough, even for a West Indian port. It was a port of call for countless ships, and what with discharges, illness, and desertion, it had acquired a floating population of characters regarded as desperate even by mariners, and no seafaring men in 1770 were fragile and delicate. Prudence counseled every captain never to start trouble in Tobago if it were humanly possible to avoid it. But Captain Paul applied the law, and the law applied the lash. Then he ordered the fellow off his ship.

Maxwell went ashore raging and determined to apply a little law himself. The law, in such cases, was represented by the Court of Vice-Admiralty, of which one James Simpson was surrogate in Tobago. To this magistrate the infuriated carpenter applied for action against the Captain, and Paul was accordingly summoned and required to give an account of the affair, which he did, "at the same time," said Simpson in a later report, "declaring his sorrow for having corrected the complainant." The surrogate had Maxwell bare his back and found evidence that he had caught the lash all right; but the beating did not seem to have been excessive, and the Captain clearly had the right to inflict it, so he dismissed the complaint.

This affair was annoying, but what seemed to John Paul a much more serious threat to his future soon appeared in the form of rumors that Currie, Beck & Co. were about to suspend business as far as the West Indian trade was concerned. "Should that really prove the case," he wrote in all haste to Craik, "you know the disadvantages I must of course labor under." The worst of it was that he had just turned down a chance to secure an interest "in a large ship out of London." Troubles were thickening upon the young captain as he made for Kirkcudbright again toward the end of 1770.

But he didn't know the half of it until he landed after what he considered a fairly successful voyage. Currie, Beck & Co. were, in fact, closing out, and the *John* was up for sale; but that was nothing in comparison with the truly appalling news that awaited him. He was indicted for murder!

Mungo Maxwell, the ship's carpenter, having received cold comfort from the magistrate, hung around the water front for a month or six weeks, then shipped on "the Barcelona packet," a vessel trading among the islands. Four or five days out he came down with what the captain of the packet described as "a fever and lowness of spirits" and died. Word of the beating and his subsequent death had reached Scotland.

His father, Robert Maxwell of Clonyard, near Kirkcudbright, not unnaturally connected the two events and laid before the Vice-Admiral of Scotland a furious information alleging that Mungo "was most unmercifully, by the said John Paul, with a cudgel or baton, beat, bled, and bruised, and wounded upon his back and other parts of his body, and of which wounds and bruises he soon afterwards died." So a warrant was out for the Captain when he landed.

The prosecution was bad enough, but worse was the public scandal. Robert Maxwell told his story long before John Paul could arrive to contradict it; and as it passed from mouth to mouth it is certain that it lost nothing in the telling. Without knowledge of the circumstances, the Captain's friends were helpless. There was no doubt that Mungo was dead, and his father's account was so circumstantial that nothing short of the complete details could clear the matter up. So on landing John Paul found himself no longer the boy hero of Kirkcudbright, but the brutal martinet who had beaten one of the town lads to death. Even William Craik was, John Paul said, "ungracious." Probably he was. Without doubt the Laird of Arbigland knew the Maxwells, and Mungo had sailed with a man who was in some sense the Laird's protégé. Craik was probably in an embarrassing position and not disposed to thank the Captain for having put him there.

The prosecution did not come to much in and of itself. Paul was admitted to bail, but cautioned not to leave Scotland for the next six months, so he had to suspend his seafaring career while he prepared his defense. It was abundantly good. Simpson, the surrogate, readily made a deposition that he had examined Maxwell's stripes and found them so little dangerous that he had dismissed the complaint as "frivolous"; and that he was satisfied the beating had nothing to do with the man's death. James Eastment, captain of the Barcelona packet, swore that Maxwell had come aboard his ship apparently in good health and had attended to his duties four or five days before being taken ill, and that at the time it never occurred to him that the man died of anything but "fever and lowness of spirits," a fate all too common among sailors in those seas. The court was satisfied and the indictment was quashed.

But spiteful gossip kept the story alive, and from time to time it was revived to plague John Paul Jones all the rest of his life. He was maturing the hard way. Here he learned one lesson that a man must know before he is master of himself—that one may act entirely within his rights and yet gain the reputation among his neighbors of being a low swine.

He accepted the teaching with no good grace. He regarded himself as extremely ill used, and wrote to his mother and sisters about it in rather turgid phrases even two years after it was all over: "My life has been thirsted after, and, which is much dearer to me, my honour by maliciously loading my fair character with obloquy and vile aspersions." Worst of all, apparently, was the defection of William Craik, to whom, he said, he was sending copies of the documents in the case, "as his nice feelings will not perhaps be otherways [sic] satisfied. . . . His ungracious conduct to me before I left Scotland I have not yet been able to get the better of. Every person of feeling must think meanly of adding to the load of the afflicted. It is true I bore it with seeming unconcern, but Heaven can witness for me, that I suffered the more on that very account." His relations with Craik thereafter were never more than formally polite, although years later, when Jones was being denounced in unbridled terms through all Great Britain, the Laird sturdily declared that the Mungo Maxwell story was a tissue of lies.

While he was busy clearing himself of the legal charges against him—perhaps by way of supporting that effort—he made application for membership in the Masonic lodge of St. Bernard, Kirkcudbright, and received the second degree on February 1, 1771. As he attended at least one other meeting after that, Lorenz is sure that he received the third degree also, although the records are missing. The records that do exist, however, show two interesting features. An application for membership, to be considered, had to be supported by a member in good standing. John Paul's application was thus supported by one James Smith, thought to be a brother of the junior member of the firm of Hewes & Smith in Edenton. Then the minutes of the lodge dealing with his admission bear the notation, "Paul Jones entered." There is no means of determining when this notation was made; perhaps it was years later, but if not it is the earliest mention of the name "Jones" in connection with him.

Once clear of his entanglement with the law, or perhaps in the course of that clearance, the harried young captain temporarily forsook the career of a deep-water sailor and served a while on boats plying between England and the Isle of Man. It was a stopgap job, accepted to tide him over until he could secure another high-seas command, and without doubt he looked upon it as an ordinary, commonplace, humdrum sort of job, which he was glad to drop at the earliest opportunity; and there is no indication that anyone else regarded it otherwise at the time. But it was the man's singular fate at this period to touch nothing that did not recoil upon him, soon or late. It was while he was engaged in this trade that the Isle of Man was formally annexed by Great Britain and the first entry of a cargo in the customhouse at Douglas was made by Captain Paul.

But one reason for the annexation was that the island had from time immemorial been a notorious nest of smugglers, who ran all manner of contraband into the Solway. Therefore when the British were searching earnestly for any sort of mud to throw at the man who had become the terror of the seas, it was remembered that he once traded to the Isle of Man. Therefore he was promptly exalted *ex post facto* into a sort of King of the Smugglers with nothing to support the story except the fact that he did ferry a number of cargoes back and forth.

By the latter part of 1772, however, his affairs were in much better shape. For at least two years he had been negotiating with a group in London that controlled a ship to which he had taken a liking, the *Betsy*, somewhat larger than the *John* and well adapted, as he believed, to the West Indian trade.

Details of the transaction are not clear, but it seems to have been some form of charter arrangement. The Captain not only commanded the ship, but also owned a large part, perhaps the greater part, of her cargo. He had become a merchant adventurer as well as a seaman, which enormously enhanced his chances of profit, but which also added immensely to his worries and responsibilities.

However, he was not the man to shy away from responsibility, and his energy was boundless. As he set his course for the West Indies it must have seemed to him again a pretty good world. At twenty-six he was master of a ship and trading on his own. He knew what his skill and industry could accomplish in that sort of business. He now had excellent connections in London, and he knew the western side of the Atlantic thoroughly. Still well short of thirty, he was already on the road to fortune, and there was no apparent reason why it should not be an immense fortune. If he had visions of himself as one of the leading merchants of London in another twenty years, with a fleet of ships, agents in every port in the world, his country seat, his carriage, his town house thronged by the nobility and gentry, why not? Others had done it. Some had done it who at twenty-six were in far worse position than his.

It would require diligent application. He had no illusions about that. But who was more capable of diligent application than the gardener's son who in fourteen years had already made himself captain of a ship and a merchant of substance? He was always a man of soaring imagination combined with hardheaded practicality. He reveled in the society of beautiful women and distinguished men, but with a liverish, splenetic West Indian trader, a shrewd Virginia tobacco planter, a hard-bitten Connecticut Yankee, or the toughest British bo'sun that ever swung a belaying pin, he was at ease. He could deal with any of them and hold his own, and he knew it. For such a man dreams of fortune were no idle reveries; it was within his power to realize them.

For the first months of the voyage he began to realize them. He was no Dick Whittington, to acquire a chest of jewels in exchange for a cat, no Sinbad, measuring his diamonds and pearls and rubies in bushel baskets; but he was doing pretty well. Toward the end of 1773, after gradually disposing of his cargo as he moved from port to port, he had a balance on the books of various agents of some £1,190 in addition to some goods still unsold and a shipment of Madeira wine already sent back to England. This should be regarded as considerably more than $6,000 in available cash, for the value of money was materially greater in 1773 than it is today. To be in an equivalent financial position a man now must have two or three times as much. John Paul was doing very well indeed when his ship dropped anchor once more in that place of ill omen, Rockley Bay in the island of Tobago.

And then once more everything was ruined in a flash. He had learned something from his experience with Mungo Maxwell. All hands agreed that the martinet had been suppressed. The captain of the *Betsy* was no bucko, no matter what might be said of the captain of the *John*. There was no talk of flogging or other brutality on that ship.

But John Paul had not learned enough. He was still too much disposed to stand on his legal rights, even when they came into conflict with human rights. He had a legal right to delay paying off the crew until the end of the voyage. Since he was merchant as well as captain, it was to his interest to do so, for he needed all his available cash to purchase cargo for the return trip.

But because he was a merchant this voyage had been prolonged beyond the crew's expectation. When they signed on for a voyage to the West Indies, most of them undoubtedly assumed that it was to be a matter of six months at most; but the *Betsy* had now been out fourteen months, and she was still three thousand miles from home. The crew became more and more restive. They began to demand their pay, or at least part of it. Legally they had not a leg to stand on, but morally there was something to be said for them. For one thing, some of them were in rags, having worn out the clothes with which they started from England. Even the Captain had to admit that this was intolerable, so he issued clothing at his own expense to those who were in most need; but with regard to pay he was adamant.

In some measure he was justified. Had he paid the men all that was due them, the chances are that he would have ruined his whole enterprise, for any number of them would have jumped the ship then and there, and the *Betsy* might have been stuck in Tobago without hands enough to bring her home; but a sailor was slow to desert while his pay was still due. Yet to refuse any payment at all was a mistake. An older and wiser captain would have yielded something of his legal rights and reached a compromise that would have suppressed disaffection.

But John Paul was still young and headstrong. One reason that may have stiffened his attitude was the fact that the leader of the agitation had no cause for complaint. He was not one of the Kirkcudbright men who had been with the ship more than a year; he was a drifter whom Paul had picked up in Tobago and signed on quite recently. He was a surly brute, one of that type dreaded by every efficient officer and called "a sea lawyer." Although, having just signed on, he had no grievance himself, he busied himself stirring up trouble among the other men and constituted himself the ringleader.

All the available evidence indicates that the Captain exhibited remarkable patience with this fellow. They had several arguments in which the sailor became more and more insolent; but John Paul did not employ the cat in this case. He contented himself with explanations, which did no good.

Matters came to a head one day in December under circumstances all unfavorable to John Paul. The first mate had gone ashore on business. The second mate was sick in his bunk, as were several of the Kirkcudbright men most loyal to the officers. The agitator seized the moment to renew his demands, and this time he was more than insolent; he became menacing, and in the end he actually struck at his commanding officer. This, of course, was flat mutiny and made the man instantly an outlaw. All captains in those days habitually went armed, so Paul whipped out his sword and fended the man off with the point. But witnesses agreed that he did not lunge. On the contrary, he stepped backward toward the door of his cabin, plainly trying to avoid an affray. Unfortunately, the sailor by this time was completely maddened; he snatched up an ax that happened to be lying on the deck and whirled it above his head to strike, whereupon the Captain let him have it.

Even so, the thrust may have been involuntary. He always maintained that stepping backward he brought his heel against the hatch combing, which made him stop, and the sailor rushed upon the point. Be that as it may, there was nothing lackadaisical about the job. It was grimly efficient. The mutineer was as dead as a mackerel almost before he hit the deck, and his companions, appalled, shrank out of the Captain's way.

But John Paul had cut down far more than a mutinous sailor. He had cut down his own fair fame, his prosperity, his future career, and all prospect of wealth and power among the great merchants of London. In the twinkling of an eye he was a ruined man.

It wouldn't have been so bad if the affair had taken place anywhere except in Tobago. But it was only a little over two years since this same captain had been accused of killing another sailor in the same port. Twice was too much. John Paul's best friends shook their heads and regarded the future apprehensively.

He went ashore immediately and gave himself up to a magistrate. This official summoned the witnesses and made a preliminary, but apparently thorough, investigation that convinced him that it was a clear case of self-defense; nevertheless, it involved death by violence, which meant that there must be a judicial inquiry by a higher authority than the magistrate. The evidence did not justify holding the Captain for murder, but he could not be cleared by anything less than a court of admiralty, and no such court would sit in Tobago for some months. The magistrate accordingly released John Paul on his promise to appear before the court in due time.

But while this satisfied the law, it did nothing to appease the lawless. Tobago was not Scotland. Its water-front population included not only the usual contingent of deserters, crimps, and footpads, but plenty of men who were more than suspected of having sailed in pirate ships. Many a hard-fisted bo'sun or mate or captain had died there of something more sudden than even yellow fever. It was nothing unusual for an unpopular officer to be fished out of the harbor, or picked up in a dark alley with a knife hole in his back, and with no evidence that would bring the perpetrators of the crime to justice.

James Simpson, no longer surrogate but still a friend of John Paul, and Lieutenant Governor William Young both advised him not to wait for the court in Tobago. All his friends agreed that if he stayed there his chances of living to stand trial were not good; they all told him to move and to move fast, and the advice unquestionably was good. He could find out when the court was to sit and come back for the session, which would meet the requirements of the law.

They urged him not to wait even for the time necessary to settle his business affairs. Accordingly, he entrusted his interests to various businessmen, principally to one Ferguson, of Orange Valley, who, incidentally, turned out to be a crook. All the cash his friends could raise at the moment was fifty pounds; with this, and on a horse that someone lent him, between dusk and dawn one night he rode off into the darkness, never to be seen in Tobago again.

John Paul, indeed, was never seen again anywhere. Some twenty months later one John Paul Jones appeared in Virginia in the turmoil immediately preceding the Revolution, when all sorts of odd characters were appearing from nowhere, some to offer their services to the colonists, some merely to fish in troubled waters. It was not the mode, in those days, to inquire too carefully into the antecedents of a man capable of bearing arms and willing to do so. If a man could and would strike a blow for liberty, he could call himself anything he pleased, and welcome.

This newcomer was the same man as John Paul biologically, but not in any other respect. Psychologically, John Paul disappeared into the darkness that night on Tobago and never reappeared. How could it be otherwise? When a man has not only ruined himself, but horrified himself by his own act, he does not emerge from the experience the same man. John Paul was not a killer by nature. On the contrary, he was a romantic and somewhat sentimental youth, inclined to attach too much importance to wealth and position, but far from cherishing contempt for human life. When that man fell dead before him he was shattered; and when he pulled himself together again he was a different man.

Where he went and what he did during those twenty months the world has never known and will never know, for he took the secret to the grave. The assumption is that he crossed the island and got some fishing boat to take him away, probably to Trinidad, possibly to Grenada; but from there it is impossible to make even a reasonable guess. Malice came forward to fill the gap, of course, and speculation has busied itself endlessly, sometimes to attack the man, sometimes to defend him, but with equal futility either way.

What does it matter? Even though we have no geographical data, we know where he was, all right. He was going through his own private hell and in what part of the earth he found it is of no significance. He must have taken to the sea, for that was his trade, and eventually he turned up in a different part of the world. He may have resorted to some pretty desperate expedients. There are legends of service on Spanish ships, on smugglers, on slavers. His enemies declared that for a while he turned pirate, certainly no physical impossibility, for piracy was far from unknown in the Caribbean at the time.

In all the mass of gossip, perhaps the story that comes nearest to having something like authenticity is the yarn told by Thomas Chase, a seafaring man from Martha's Vineyard, and written down many years later by his grandson, first a clergyman and then a lawyer of Maine. Thomas Chase, no more than a lad, was on the beach one day when a black, rakish ship came sliding into Holme's Bay and lowered a boat, which Chase went to meet. It was rowed by Spanish and Portuguese sailors, but was commanded by an officer who spoke English, and it contained a dead man. The officer explained that it was the body of a member of the crew who had died at sea, but wished to be buried ashore; and he asked for Chase's assistance.

Martha's Vineyard was a long way from Tobago and in a quieter part of the world, but in the eighteenth century islanders everywhere were wonderfully discreet when strange ships slipped into lonely harbors. Thomas Chase, looking at the sailors, looking at the ship, and looking at the officer, decided that politeness was strongly indicated, since he had a decided objection to having his throat cut. He therefore rendered every assistance, making a coffin with his own hands and helping with the burial. He even tendered the officer the hospitality of his own house, and they got along amiably enough, but Chase asked no questions. The officer was not a large man, and there seems to have been nothing particularly ferocious in his countenance, but—well, Chase asked no questions. It was plainly better to be incurious.

The ship went on her way and years passed. The Revolution came, and Chase, a seaman now, was captured on an American privateer and thrown into a naval prison, where he languished until the famous—or notorious, but certainly tremendous—Captain John Paul Jones had captured so many thousands of British that an exchange had to be arranged. Chase was sent to France, where he was offered an opportunity to serve with Jones on a new ship he was fitting out, called the *Bon Homme Richard*. He accepted, and in the new commander instantly recognized the officer of the burial party at Martha's Vineyard.

If this romantic tale is true in every particular, it doesn't convict John Paul Jones of piracy, but it does raise some questions. If he was at this time an officer of an honest ship, engaged in legitimate trade, why didn't he say so later? This is the only period of his life about which he always refused to give any information whatever; it is an inescapable inference that it must have been a bad time. We know that he fled from Tobago with only fifty pounds in his pocket, and he could hardly have subsisted on that for twenty months. What he did to secure money we do not know, but we do know that he did not choose to talk about it. A desperate man, a fugitive and penniless, or nearly so, is not likely to be fastidious about his employment. This one may not have descended to actual piracy, but he certainly did nothing that he was proud of, or he would not have concealed it.

In the complete absence of reliable information, it is nonsensical for a biographer to undertake his defense. He needs no assistance. He cleared his own character. Whatever he may have been at this time, he was for twenty years after an honorable and distinguished officer, which is the one irrefutable proof of moral power. A man who has never been in the gutter may, indeed, be a strong character; but on the other hand, he may be no more than a mediocrity who has had the luck never to be caught in a really tight place. But a man who has been definitely, unmistakably down and out, yet has dragged himself by his own efforts back into the respect and admiration of the world, is strong beyond peradventure.

It is the eternal frustration of biography that in describing the life of almost any great man the critical part is precisely the part that can never be told. John Paul Jones always lived dangerously, but it was usually physical or economic or political danger. This is the moment in his career when he came closest to moral ruin, the moment when he demonstrated possession of the quality that makes a man great—and we know nothing about it.

It is as certain as anything in the realm of the spiritual can be that a little more pressure at this time would have sent him down for the last time, as even less pressure has sent many a man down to end in the gutter—to die of delirium tremens in some drunken beachcomber's haunt, or in a tavern brawl, or even on a gibbet at the hands of the law. It is just as certain that, having had the force to straighten himself up against this pressure, he was thenceforth bound to become a man of distinction. His world-wide fame was perhaps somewhat fortuitous, but he would have made his mark somehow, somewhere, and to some extent. The turning point, the illogical thing, the thing for which there is no explanation, was reached in the darkness of these twenty months; what followed is all logical enough, but what can never be explained is the strength that enabled this man, apparently headed straight for ruin, to turn about and head the other way.

But one thing is plain enough. It was at this very time that John Paul Jones began to qualify morally, if not in skill and intelligence, to become the instructor of future naval officers. For it was at this time that he attained emotional maturity. No man can be truly wise until he has discovered by bitter experience what an appalling fool he is capable of being. No man is fit for command until he has learned how easy it is to lose command of himself and how surely fatal is that loss.

When he plunged into the darkness on Tobago and through all the months that he wandered nameless up and down the world, this man carried with him the knowledge that he, who fancied himself so shrewd and wise, had played the giddy goat and thereby ruined his own prospects. He, so proud of being captain of a ship at twenty-one, had lost his head like any homesick ship's boy, and therewith had come near losing his life as well, saving it only by ignominious flight.

It was gall and wormwood to a proud spirit, but it was fact; and in this period it soaked into him, it permeated him, it became part of his very fiber, and if he had been a weak character, undoubtedly it would have destroyed him. But he was not weak. Somewhere within him was the indomitable streak, the core of steel that is, in the final analysis, the indispensable requisite of the great man. Nobody can describe it exactly, but its presence can never be missed. It certainly does not consist of intelligence alone, or of skill, and certainly not of morality, for many good men have not been great, and not a few have been great who were far from good. A man has it or he doesn't; and no one knows until some crisis develops of sufficient magnitude to demonstrate conclusively either its presence or its absence.

The blank twenty months were that crisis for this man. It would be interesting and informative, perhaps, to know how he occupied himself in that period; but it might not tell us anything important that we do not already know. For about the really important thing, the supremely important thing, there is no obscurity at all. This is the fact that from the darkness John Paul Jones emerged into the light again master of himself. He was not stripped of folly. He could still act on misinformation and act as insanely as any idiot. But he never again acted on a misapprehension of his own strength, which was the supreme folly. He could still make a fool of himself over a woman. He was still capable of mistaking a traitor for an honest man and vice versa. But about one man he was mistaken no more. Never again could he believe that John Paul Jones was either Hercules or Nestor. Whoever else might escape him, that man was ever thereafter under his control.

Therefore he was ready for command. He was ready for more than that—he was ready to demonstrate what command should be.

CHAPTER III.

I.

THE FACT that Mr. Jones, who seemed to have no fixed abode, was a brother of that Mr. Paul who used to live at Fredericksburg, but who had died in 1773, seems to have aroused no undue curiosity in Virginia in 1775. If they thought about it at all, people doubtless assumed that they were half brothers, sons of the same mother but different fathers; but the chances are that nobody thought about it.

Why should they? Mr. Jones was an affable gentleman, yet showing withal a remarkable propensity for minding his own business, a quality highly valued in all frontier communities. He was said to have been a sea captain, and certainly he could talk familiarly of various corners of the earth and of all sorts of people; which was doubtless one reason why Dr. Read, of Goochland, took such a fancy to him.

Not that there was any accounting for the tastes of John Read, to be sure. He was a good enough doctor, no doubt, but, in the estimation of the country people, rattle-brained. Always gadding about the country, he would take up with anybody whom he found interesting and amusing, high or low. He was a nephew by marriage of Old Man Franklin, up in Pennsylvania, and seemed to have acquired by association some of the old fellow's breezy manners and insatiable curiosity about everything on earth.

The country people would admit, though, that Dr. John in his time had picked up worse than this Jones. He was at least a civil-spoken body and no braggart. In fact, he said so little about himself that people didn't know exactly where he stayed. Some said he lived in Fredericksburg over the tailor shop that had belonged to his brother—or was it his half brother?—that William Paul. Others said he had bought a place up one of the creeks somewhere and was raising tobacco. It was generally understood that he was doing a little trading here and there, especially around Norfolk and down in North Carolina, and he seemed to stand in especially well with the Hewes & Smith outfit at Edenton; but nobody knew much about it.

Still, Dr. Read liked him, and when John Read liked a man he could never do enough for him. For one thing, the fellow was a Freemason, as was the doctor. Indeed, one might emphasize that strongly. It was the opinion of the farmers that if the doctor would pay more attention to his pills and plasters and less to running Masonic affairs everyone would profit. He was then within a few years of becoming Grand Master of Virginia and was extremely enthusiastic about the order. It was quite possible that through some emblem or secret Masonic sign he had first made the acquaintance of Jones.

This was certainly nothing against a man in the Virginia of 1775. The Masons had their critics, to be sure, but the criticisms were not very searching. To the nostrils of the devout there was a slight smell of hell-fire about them, for they included plenty of freethinkers, and there was more than a hint of snobbishness in the way they stuck together. But all the great names of Virginia were carried on their rolls—the Lees, the Byrds, the Randolphs, the Carters, the Jeffersons, the Washingtons all had representatives among the Masons, and the representatives were usually not poor relations, but grandees of the first order. Read certainly took John Paul Jones to lodge meetings, and the sailor's acquaintance spread rapidly among the eminent men of the colony.

Yet perhaps it is not quite accurate to describe him as a sailor at this time, for he was no longer thinking of himself in that character. He thought that he had come ashore definitely to rehabilitate himself as a landsman. It was his purpose to follow William's example, to acquire land and become a freeholder, although he had far loftier schemes in mind than had ever occurred to plodding William. A place among the sturdy yeomanry had no attractions for him; he would become a country gentleman, spending the rest of his life placidly philosophizing on his broad acres.

Taking his pleasures sadly, like a true Scot, John Paul Jones had become passionately addicted to that somewhat dismal poet James Thomson, and habitually carried a copy of *The Seasons* with him wherever he went. In that composition is a line that for some reason beyond the power of rational thought to explain stuck to his mind all his life, to be produced over and over again in the oddest connections. Thomson is describing the existence of the Arcadian philosopher,

> who far from public rage
> Deep in the vale, with a choice few retired,
> Drinks the pure pleasures of the rural life
> In calm contemplation and poetic ease.

The expression "in calm contemplation and poetic ease" rang a bell somewhere within John Paul Jones's intellectual and emotional structure. He could never forget it. In time he came to regard it as the summation of all that his soul yearned for, and for years he would occasionally startle and mayhap embarrass his friends by solemnly intoning it as the expression of his deepest desire.

The truth is, of course, that if one were to search all American history for the man least fit for "calm contemplation and poetic ease" he might reasonably be first choice. Yet to denounce his tag line as fraudulent would be altogether beside the mark. Every vigorous man has moments, especially when he has driven himself, mentally or physically, beyond his limit, when he thinks that he really wishes to be the opposite of what he is.

Besides, and possibly even more to the point, this way of speaking was the fashion of the day. The English-speaking world of the moment was working itself up into the sentimental orgy that was to culminate fifty years later in Byronic romanticism. In Virginia, as well as in England, young men in particular were giving themselves up to voluptuous wallowings in baths of slush such as the modern generation contemplates with stupefaction and total incomprehension. Only a few years earlier as powerful an intellect as that of the young Thomas Jefferson was construct-ing in praise of his "Belinda," his "Bell-in-day," his *campana in die*, his Adnileb—whose real name, by the way, was Becky Bur-well—such turrets, battlements, and towers of pure marshmal-low as Rudel hardly built to the Lady of Tripoli. If Jefferson went so far, imagine the state of lesser minds!

John Paul Jones was never critical of literary and social fash-ions. In such matters he habitually observed, accepted, and went along for the ride. If languishing were the thing to do, he would outlanguish the most languid. On the other hand, if brisker action seemed the logical requirement, he would cheer-fully and promptly punch the nose of a British officer and almost precipitate an international incident. In whatever case might arise he was always willing to oblige; so he was a social success.

The unfortunate Briton was encountered at a dance in Nor-folk one night before the outbreak of hostilities, when a British man-o'-war was lying in the harbor. Being quite evidently very young and very inexperienced, he visited the punch bowl rather more frequently than was expedient; and thereafter was moved to give utterance to certain observations more candid than flat-tering upon the appearance, dress, and demeanor of American ladies. At that Mr. Jones, being within earshot, floored him; this was, of course, a flagrant insult to the British uniform. In the ensuing hubbub Mr. Jones proclaimed the happiness it would give him to afford satisfaction to the prostrate officer at dawn with any weapons the offended party cared to name; and formal arrangements were made on the spot.

At this juncture certain senior officers of the warship took a hand. Their inquiry convinced them that their youthful col-league really had been tight and really had grown offensive. Accordingly they ruled that any stain upon the uniform had been put there by the officer, not by the civilian who knocked him down; and they prohibited a duel.

In the perspective of a century and three quarters it seems to a disinterested observer that John Paul Jones was a little less than fair about this business. Some years afterward he cited it—in the heat of war, to be sure, and at a moment when he was being savagely attacked by the British press—as evidence of the arrogance and insolence of the British service. But all it really proves is that, even in the British service, a young man who takes on more of a load than he can handle is pretty sure to make a fool of himself; which needed no proof.

If it proves anything else, it establishes that the older and wiser British officers could be relied on to take a sensible view of such matters; and that they were not disposed to permit an officer who had behaved badly to claim that his uniform had been insulted when he got the treatment he had been asking for. If it is a deep disgrace to any service to include an occasional indiscreet junior officer, then it may be said at once that all services are equally disgraced, for they all have them; for the rest, the British service actually came out of this business pretty well.

Yet even the young man exalted by alcohol should be viewed somewhat leniently, considering the time and the circumstances. For tension in Virginia was already great and was growing daily, almost hourly. Older and presumably wiser men than young naval officers were losing their heads and hurling charges and countercharges. If a boy got drunk and said what he shouldn't, he did no more than graybeards all around him were doing cold sober. The crash was coming, and all men could see it. The difference between them was that some welcomed it while most dreaded it; but that it was close at hand nobody doubted, which meant that excitement ran high and speech was quite commonly far from judicious. No, the young officer's false step was anything but an outstanding scandal in that place and at that time.

As for John Paul Jones, in the beginning he considered himself involved in the political storm more or less fortuitously. He explained his own purpose at the time quite clearly, and there is no reason to doubt his explanation. "It had been my intention," he said, "from the time of my misfortune to quit the sea service altogether, and, after standing trial, as I had the means, to purchase some small tracts of Land on the Continent, which had been my favorite Country from the age of thirteen, when I first saw it. I had settled my future place of retirement in 'calm contemplation and poetic ease.' "

Yet however high-minded, he was nobody's fool. It was his purpose to return to Tobago and clear his name; but he was keenly aware that the man who goes into court with the best of causes should nevertheless put money in his purse. That twelve hundred pounds lying to his credit there would be very useful, and he made repeated efforts to get hold of it, or of some part, but without success. It was two years before he discovered the reason—Ferguson had absconded, not only with his money, but also with funds belonging to his employer in England. Before the victim had realized what was wrong the political situation was in a turmoil, the customary traffic lanes were disrupted, and a journey from Virginia to Tobago was out of the question. Then he began to be drawn into the current excitement on his own account.

II.

Nor were his interests exclusively confined to business and politics, for it was in this period that romance entered John Paul Jones's life for the first time, or certainly for the first time in a serious way.

The lady was Dorothea Spottswood Dandridge, and she was a charmer. Say this for the man—his loves were light, and he was drawn to women of various types, but never in his life did he love a vapid, commonplace creature simply because she had a pretty face. Dorothea Dandridge, indeed, was considered a beauty, but it is evident that she had more than good looks; she had something of her suitor's own quality in that she was never known to give encouragement to a dull fellow.

For the rest, she was most decidedly a lady of quality in the Virginia sense. Her father, Nathaniel West Dandridge, had held His Majesty's commission in the British navy. The ancestor from whom she took her middle name was the famous Governor Spottswood. Martha Washington was a cousin. She was heiress to a pleasant, if not imposing, fortune and to a social position eclipsed by none in Virginia. Her father's estate lay in Hanover County, near that of his friend and attorney, Patrick Henry.

This was aiming high for a Scotch gardener's son with a shadow on his name, no money that he could lay his hands on, and a dubious future. One wonders how John Paul Jones hoped ever to explain to a veteran of the quarterdeck the embarrassing brevity of his stay in the British navy, not to mention such items as the slave ships and two legal processes involving charges against his conduct as an officer. They were not things that an old navy man was likely to overlook in a prospective son-in-law.

Nevertheless, there seems to have been a time when Read, at least, had an idea that he might make it. If the lady had been utterly cold the sophisticated doctor would not have failed to note it, for he was too much the man of the world to have been fooled on such a point.

The period of its prosperity was brief, however; indeed, it was so fragile a romance, such a ghost of a romance, that one hardly knows how to treat it without exaggerating it out of all proportion to the truth. What blighted it we shall never know. Possibly the spirit of the quarterdeck rose again in Father Nathaniel and he rushed to repel boarders; possibly it was simply that another sail hove in sight; possibly, although this seems unlikely, the pursuer's heart failed him at the last moment and he dared not close and grapple.

At any rate, it all came to nothing. Charming Dorothea unquestionably figures in any adequate life of Paul Jones, but how lightly, how delicately! A whiff of perfume rising from the page, a ripple of teasing laughter, a momentary clicking of high

heels and the flirt of a fan, a lovely face glimpsed only as it van-
ishes—that's Dorothea.

For a great wind roared through the land, driving men and
ships and kingdoms and empires like chaff before it; is it to be
wondered at that a dainty, small romance should be whirled
away? A great voice roared through the land, and statesmen
and generals leaped at its electric shock, while down the long
corridor of the centuries its echoes still reverberate in the ears
of men; is it to be wondered at that one exquisite lady should
be electrified too? "Is life so dear, or peace so sweet, as to be purchased at the price of chains and slavery? Forbid it, Almighty
God!"

When the blast those words set off had passed, Paul Jones
was blown far out to sea, and as for Dorothea—well, she became
Mrs. Patrick Henry.

Sigh for romance, if you will, for he who would deny it the
tribute of a sigh must surely be a hardhearted wretch. Dr. John
Read, sad to say, appears to have been just that, for he viewed
the whole business somewhat jocosely. Writing to Jones in 1778,
he spoke of that project of a Virginia estate, adding, "but some
more agreeable idea will I fear call you off and deprive us of
you. Miss Dandridge is no more, that is, she a few months ago
gave herself into the arms of Governor Henry."

Probably there was a true word spoken in jest. Much as the
suggestion may shock the romantic, it is by no means unbelievable that for Paul Jones there was one "more agreeable idea"
even than the arms of Dorothea, and that was the idea of "a tall
ship, and a star to steer her by." For John Paul Jones to marry
any woman would have been something akin to bigamy. His
true love was the sea, and probably no woman on earth could
have held him back when the sea called.

He never admitted it, perhaps he never realized it, but it was
true. He insisted that Dorothea broke his heart, but what she
actually did for him was give him a lifelong excuse for backing
gracefully out of any entanglement that threatened to become

too confining. Could a woman afford to resent it if her encouragement was declined by a man whose heart was notoriously broken?

Long years afterward the Terror of the Seas was being lionized in a Parisian *salon* when one of the adoring ladies asked, "Chevalier, have you ever been wounded?"

"Never on the sea, mademoiselle," was his answer, "but on land I have been bled by arrows that were never launched by the English."

Charmed by the answer, she promptly pinned a rosette upon his coat. He carried it off, but by right it was a decoration for Dorothea.

III.

But the great wind roared and the great men roared, and presently Paul Jones, along with everything else that was loose, was swept into the vortex, which was Philadelphia. There the Continental Congress sat, laboring at it knew not what, but laboring prodigiously.

In 1776 Philadelphia was a great city. This statement may be challenged by those whose minds are cribb'd, cabin'd, and confined by census reports, seeing that as late as 1780 it numbered no more than thirty thousand souls. But greatness is not statistical. Even in numbers, Philadelphia in 1776 was as large as Athens under Pericles, and relatively to its rivals it was larger, for Athens did not overshadow Sparta as Philadelphia did Boston, New York, and Charleston, its only American challengers.

Certainly it was not another London. The city of London even then had a quarter of a million people, with perhaps three times as many more living in the circle of cities that surrounded it. Philadelphia was nothing like that. In the eyes of British officers fresh from London, it was a sprawling, overgrown village along the banks of the Delaware. It seemed sprawling to them because, by comparison with European cities, it was full of light and air.

Already the city was largely built of brick, but two-story

houses were the rule and the dwellings were usually set apart, with some space around them, frequently a considerable plot of ground protected by a whitewashed picket fence. True, only one or two of the principal streets were cobbled, the others being deep in dust in dry weather and almost bottomless sloughs in wet. Still, Philadelphia considered itself advanced, and not without reason. Even in the outlying districts there were stepping-stones at every corner by which it was possible to cross without going over ankle deep in mud; and the downtown thoroughfares had street lamps, maintained by the municipality, almost as rare a thing among cities then as a tax-supported symphony orchestra is today.

But perhaps the most conspicuous proof of the aggressive and progressive temper of the place was what its more reactionary citizens regarded as its white elephant, the municipal auditorium known today as Independence Hall. It loomed above two-story Philadelphia even more portentously than Faneuil Hall did above Boston, and if it owed to Wren or Palladio or perhaps the Adam brothers a lightness and grace that Faneuil Hall could not match, still it was an extravagance for a town of that size.

The white elephant came in handy, though, when great events were toward. Aside from the fact that the colonials would have to break through a hedge of British bayonets to get into Boston, the size and location of Independence Hall rendered it the obvious place for a gathering of national importance; and Congress gravitated toward it naturally.

To visiting British officers it may have seemed an incomprehensible setting for deliberations concerned with the erection of a nation; and so it would have been had the task in hand been the erection of a nation comparable to the British monarchy. What the visitors overlooked was the fact that the task was quite different. The overgrown village sprawled, no doubt; but for that very reason it let in light and air, as close-built London and Paris did not. So it was appropriate to the creation of a government committed to the principle of the free circulation of ideas, a government open to every wind of doctrine that blew.

Philadelphia regarded itself as sophisticated. Already it was making vigorous efforts to eliminate the circulation of domestic animals, at least of the bulkier type, through the streets. As for hogs and chickens, of course, there didn't seem to be much that one could do about them; but the citizen making his way home even after nine o'clock at night was in relatively little danger of falling over a cow or a mule sleeping in the dark streets.

But Philadelphia had not attained, nor did it ever attain, the degree of sophistication that in London and Paris reduced certain classes of the population almost to the status of domestic animals. Anything that could pass for a man circulated freely in any part of the town. Shaggy trappers from the wilderness beyond Pittsburgh strolled at will through Independence Hall itself, nor was there any section of the town too hallowed to be pressed by the foot of a farmer with the clay of Lancaster County clinging to his cowhide boots, or that of a charcoal burner who supplied the iron furnaces, or of a carpenter or wheelwright or brickmason, or of a sailor from any maritime nation.

It was conspicuously an open town, and not in its physical make-up alone—an open town in which there was being erected a new kind of nation, an open nation, in which men and ideas were to circulate as freely as hogs and chickens did in Philadelphia, much more freely than cows and mules.

Not that anyone fully understood this at the time—on the contrary, the more influential men there present were convinced that nothing sensationally new was projected. They were merely exercising the ancient right of freeborn Britons to protest against misgovernment; or at least that is what they thought in the beginning. So they labored and, having nothing to conceal, cared not at all who looked on.

Everybody was there, because the storm had compelled the thirteen colonies to go into a huddle, something they had successfully avoided doing since John Smith and his companions landed in 1607. Everybody was there, so the presence of one slightly undersized, slightly pug-nosed Scotch sailor more or less was no great matter. Everybody included, of course, Dr. John Read's uncle, and one would suppose that Paul Jones must have had a letter to him; but they seem to have had little to do with each other at this time. It is possible that the sailor stood somewhat in awe of the scandalous old man; plenty of others did. His bright suggestion that perhaps their toil was the labor of Haman, every man building his own gallows, was enough to take the starch out of the humorless. For obvious reasons the humorless never really liked Benjamin Franklin, and there were many of them on hand.

In 1775 and the early part of 1776 the Continental Congress labored more than diligently. It labored frantically. A congregation more frankly terrified probably never has assembled on the continent. They were men who saw the whole fabric of civilization collapsing before their eyes, and there is nothing better designed to affright and dismay.

We do less than justice to the Founding Fathers when we assume that their terror revolved around the peril, the very considerable peril, that as a result of their collective acts they might individually be shot or hanged by the British. This was serious enough, in all conscience, but it was an old, familiar fear that men have had to face since time began. Had that been their only or their principal dread, they would deserve little consideration, for there is no excuse for a man's becoming completely unstrung merely because he is risking his life.

But it is quite possible for grave burgesses, as well as damsels in distress, to confront a fate that is worse than death. This fate is the necessity of doing something unheard of, something without precedent, and the outcome of which cannot be predicted with any sort of assurance. Such was the necessity facing the assembly at Philadelphia, and that, not mere death, was the grisly terror that hung over its members.

This is not a feeble attempt at satire; it is a sober statement of fact. Its truth needs only a moment's consideration to become evident. The members of the Continental Congress were genuinely patriotic, and has anyone, above all anyone of the generation that lived through the years from 1941 to 1945, the hardihood to say that patriotism is only a word? In those years we found men, not among the rare elite, but by millions in every walk of life, who went briskly into battle without being driven, not because they were without fear of the enemy, but because they harbored another fear that was very much greater. This was the fear of seeing their country overwhelmed by the savage and the brute.

It was under this fear that the Continental Congress really quaked. Tyranny already was upon it, but all history taught that the recoil from tyranny drove straight into anarchy. Its task was to find the middle way, which nobody had found yet. That was the unheard-of thing, the thing without precedent and without predictable outcome, which it was called upon to do. Let it fail, and it would have taken the country from under the lash of the king only to put it under the whip of scorpions wielded by some dictator.

Everybody was there, for the crisis had summoned all talents and the roll of that Congress today is a roster of the illustrious such as is rarely to be found in the annals of any country. But not only were the Founding Fathers there; among them also were unbidden presences, not manifest in the flesh, but haunting the mind of every man among them, terrible presences that made a patriot's blood run cold. Let the Congress do the wrong thing, and none doubted that these apparitions would materialize with dreadful speed—Gaius Marius with his bloody ax. Sulla with his rolls of the proscribed, Caesar and Cromwell. Each had been the dreadful outcome of a revolt against tyranny, each in the beginning had claimed to be the herald of the people's rule. In all history no rising of the populace hitherto had ended in anything else; except that sometimes it had been a smaller Marius, a tin-pot Caesar, bringing upon the stricken country ignominy as well as woe.

A Scotch sailor hanging around, seeking an opportunity, and observing all this could hardly fail to gain a pretty clear understanding of the structure of this country. He knew how it was made, for he had been there and seen it in the process of being put together. The herculean labors of the Continental Congress were performed under his eyes. He could hardly have been acquainted with many of the minor details, but he knew exactly why the main struts and trusses were placed where they were. He understood the genius of our government; and on that point he was never mistaken thereafter.

His was the opportunity, too, to observe in action most of the men who were to figure importantly in the history of the country for the next twenty years. He saw them under stress, which is to say he saw them stripped down to their essential natures; and among those who were here at this time he made few mistakes afterward as regards judgment of character.

Of course this is not to be construed as even a suggestion that he fully understood what was going on. Who did? If it comes to that, who does? It is getting close to two hundred years now since this session of the Continental Congress, yet its work is still unfolding and its final flowering remains even for this generation "the substance of things hoped for, the evidence of things not seen." All who sat in that congress, all who, with John Paul Jones, looked on, had been in the grave long years before the world began to suspect how great had been its work.

A city of confusion and dread was Philadelphia as the year 1775 drew toward its close. Divided counsels, contending interests, minds of disparate weight, and hearts not all courageous made the deliberations of the Congress a bedlam from which many good men despaired of seeing any intelligent issue. Yet time was of the essence. Events were moving with torrential speed. Already the north was all aflame; Boston was pinned down by bayonets, and like a swarm of hornets all around it the Continental forces hemmed in the king's men. It was war, declared or not. No matter how the pen might lag, the sword was already drawn, and the counselors were being rushed to a decision under penalty of the execration of all generations of men if they decided wrong.

The great wind roared, and even men of weight and sub-

stance were driven before it. Consider, for example, John
Read's uncle. What was an Industrious Philosopher doing in
this madhouse? Benjamin Franklin's allotted earthly span was
up before this congress was half done. He was already sixty-nine
when its sessions began, time for a man to retire to the chim-
ney corner, time for him to be done with challenges and de-
fiances and the clash of earthly ambitions. That bald dome was
stately enough, but none would ever mistake it for a martial
crest, nor would one look for an eagle eye behind bifocal glasses.
Once, indeed, he had been a powerful man, and he still had
the broad shoulders of the expert swimmer; but his physical
prowess was of the long ago. For years he had been striving manfully to withdraw from public life except as the work of a scientific investigator is always in a sense public life. He wished to
study physical, not political, earthquakes, storms, and electrical
discharges; he had invented the lightning rod, but he knew he
had made only the slightest of approaches to the problems of
electricity. At sixty-nine he had earned the right to work at
what he pleased.

But the great wind swept him along, swept him into the very
vortex. Civilization itself was disintegrating and Pennsylvania
needed him, America needed him, so what did the wishes or
the rights of Benjamin Franklin matter?

As regards most national heroes, the passage of time enhances
their glamour and dims their humanity, but as regards Franklin
the reverse is true. Americans have always loved him for his wit,
his shrewdness, his good humor, and his very impressive intellectual attainments in widely separated fields. At once the first
great national manufacturer of pungent aphorisms, what a later
generation calls "wisecracks," and the first American to gain an
international reputation in scientific circles on the one hand
and in diplomatic circles on the other, he could not fail of popularity.

But his colorful personality, his homely common sense, and
his mental vigor have combined to obscure our perception of
the fact that this same Franklin was among the bravest of the

brave. Beginning at sixty-nine he cheerfully risked the hangman, he risked the hardships and hazards of the sea in the day of sailing vessels, he ran the blockade of the British fleet, he risked betrayal and possible assassination for seven long years. But in addition to this physical courage he exhibited a moral courage that was even higher—as an old man he was brave enough to face up to new conditions and new ideas.

John Paul Jones is the conventional hero, and worthily so, as nobody can deny. He fought intrepidly, skillfully, and successfully against great odds. With poor ships and worse crews he met and defeated the enemy's finest, which is superb. Note well, though, that he was a young man, just coming to the peak of his physical and mental powers. His eye was keen and his hand was steady. He was the best man-at-arms on any of his ships—a competent swordsman, a fine rifleman, and one of the best gunners afloat. One hesitates to claim for him courage any more dashing, dazzling, blinding than belonged to the old baldhead, sick with the stone and feeble with the years, who tottered out to smite the King of England with a lightning rod.

But if American age could not resist the blast of the great wind, youth was spun along as dizzily. When the Congress met there was one delegate nearly two years less than half Franklin's age who was also destined to affect John Paul Jones's career strongly, although we do not know that the two men met at this time. A long, loose-jointed, slab-sided mountaineer from Virginia, with a mop of sandy red hair and a face that not even a mother could have called handsome, he made no wisecracks and told no bawdy stories; he did not even give the impression of extreme busyness, but he got things done. In response to no apparent effort on his part men gravitated toward him, and the last thing they thought of in 1775 was that Thomas Jefferson was only thirty-two.

Perhaps the reason was that he was one of the very few men in the assemblage who were not perturbed. It was not the valor of ignorance; he knew as much about Marius and Sulla, Cromwell and Caesar as any man there, and a great deal more than most. He understood as clearly as any that at least since Alfred's time, and that was a thousand years earlier, Englishmen had found only one political system capable of affording that stability and order essential to civilized living, not to mention political liberty. In the course of that millennium they had tried various expedients, but they had always come back to the only one that had worked reasonably well, to wit, monarchy. Now monarchy was crumbling under their eyes, indeed, had already crumbled to the point at which it was no longer tolerable.

The lanky Virginian knew all this, and yet he was not profoundly disturbed, because to him, and almost to him alone in that gathering, the upheaval was not a reversal but the restoration of the order of nature. He was no soothsayer. He could pierce the veil of the future no further than the next man. But somewhere, somehow he had developed a firm conviction on which his whole policy was based, but which he did not express perfectly until fifty years later, when as he lay dying he paraphrased old Richard Rumbold by declaring his faith in "the palpable truth that the mass of mankind has not been born with saddles on their backs, nor a favored few booted and spurred, ready to ride them legitimately, by the Grace of God."

We forget that up to 1775 this truth had been anything but palpable. What men regarded as the palpable truth, indeed, was the reverse—the mass of mankind always had been saddled and bridled and a favored few always had been booted and spurred to ride. Thus the secret of Jefferson's inner calm was hidden from his contemporaries; but the fact was evident, and in any great tumult the man who is patently tranquil amazes and impresses his fellows. What were years at a time like that? Mr. Jefferson might be only thirty-two or he might be older than Dr. Franklin. That was irrelevant. What was important was that where the others were bewildered, Mr. Jefferson was certain; where the others were apprehensive, Mr. Jefferson was hopeful; where the others, witnessing the collapse of the old order, were horrified, Mr. Jefferson was satisfied; where the others wavered, Mr. Jefferson went straight to his mark.

John Paul Jones could not know it, but as he watched the tranquil mountaineer moving about the crowded floor he was looking on at the first steps in the weaving of the mightiest spell that has ever been cast upon the minds of the American people. For this was the magician who was to exorcise their doubts of their own capacity. Of course, they have held him in memory as a mighty man ever since; for who is greater than a man whose wizardry can make his people believe that they are great themselves?

The spinning vortex in Philadelphia swept them in from the north, too. There were the Adams pair, from Massachusetts —Adams of Braintree, later to be known as "Honest John" and to become familiar with Paul Jones, not altogether to the comfort of either; and Adams of Boston, never to be known as "Honest Sam," but still worth while. No matter how much of a trial he may have been to his creditors, he was a valuable man here, a strident man, hateful to the lethargic, appalling to the fearful, the gadfly, the spur, the certain assurance against things' settling down. Perhaps he was the only simon-pure revolutionist in the group; for he was the sort of man to whom turmoil is the breath of life and tranquillity is but life-in-death. Perhaps he was also, and by the same token, more nearly innocent of any sort of political philosophy than any other.

If Sam was to be named Adams, Honest John should have been called something else, for never were kinsmen more dissimilar. Stumpy, cherubic, and greatly displeased, Mr. Adams moved through the Continental Congress as he moved through life, taking no joy in it, expecting no good of it, but sternly resolved to make the best of a bad matter. With that small but balloon-like figure, he should have been jolly, if rather brainless; whereas he was actually sour and extraordinarily able.

After an eclipse of a hundred years John Adams began to rise again in the estimation of historians, until within this century they have begun to rank him among the half-dozen greatest men in that great congress. But to this day they seldom give him credit for one claim he has upon the sympathy of all posterity.

He was a great sufferer. It was not by reason of wounds or contusions or painful disease that he agonized, but because of the incongruity of his nature and his appearance; for it is the perception of incongruity that stirs risibility.

Had he looked like John Randolph of Roanoke, that walking cadaver, men might have averted their eyes as he passed, mumbling incantations. This would have been far from adulation, but it would have been a tribute of sorts and might have gratified his somber spirit as an attitude appropriate in sinful men toward one whose voice was an echo of the wrath of God. But he didn't. He looked more like Mr. Pickwick, and when Mr. Pickwick took a high and solemn tone a perverse and stiff-necked generation didn't quake. It laughed.

Even after a hundred and fifty years there remains some spice of the comic in the country's memory of "His Rotundity." But a man whose vanity is constantly lacerated is a man in torture. If he is a weak man, the incessant irritation may eventually turn him into a snarling misanthrope, useless for any social purpose. One proof of the essential greatness of John Adams is the fact that the stings he received daily did not prevent him from being one of the most useful men of his generation, one of the most useful the country ever had.

Still, his greatness did not prevent him from always regarding John Paul Jones as a meddling interloper, intent on stealing credit from New England men; so if the sailor never was able to see Honest John as a very great man—well, one can only regret the blindness that great men often show with regard to each other's good qualities.

With the great wind bringing down the ancient fanes about their ears and blowing the dust of every ancient prejudice, every world-old passion into their eyes, it is no wonder that the men of the Continental Congress worked hard, but without knowing too well what they were about. Not all of them by any means were philosophers; probably a majority had but a scraped acquaintance with the theories of the ingenious Mr. Locke and the abstruse M. Montesquieu. Burly John Hancock, for instance, was neither an idealist nor an ideologist, but he had a sharp perception of the advantages of throwing off British restrictions on trade, being in the importing and exporting business himself. The subtle lawyer George Wythe and the scholarly James Wilson may have been fascinated by the legal complexities of the situation, but it was a legal simplicity that brought the fabulously wealthy Mr. Carroll into strange company for the third richest man in America. Mr. Carroll was something of a precisionist, as his signature attests; this was not Charles Carroll of Homewood, or Charles Carroll the Barrister, but Charles Carroll of Carrollton—a distinction important in his native Maryland. Well-dressed, thin-lipped, silent, and a little aloof, Mr. Carroll may have looked a bit icy, but he seethed within. Highly educated, prepared for the bar at the Temple in London, Mr. Carroll could not practice law in the colony founded on the principle of religious toleration because he was a Catholic. Mr. Carroll was rich, and rich men usually adhere to the existing order; but the insolence to his faith set him among the rebels. Taking advantage of the uproar created by Tom Paine and others bawling for the rights of man, he struck a blow for the dignity of Our Lady.

But in the midst of the cross-purposes, the confusion, the obscurity, and the din, work was done. A shape began to emerge, a pattern was slowly imposed upon chaos. For if doubt, fear, and perplexity were there, so also were courage, patriotism, and keen intelligence, and these were ever fine catalysts. The shape took form around an idea and a man. Neither was perceived at first, or, if perceived, only vaguely noted among other ideas and men that seemed as well worth attention. But as the months wore away and events drove on relentlessly, all the others gradually faded into the background and these two stood forth as dominant.

The idea in its final statement was "that all men are created equal, that they are endowed by their Creator with certain unalienable Rights." In the end the Continental Congress proclaimed this to be self-evident, and from it stemmed the whole political structure that became the United States of America. The man was Washington. He was not there in person. He had left the Congress in 1775 to try to beat out the flames in the north; but he dominated the assemblage more completely than did John Hancock, sitting in the president's chair. For he was the one man among the leaders who was facing the ultimate reality of war, and he was facing it with calm confidence. Here was the fixed, immovable man, the massive man who was a rock when others were chaff before the wind.

So the storm-beaten congress, laying firm hold upon a great idea and a great man, came out of its confusion, shook off its bewilderment, and did the work men thought could not be done, defied the terror that had appalled the boldest, achieved the unheard of, created the unprecedented, acted without knowing the outcome. And when it had looked upon the work, it had the manhood to declare to the world that in its support "with a firm reliance on the protection of Divine Providence, we mutually pledge to each other our Lives, our Fortunes, and our sacred Honor."

IV.

The culminating act of the drama was played on July 4, 1776, just two days before John Paul Jones's twenty-ninth birthday, but he was not there to see it. By the time the Declaration of Independence was signed he had already participated in one successful raid on British territory, had fought one British man-o'-war, and had run the British blockade two or three times.

This he had accomplished by assiduous cultivation of two men, one of whom is utterly forgotten and the other rated distinctly below the giants of the Congress, but both of whom were highly important at the time. They were Joseph Hewes and Robert Morris.

Schoolbooks have to cover so much ground in so little time that they are doubtless justified in discarding this pair, but any man who wishes really to understand how things happened in this country will be well advised to study them both; for they represent types very familiar in our political life, not merely at the Revolutionary crisis but throughout. It probably would require no extraordinary discernment to perceive their like in Washington today.

All things considered, Robert Morris has been pretty justly treated by history. He may be described briefly as the patriot who was invariably exonerated by the investigating committee; so history speaks of him with an enthusiasm markedly restrained.

He was a merchant and banker in Philadelphia, having come up as a boy from Oxford, Maryland, where his father had set up in business after bringing the family from Liverpool. Robert was something for which they had no name in his day, but which Wall Street, five generations later, was calling a Wonder Boy. He secured a junior clerkship in the somewhat staid but intensely respectable commission house of Thomas Willing, and within seven years had made it into Willing, Morris & Co. Then for twenty years he put it through a series of financial gyrations that kept Quaker businessmen gasping and blinking. As a financier, Robert Morris had the nerve of D'Artagnan and the luck of the devil; his partners ran a grave risk of death by heart failure, but if they survived they got rich.

From about 1773, when law and order were obviously falling to pieces in all directions and it was increasingly clear that the whole system of government might come down at any minute, American bankers and other capitalists reacted as financiers usually do in similar circumstances. Their knees knocked together, they sweat profusely, and, almost to a man, they ran to buttress the shaking timbers of the old order with any materials on which they could lay hands. Some among them who were strong for liberty and the rights of man, in theory, recanted and turned Tory when law and order began to give way.

But Robert Morris was not the conventional type of financier. He had made a fortune by his ability to descry the profit in what seemed to the others merely a desperate gamble. Here was the biggest gamble of all, and he was not the man to blench.

Long before independence, when revolutionary activities were still indubitably high treason, he was secretly fitting out ships for the Committee of Safety. When war finally emerged into the open, he undertook the financing of the new government.

He did the most magnificent job of his career and one of the best in the history of finance. He worked prodigiously—and he also collected a prodigious profit. He emerged from the war immensely rich, and he would have amassed the most colossal fortune in America except for the thing that usually brings down a successful gambler in the end—the entry of a dark horse. Robert Morris, with all his genius, did not foresee Napoleon. He invested his war profits in western land and would have cleaned up had not the Napoleonic Wars choked off immigration for twenty years. But they did, and he was caught over-extended. He died impoverished.

Nevertheless, although he lost it, he once enjoyed it. He was the patriot who collected his bill; and although repeated investigations never showed that he took anything illegally, America has always felt that for his admittedly great services he was paid off and there is nothing left owing to him.

To this man, as to others influential in Philadelphia, John Paul Jones was recommended by an old acquaintance, the merchant from Edenton. Joseph Hewes had been sent to the Continental Congress on merit, not out of local pride, for he was not a native of North Carolina and had been a resident there certainly less than twenty and perhaps not more than a dozen years. But he had integrity, he had intelligence, he had good sense and good humor, and the state, with rare political sagacity, decided that these things were more important than local birth.

What took Hewes from his native place, Kingston, New Jersey, to Edenton, North Carolina, is not known definitely, but it was probably his interest in the West Indian trade, for which Edenton was a convenient port. At any rate, by the time the great wind began to roar in earnest the firm of Hewes & Smith was well established in the business world and its senior partner even better established in the estimation of the town as a gentleman of high attainments and unimpeachable character.

Here he may have met John Paul in the years before the blank twenty months, but as far as anyone is aware he never said so. He wouldn't. If a friend whom he had known in other days as Paul suddenly showed up as Jones, why, Hewes was the sort of man who would assume that he had a good reason for doing so and say nothing about it. We do know that in 1775 the sailor was treating the merchant as if he were an old friend, but that is not conclusive, for Hewes was the sort of man to whom strangers gave their confidence with remarkable speed.

In any event, when naval warfare began to be seriously considered Hewes was put upon the committee to deal with maritime affairs, and thus he became for the time being the most important man in John Paul Jones's life. It was a contact fortunate for the sailor in more ways than merely in that it opened the way to a commission. It was contact with a man whom it was good to know.

If there was a purer patriot in all the Continental Congress than this Joseph Hewes, he has yet to be brought out of obscurity and exhibited to the public gaze. Although a businessman, he had opposed the Stamp Act. Although an importer and exporter, he had supported the nonimportation movement. Although a gentleman of birth and fortune, he had advocated the rule of the people. Finally, although emotionally a loyalist, when he was outvoted he accepted the decision good-humoredly and thenceforth worked as hard for the common cause as the noisiest antimonarchist.

In the Committee on Maritime Affairs he drew one of the wickedest assignments imaginable, for everything was to be done and nobody was disposed to help except Robert Morris, who was disposed to help anything in which a commission was involved. But Hewes threw himself into it energetically. The bibulous and erratic Stephen Hopkins was chairman, but of small account. Hewes worked steadily twelve hours a day, even though it was a drain upon his physical strength that he was ill prepared to stand. In fact, three years of it finished him. He had to withdraw on account of illness. But there was nobody to take his place. After a few months, being re-elected in spite of his physical condition, he assumed the burden again, returned to Philadelphia, went to work as hard as ever, and in 1779 died there—as certainly a war casualty as Pulaski or De Kalb, but never so acclaimed.

By working in close collaboration with this man through several critical years, John Paul Jones became aware of a facet of American character that few foreign-born people and not too many natives ever see. Hewes was a rarity, but he was not unique. There have always been a few such men scattered through the country—men who have sworn to their own hurt and never changed; men who have voted money out of their own pockets and never filed a claim; men who have done the hard and dirty, but necessary, work and never demanded sympathy; men who at the last have died for their country and never mentioned it.

They are few, but thus far they have been sufficient to refute the argument of political philosophers from Plato to Thomas Hobbes—or to Friedrich Nietzsche, if he was a political philosopher—that democracy must inevitably fail because the masses are incapable of producing men who can and will consistently put the general welfare ahead of their own interest unless they are well paid for it, in acclaim if not in cash. Well, here was one. There have been others like him. There are still others. Their existence is one reason and it may be the main reason why the logic of the philosophers has proved fallacious and the democracy that Hewes helped frame, after the battering of a hundred and seventy years, has not collapsed, but stands stronger than it was when it was brand-new.

It was good for one who was to serve the republic in many tight places to know that. Long after he was dead the memory of Joseph Hewes must have helped keep John Paul Jones from despair more than once when he found himself surrounded by Americans of a very different sort—swindlers, traitors, poltroons, self-seekers, frauds and fakers and plain thieves, all the rout of Gadarene swine that have often dragged America down steep places to dishonor and almost to destruction. They were enough to make a man despair; yet, on the other hand, there was always Joseph Hewes to be considered, and always Captain Jones thrust despair from him and tried again.

The work of the maritime committee must have been hard and tedious in any case, but it was not made less difficult by the colleagues Hewes found given him. Of these the outstanding two were John Adams and Stephen Hopkins, of Rhode Island— as difficult a pair as ever a reasonable man had to handle.

It was not that they lacked ability. On the contrary, Honest John was intellectually of the first order, and while Stephen Hopkins was a smaller man, no one ever denied that he had brains. But they were spiky. No one could come near them without being stung, frequently stung to fury. They were both tremendously energetic, but their energy all too often was directed at pulling to pieces all that the other members, Hewes in chief, had carefully and laboriously put together.

Hopkins was notorious as a stormy petrel before the first Continental Congress assembled. He had been half a governor, or governor of half a state. He assumed the title of Governor of Rhode Island, but there is a good deal of evidence to support the contention that he was in fact governor of Providence only and satrap of Newport. For years he was the leader of one side in a factional quarrel that more than once brushed the edge of civil war, and like all effective factional leaders, he was, or he came to be, a man of violent prejudices. It is rather too extreme to say that he was an eighteenth-century Huey Long, but the Louisianian's notion that the state was an instrumentality created for the use of Huey and his friends was not far from Stephen Hopkins' attitude toward Rhode Island. He held quite completely Long's profound distrust of anyone on the other side, and a taste for revelry surpassing that of the Kingfish.

American naval operations actually began without benefit

of Congress. In August 1775, Washington, operating around Boston, found it desperately necessary to acquire some kind of support by sea, and tried various expedients. The most successful was the work of John Manley, a Marblehead fisherman who did some smart raiding, but whose vessels were too small to take on anything carrying a considerable weight of metal.

Manley was bold, resourceful, and a first-rate seaman, at least for the limited tasks he was able to undertake; and unquestionably he did the first shooting at sea. To this extent, but only to this rather small extent, the claim made in later years that he was the father of the American navy is substantiated; and this should be acknowledged with especial care in a book that gives the greater part of the credit to another.

In Congress it was John Adams who made the motion for the first committee of the sort that we now call the Committee on Naval Affairs; and he was named on it with John Langdon of New Hampshire and Silas Deane of Pennsylvania. A little later he gave way to Christopher Gadsden of South Carolina, but a few months after that, when it was determined really to start something in a big way, Adams went back on the committee, along with Hewes, Hopkins, and Richard Henry Lee of Virginia.

It should be noted, however, that these seven men were more than the Committee on Naval Affairs. They were the whole Navy Department, lock, stock, and barrel; and, as usually happens in committee work, it fell out that most of them were merely riding along. The division of labor eventually resolved itself into Hewes—ably assisted by Robert Morris, not without a reasonable broker's commission—getting the ships, while Hopkins got the men.

The original program was for four ships—a fifth became unexpectedly available later and was snapped up—each of which was to have a captain and three lieutenants. Hopkins' method of getting these men named must have been wonderful, for it actually mellowed John Adams! "The pleasantest part of the labors from 1774 to 1778," he wrote years later, "was in the

Committee on Naval Affairs. Mr. Lee and Mr. Gadsden were
sensible men and very cheerful, but Governor Hopkins of
Rhode Island, about seventy years of age, kept us all alive. . . .
His beverage was Jamaica spirits and water. . . . Hopkins
never drank to excess, but all he drank was not only immediately converted into wit, sense, knowledge and good humor,
but inspired us all with similar qualities."

Ah, what a liquor was that! Wit, sense, knowledge, yes, but
the Jamaica rum that could inspire good humor in John Adams
must have been the mightiest Jamaica distilled since that island rose from the sea.

Could reasonable men quarrel with the selections of such a
host? They didn't—or not much or for long. Only Robert Morris did, but he screamed. Perhaps he hadn't been invited to
dinner, or perhaps he drank brandy, or perhaps he wasn't a
reasonable man.

Yet the original list was one to startle a Pennsylvanian, or
almost anyone in modern times. As first submitted, it read: for
commander in chief, Esek Hopkins, brother of Stephen; for
ranking captain, Dudley Saltonstall, brother-in-law of Deane
and relative of John Adams; for second captain, Abraham
Whipple, cousin of Stephen Hopkins; for third captain, John B.
Hopkins, nephew of Stephen and son of the Commodore; and
for fourth captain, one Hazard, who must have been an accident, for he seems to have been kin to nobody. This was the list
of the chairman of the committee, the technical, although not
the actual, head of the United States Navy. Except for its gender
it ranks with the achievement of that later sea lord who extorted
tribute to

> His sisters and his cousins, whom he reckons
>   up by dozens,
> And his aunts!

The committee passed it, but when Robert Morris saw it he
went into a spinning, howling war dance that would have astonished Prince Igor. What shocked him was not the nepotism;

what harrowed his soul was the fact that he had worked like a dog with Hewes getting the ships, yet there was no *quid pro quo* for Pennsylvania. Four of these officers were from Rhode Island and the other from Connecticut. An agent who is an agent by nature as well as training when deprived of what he regards as his just commission is as terrible as an army with banners; it soon became clear to Hopkins that Morris had to be appeased or he would inevitably upset the applecart. So Hazard was temporarily chucked overboard and it was agreed that Pennsylvania should have the third captain. Morris, mollified, then named Nicholas Biddle, who turned out to be one of the best naval officers serving in the Revolution.

Hardly, however, had Hopkins subdued this trouble than the woods took fire behind him. Suddenly the mild, the innocuous, and the hitherto unnoticed Mr. Hewes blew up; and if an agent whose commission is withheld is a fearsome object, the wrath of a patient man is also dreadful to behold. Hopkins had to deal with this rebellion, too.

Mr. Hewes, it appeared, had thus far gone along quietly because he understood there was a gentlemen's agreement that since Virginia had already taken the army, it was but just that New England should have the navy. However, if that principle were to be abrogated in favor of Pennsylvania, then by the Sacred Sands of Currituck he swore that North Carolina should have representation too, and in defense of that principle he was ready to fight, bleed, and die all over the floor of the Continental Congress.

One wonders if Mr. Hewes was not just a trifle disingenuous in this. In the first place, Virginia had not actually taken the army. In New England itself, for instance, Washington had already found both Benedict Arnold, to his subsequent sorrow, and Nathanael Greene, to his great comfort. But it was indubitably true that Virginia, as the largest of the colonies, had been throwing her weight around considerably; and perhaps Mr. Hewes, as a representative of the third largest, had no great objection to seeing her reminded that there were others. It is also certain that he very much wanted to name one captain but had seen no opportunity to do so, up to this point; his indignant championship of North Carolina, therefore, is a little suspect. There is a suggestion of the synthetic in his wrath.

But it was fiery enough to appall Hopkins and set him to thinking fast. After a long struggle, although he wouldn't give up another captain, he agreed that Mr. Hewes should be permitted to name the ranking first lieutenant; and Mr. Hewes promptly named John P. Jones.

At first they thought it was some sort of joke. They suspected the Tarheel of trying to secure a blank commission, something resembling a "John Doe warrant," which an officer takes out when he is not quite sure whom he is going to arrest, but which he can use on anybody. They didn't believe there was any John P. Jones, but on Hewes's solemn assurance that the man existed, they let it go.

So the first roster of the officers of the United States Navy appeared bearing the name of Lieutenant John P. Jones of North Carolina. Did a great sea fighter ever begin his career under auspices more bizarre? He landed his commission, not on merit, but on political blackmail, but there he was, and in part he was authentic. Lieutenant John P. Jones of North Carolina wasn't Jones and wasn't of North Carolina, but all the subsequent history of naval warfare attests that he certainly was a lieutenant —and what a lieutenant!

CHAPTER IV.

I.

"I HOISTED with my own hands the flag of freedom the first time it was displayed on board the *Alfred* in the Delaware."

So wrote Paul Jones, to the vast indignation of Honest John. He was equally perturbed over Barry's claim that the first British flag was struck to him. "It is not decent or just," snorted John Adams in 1813, "that those emigrants, foreigners of the South, should falsely arrogate to themselves merit that belongs to New England sailors, officers and men."

What Adams had in mind was that Jones's flag-raising took place on December 3, 1775, while Manley and another New Englander, Broughton, had been to sea before that, and Manley, at least, had captured some British trading vessels. But their ships flew either the flags of the colonies to which they belonged or the Pinetree or Rattlesnake flag, neither of which was ever formally adopted as a national ensign by the Continental Congress.

The flag that Jones ran up at the command of Commodore Hopkins—for Captain Dudley Saltonstall, "that sleepy gentleman," as Jones characterized him, had not troubled to come down for the ceremony—was the emblem of the Congress and not of any individual colony; but it was not the Stars and Stripes. The colonies had not yet denied their allegiance to the British Crown; on the contrary, they were still proclaiming it with a vehemence that seemed to increase in direct ratio to the increasing doubtfulness of the claim. What they had denied was their subjection to the British Parliament. They raised no objection to being British; but they did object to being bondmen, and this flag was the emblem of their objection. It would seem, therefore, that Paul Jones showed a nice discrimination in his choice of words—it was not the flag of the United States that went up at Esek Hopkins' word, but it was the flag of freedom. More than that, this was the first occasion on which it was displayed over armed forces by land or sea, for Washington up at Boston did not receive the one they sent to him until nearly a month later, and flew it for the first time on January 2, 1776.

The surviving descriptions of this flag are none too exact, but we do know that the canton carried not stars, but the saltired cross of Great Britain; but whether the field was white with six red stripes or red with six white stripes is disputed. In any event, the effect was of thirteen stripes, alternately white and red. The whole device was the old flag, the Union Jack, imposed upon a striped field. The solemnity of the occasion is attested by the fact that the commander of the squadron uttered the command, and no petty officer but the first lieutenant himself handled the ropes when the flag was hoisted for the first time.

There is a tradition that the first naval squadron that was distinctly and formally American, as contrasted with Virginian or Pennsylvanian or New Englander put to sea under the Rattlesnake. So indeed it did, in a way, but not as its national emblem. That was the personal flag of the squadron's commander, hoisted on the flagship when he came aboard. It had been sent to Commodore Hopkins by Christopher Gadsden shortly before the squadron sailed; the device was a coiled serpent with the motto "Don't Tread on Me."

But although the flag went up with proper ceremonial on December 3, 1775, it was reflected only in the waters of the Delaware River for a long time thereafter. Congress and the country were exceedingly anxious to have it at sea, but to get Esek Hopkins in motion was a task beyond the ability of both Congress and country.

II.

In the Book of Genesis, twenty-sixth chapter, twentieth verse, it is recorded that "the herdmen of Gerar did strive with Isaac's herdmen, saying, The water is ours: and he called the name of the well Esek; because they strove with him."

Esek, the Well of Strife, was no inappropriate name for the first American admiral,* for he was productive of strife in abundant measure. In the end he was cashiered, for good and sufficient reasons, and generations of schoolboys, if they heard his name at all, were taught that he was about the most incompetent officer in the history of naval warfare.

But that was never the opinion of John Paul Jones, who was there, who was the best possible judge, and who quarreled violently with Hopkins and so was not likely to be tender with his reputation. Jones's opinion of Hopkins as a man was blistering; but as an officer he considered him not so bad—a bleak tribute, to be sure, but an improvement on what less qualified critics have said.

The fact is that poor Esek was facing a situation with which only genius could have coped successfully, and he was emphatically no genius. His appointment, practically dictated by his brother, was scandalous, but on account of the relationship, not because Esek was conspicuously worse qualified than other possible choices.

He was not only a good seaman, but he had had experience in naval warfare. During the French and Indian War he had commanded a privateer with notable success; and, as a matter of fact, in the eighteenth century every deep-water captain had to know the rudiments of gunnery and fighting tactics as a matter of protection against the swarming pirates. In these matters Hopkins was probably better than average, and as captain of a

---

* The title formally conferred upon Hopkins in the Congressional resolution of December 22, 1775, appointing him and the other officers, is "Commander in Chief of the fleet," and he is usually referred to in letters and reports as "Commodore," but as the highest ranking officer in the Navy he was certainly the equivalent of an admiral, so the modern title is used here.

single ship, a frigate or possibly a ship of the line, he might have made a good or even a distinguished record.

But a flag officer is not a captain. If Paul Jones did not know it before, he was to learn it now at most uncomfortably close quarters. One of the striking things about this man's career was the terrific effectiveness of the methods by which he was educated. He learned everything the hard way. An understanding of the qualities of a ship's officer he had burned into him as with a hot iron at Tobago. An understanding of the essential structure of the American government he gained by watching it being painfully put together even as the old order was falling down. Now he was to learn the immensely important difference between a captain and a flag officer by watching a good captain but a bad flag officer making one blunder after another, each of which came shudderingly close to landing John Paul Jones, among others, either in a military prison or at the bottom of the sea—if not, indeed, at a rope's end on Execution Dock, where they hanged pirates in London. What a man learns under such circumstances doesn't pass out of his mind the next day; it stays with him.

Esek Hopkins was fifty-seven at the time of his appointment, which in modern times is no unreasonable age for a man to reach flag rank, to say nothing of being Commander of the Battle Fleet, Chief of Naval Operations, and all the bureau chiefs rolled into one. Yet the impression he made upon all beholders at Philadelphia was one of extraordinary antiquity. Lorenz quotes a newspaper correspondent, evidently meaning to be friendly, as calling him "a most experienced and venerable sea-captain," and General Knox, aide-de-camp to Washington, was even more explicit: "He brought to my mind Van Tromp, the famous Dutch Admiral. Although antiquated in figure, he is shrewd and sensible. I, who you think only a little enthusiastic, should have taken him for an angel, only he swore now and then."

Well, there is something for the record. The United States Navy can safely defy any other service in existence to show that it first put to sea commanded by a venerable and cussing angel.

But the Venerable Angel had a completely hellish job in getting to sea at all. The flag was hoisted on December 3, but before the fleet could get down to the mouth of the river the ice caught it and it was frozen in for six weeks.

It was not all Hopkins' fault, by any means. Nobody knew how to do anything. Least of all did the honorable members of Congress know how to back up an officer struggling with the problems of personnel, equipment, and supplies. Had they been aware of their ignorance it would not have been so bad. But they were not aware of it at all. On the contrary, they were bursting with bright ideas, which they promptly enacted into legislation, frequently without consulting the Commander of the Fleet, or disregarding his advice when they did consult him. And frequently these bright ideas were like so many grenades tossed down his hatches.

For one thing, there was the matter of letters of marque and reprisal. Congressmen had a great fancy for issuing these documents, which converted any ship into a privateer. Congressmen argued that one of the objects of naval warfare was the destruction of enemy shipping, and how get it destroyed faster than by making it profitable for all mariners to join in the destruction?

Congressmen overlooked the fact that whatever a privateer seized belonged to her owners and her ship's company. A successful cruise might result in so many prizes that even an ordinary seaman's share would be more than the salary of the Commander in Chief of the Fleet for a year—which was $1,500. A naval vessel, on the other hand, when she took a prize had to hand over two thirds of its value to the government. Furthermore, she could take prizes only in her odd moments, so to speak. Her business was to fight. She cruised, not where the rich prizes were thickest, but where the hard-hitting enemy men-o'-war were thickest. Her company could expect more blows than booty.

Then Congress insisted on calling loudly for men to serve on privateers as a patriotic duty. If a sailor were offered two ways in which he could do his patriotic duty, one with the possibility of getting rich attached, the other with a much greater possibility of getting shot attached, who could blame the sailor for choosing the former? In any event, they did it, and not even the opportunity to serve under a venerable angel could persuade them to do otherwise.

Thus it is not surprising to learn that it took Hopkins an interminable time to fill his ships' complements. Even when he had secured a man his troubles were not over, for there remained the problem of holding him. Privateers did not hesitate to raid the fleet if they could secure experienced mariners in that way. There is a grim note on this in John Paul Jones's journal. While the ships were frozen in at Reedy Island, he says, he "and the other lieutenants stood the deck, watch and watch, night and day, to prevent desertion; and they lost no man from the *Alfred.*" The implication, supported by independent testimony, is that the other ships lost plenty.

Supplies, also, were slow in arriving—not merely ordinary ship's stores, but such essentials as rigging and armament. Esek Hopkins learned a great deal about the rascality of contractors during these weeks, and the fleet learned how hard it is to have a top officer who doesn't know how to throw the fear of the Lord into ship chandlers.

The delay was the more exasperating because a little to the south of Delaware Bay, just within the Virginia capes, there was a fleet operating under command of one of the minor misfortunes of the British empire, John Murray, Lord Dunmore. Murray was a belted earl, but he was also one of the prize jackasses of all history. He had been given the governorship of Virginia, largest, richest, and most conservative of all the thirteen American colonies, the one that should have been the chief support of the Crown against the subversive element in Massachusetts; but by a policy so devoid of intelligence that it would be flattery to call it half-witted he had converted Virginia into a roaring furnace of rebellion.

Dunmore was an almost perfect specimen of the worst type of British administrator, the man who holds all humanity beyond his native island in unconcealed contempt. It is possible that he might have conceded that an Englishman, as long as he remained in England, was a free man with rights that the king himself was bound to respect; but he made no concession to any other race, and not even to an Englishman who had the bad taste to proceed beyond the seas. He perceived no difference at all between a colonist and a Kaffir; he was incapable of realizing that in Virginia he was not dealing with naked savages ignorant of the art of warfare, but with transplanted Englishmen who could shoot straight and who had been hardened by frontier life until they were twice as tough as Dunmore, or any parcel of cutthroats he might dredge up from the slums of London.

His culminating folly was to steal nearly the whole of the colony's supply of gunpowder and remove it to a warship. Then, with the enraged populace upon him, he had one flash of common sense—he suddenly realized that unless he moved and moved fast his life would last just as long as it took the mob to reach a tree and knot a rope. He made the ship just a jump ahead of the posse, but he made it.

But his sanity was only momentary. Once his personal safety was assured he reverted to his fantasy that he was dealing with wild tribes hardly semicivilized. He undertook to deal with them by the method used on the Ivory Coast—he would stand in with his ships, shell the natives off the beach, drive them into the bush, and then land a few marines to burn their kraals. For months, now, he had actually been trying to bring Englishmen to heel by such tactics!

Certain furious lines in the Declaration of Independence, formally accusing George III, were really inspired by Dunmore:

"He has abdicated Government here by declaring us out of his Protection and waging war against us.

"He has plundered our seas, ravished our Coasts, burned our towns, and destroyed the lives of our people."

All those months while Esek, the Well of Strife, was striving to get started, while Lieutenant Jones walked a policeman's beat to see that such sailors as they had didn't get away, Dunmore was shooting up Virginia towns that lay within range of Hampton Roads, achieving his greatest triumph by laying Norfolk in ashes. As to relations with the mother country, this incredible fool was doing more damage every day than Pitt, Burke, Fox, Sheridan, and all the rest in London could repair in a month.

Yet the fleet stuck in the Delaware. By the time they had the absolutely necessary stores and enough men aboard to work the ships, the ice had them. It was not until February 17, 1776, that the squadron cleared Cape Henlopen and at last stood out to sea.

Once in deep water, Hopkins was presented with alternative objectives. The desirability of doing something about Dunmore was obvious; but the shortage of munitions, especially gunpowder, was acute in the colonies, and information had come through that the British were assembling enormous supplies of all kinds in the West Indies, where they were very lightly guarded. Hopkins determined to let his lordship go for the moment while the squadron made a try for the gunpowder. Accordingly, he ran south.

Later he was to be denounced for this, but not by people who understood the situation. It was a perfectly legitimate decision, probably a wise one. Dunmore at worst was a mere annoyance, although Virginians skipping nimbly out of the way of his round shot could hardly be expected to view him so lightly; while total exhaustion of the gunpowder supply would be a calamity. The squadron commander is not justly to be criticized for his choice.

But if his plan was unexceptionable, his execution of it left much to be desired. In the first place, he came careering down upon New Providence in broad day, when it would have been simple to slip in by night and take the place by surprise. As it was, the defenders had ample time to man the shore batteries and prepare to give the raiders an extremely warm reception long before Hopkins was within range. By the time he arrived it was patently out of the question to force the passage in front of Fort Nassau.

At the ensuing council of war Hopkins was for proceeding around to the southern side of the island and trying a landing there. Jones argued that as there was no anchorage there and the landing party would have to march across the breadth of the island, it would be better to slip into the lower end of Hanover Sound, seize a small outwork there named Fort Montague, and take Fort Nassau from the rear by a march of not more than three or four miles.

Hopkins objected that he did not dare bring his heavy ships up close enough to cover the landing with effective fire because the sound was notoriously full of fanged reefs and it would take skillful piloting to move safely through them. Some days previously he had captured a pair of local pilots, but he didn't trust them far enough to risk the *Alfred* in Hanover Sound under their guidance. Lieutenant Jones thereupon offered to con the ship himself from the fighting top, if the Commander would permit him to take one of the pilots there. From that height it was possible even for one unfamiliar with the locality to judge shoals pretty well.

This was a characteristic Paul Jones scheme—unconventional, daring, yet based on common sense. The Venerable Angel accepted it, but then he added a characteristic Hopkins idea, based on anything but common sense. He took the entire squadron around, leaving not so much as a rowboat to block the main entrance to Nassau Harbor.

At the other end of the sound Jones mounted to the fighting top with the pilot and instructed him to take her through. It would be a document of intense human interest if we had a record of the mental and emotional state of this man during the next half hour. It was a tricky bit of piloting in any circumstances; a very slight error of judgment could pile the ship on reefs that came uncomfortably close on both sides. But no error of judgment was permissible here. He had only to look at the man crowded close to him in the narrow area of the fighting top to know that.

We have the testimony not of one witness, but of all without exception who saw him in such circumstances that when things got really tight, John Paul Jones was a man transformed. He never was commonplace, but when all was serene he was inconspicuous—not tall, neither strikingly handsome nor startlingly ugly, not loud, not aggressive, he might easily have been overlooked among the guests at a placid dinner party, or even on a ship sailing with a fair wind on a smooth sea. But let an emergency arise, let peril appear suddenly so near and so formidable that only the lightning-like seizure of a desperate chance could win through to safety, and he was no longer inconspicuous, he was dominant. Even his stature seemed to increase as danger mounted, until in deadly crises men would have sworn that he was not five feet seven but more nearly seven feet five, and they forgot that he had any features save jaw and eyes. The jaw, thrust forward menacingly, seemed no longer flesh and bone, but the solid granite of the Caledonian hills. The blue eyes no longer suggested the azure tint of heaven, but the blue blaze of flaming brimstone.

It was an aspect that was soon to become familiar, not merely to all ranks in the American navy, but to Englishmen and Frenchmen, to Dutchmen, Spaniards, Turks, and Russians, and it impressed them all. But the first to see it was this shivering West Indian pilot. High above the deck in the fighting top, alone with John Paul Jones at a moment of crisis, the poor fellow was most literally and exactly between the devil and the deep blue sea. In that situation a man must make no mistake. He made none, and the *Alfred* slid gently to her appointed spot without so much as scraping off a barnacle.

Once the great guns were brought to bear, little Fort Montague had no chance at all. Most of its garrison, in fact, had been called to Fort Nassau at the first alarm. Then, under the protection of the ships' fire, there was staged the first of a series of assaults that were to extend through all the seven seas and down through the centuries, until this sort of fighting was to become almost as characteristic of American military history as the phalanx was of Macedonia or the legions of Rome—the amphibious assault by bluejackets and marines. Fifty sailors under Lieutenant Weaver and two hundred marines under Captain Nicholas had already been loaded into small boats. Now they dashed to the beach, leaped ashore, and swept briskly into Fort Montague.

Resistance was so completely paralyzed that not a shot was fired at the landing and hardly any effort made to prevent seizure of the fort. But Nicholas rather dimmed the brilliance of the operation by sitting down. To be sure, night was falling, but Weaver was well acquainted with the island and quite capable of guiding a column to Nassau. Nicholas should have pushed ahead, for Fort Montague was not the prize; the hundred and ninety barrels of powder at Nassau were the prize, along with what ordnance might be lying about.

Still, if the Captain of Marines erred at all it was certainly not any gross error. The next morning he drove forward vigorously enough and halfway to Nassau was met by a delegation from the town offering to surrender at discretion. But when the Americans entered the place they learned what it means to underestimate a bold and resourceful foe. Montfort Browne, the governor, had realized immediately that he was overwhelmed, and his one thought was to prevent the powder from falling into the hands of the raiders. He found a reckless sea captain, William Chambers by name, who assumed the appalling risk of running a ship loaded with gunpowder through the American fleet, and during the night they loaded a hundred and sixty-two barrels, all Chambers' craft could take, with which the daredevil stood out to sea. But as it turned out, he was running no risk at all. Hopkins had not thought of leaving even one of the brigantines to block the passage, so Chambers went serenely and sedately on his way, without even a challenge, to deliver the powder to the British authorities at St. Augustine.

If Hopkins had thought a little more, or if Nicholas had moved a little faster, the success would have been complete. Chief responsibility, however, lies upon the Commander; if his plans had been better, his subordinate's delay would have mattered not at all, and it is the business of a commander to plan so well that slight errors of judgment on the part of inferior officers will be covered.

Nevertheless, in spite of these factors, the operation as a whole must be regarded as a success. As it was, the Americans got twenty-four barrels of powder, seventy-one badly needed cannon, fifteen brass mortars, and an assortment of odds and ends of military supplies. They also carried off Governor Browne and several other dignitaries as hostages until they could get safely away.

Indeed, if the landing party had carried off no other object than the Governor himself, the operation would have been justified for its psychological effect. The spectacle of a British governor yanked off his own island and carried away captive in defiance of the British navy shattered the illusion that Britannia ruled the waves. It was so cruel a blow to British prestige that authority refused to accept it and made poor Browne a scapegoat. George Germain, the semi-imbecile whom sardonic fate had made Great Britain's Colonial Secretary, denounced the luckless governor. "There can be little doubt from the whole behaviour of the inhabitants of the Bahamas," he wrote furiously to Browne, "that the rebels were invited to undertake the enterprise."

So they were, in a way, but not by the people of the Bahamas. The admiralty had invited them. The policy of wasting swift cruisers on such idiotic enterprises as Dunmore's, while vital points of supply were left unprotected, was a virtual invitation to any bold and enterprising enemy. But with Germain, who had been formally adjudged by a court-martial "unfit to serve in any military capacity whatsoever," running the war, what was to be expected?

However, after the New Providence affair there was a hasty

scrambling to rearrange the program of naval operations. Frigates were recalled from bootless punitive expeditions and put to guarding important points. The British navy realized that it had a war on its hands, not a trifling insurrection; so it is possible that the Venerable Angel did more to relieve Virginia in the Bahamas than he could ever have done in Chesapeake Bay.

Nor is there the slightest doubt that a considerable share of the credit belongs to Lieutenant Jones. It was not his show. He was a subordinate throughout, but a first-rate subordinate. His advice in the council of war and his seamanship in taking the *Alfred* into Hanover Sound had both been excellent. He had proved himself, in other words, as a strategist and a tactician; let him now prove himself as an actual man-at-arms and he would be an all-round officer of the first quality.

But in this operation he also demonstrated his possession of another quality, which is not always granted him. He had also proved that he was capable of being a good subordinate. This was not his strongest point. He was at his best when he held an independent command, and naturally that is what he preferred. But he was not the sort of erratic lone wolf that simply cannot work with other people. If necessary, he could take orders even from an officer whom he did not greatly respect. Already he was realizing that as an admiral the Well of Strife was a pretty bad joke; but he served him faithfully while under his command.

As a sea fighter the lone wolf may be a genius—witness Richard Grenville and John Barry—but he isn't a naval officer of the first quality. The genuine, top-flight naval officer, like the top-flight soldier, is a man with a profound understanding of the value of the organization. The naval officer, especially, must always keep in mind that the battle is an incidental episode in the course of the operation; and that the operation that succeeds without a battle is better than the most brilliant victory that costs ships and men. Therefore it is of high importance for the man at the top to have and to retain the ability to accept and obey an order as promptly as the smartest young ensign in the fleet.

To the civilian it may seem worthless to labor the point that one of the men most influential in designing the American navy was a promptly obedient subordinate before he became a brilliant commander; but recent events have shown the incalculable value of this quality in the American service.

In October 1944 one of the mightiest armadas in naval history, including more than six hundred ships, carrying a vast army escorted by two battle fleets, was moving across the Pacific to a different destination when the astonishing information came that the island of Leyte, in the Philippines, instead of bristling with defenses, was lying wide open to attack. An order flashed from Washington, and within twenty-four hours the whole incomprehensibly ponderous machine had been diverted at right angles to its course and was moving toward one of the most brilliant successes of the war. This was possible only because men who wore five stars, men all of them near and some of them past the normal age of retirement, men accustomed to command hundreds of ships and hundreds of thousands of men, had retained the ability to snap into obedience at the word of command with the speed and precision of young cadets.

To put it in general terms, the capacity for subordination lends flexibility to the high command; and no student of the history of war doubts either the great value or the rarity of flexibility.

It is not unimportant, therefore, to stress the fact that John Paul Jones, while he preferred to command, knew how to obey. It was one of the elements of his greatness.

III.

The orders Congress gave the Venerable Angel before he left the Delaware were certainly among the tallest ever received by a champion sallying out to battle. He was to run down to the Chesapeake Bay, sink Dunmore's fleet, then proceed along the coast, knocking out such blockading frigates as might be hanging off the various ports, bear southeast to the West Indies and clean up all military stores collected there, and, finally, "Having completed your business in the Carolinas, you are without delay to proceed northward directly to Rhode Island, and attack, take and destroy all the enemy's naval force you may find there."

All they asked of him was that he take his five converted merchantmen and abolish the British navy!

However, Congress admitted that it was always open to reason. Notwithstanding "these particular orders," it conceded, "if bad winds or stormy weather, or any unforeseen accident or disaster disable you to do so, you are then to follow such courses as your best judgment shall suggest." The possibility that the British might interfere somewhat with this program was not even considered.

The amazing thing is how close the squadron commander came to achieving his colossal task. He did not sink any of the blockading frigates hanging along the coast, but his blow at New Providence snatched many of them off their stations and sent them scuttling to protect exposed points in the West Indies, whereupon swarms of ships dashed into the Carolina ports. The blockade was, if not lifted, so thinned as to become far less effective.

Nor did he overlook the interesting angle of prizes. British shipping was thick around the West Indies, and Hopkins sent a constant stream of captured vessels to the prize ports. This added another distracting duty to the labors of the British frigates. Their efforts to afford some protection to their own shipping weakened the blockade still further. Altogether, if the King's navy was not abolished, yet its weight upon the neck of the colonies was lessened appreciably.

But when the squadron moved north, it was getting into a far more dangerous trouble zone. Here the bulk of British naval strength in American waters was concentrated to protect troop movements; and since February it had been commanded, not by any Dunmore or Germain, but by Richard, Earl Howe, known below decks as "Black Dick," who had proved himself the worst sort of bad medicine for anything and everything that had faced him on the sea.

True, Lord Howe was handicapped, both personally and professionally. Personally, his heart was not in this job, for he didn't blame the Americans for revolting against the sort of government George III and Lord North were giving them. Professionally, he was loaded down by having Lord Sandwich as First Lord of the Admiralty and Lord Sackville as Colonial Secretary. This meant that he had Jemmy Twitcher issuing his supplies, which was a guarantee that the supplies would be short in quantity and bad in quality; and he had George Germain issuing his orders, which was a guarantee that the orders would be idiotic. No admiral could do himself justice under such conditions.

Nevertheless, he was Black Dick, and no sailor afloat, of any nation, but would have preferred to face Apollyon. As a boy he had seen the *Burford* all but shot to pieces around him at the attack on La Guayra; as a youth he had fought the Jacobites in the sloop *Baltimore*, and they said a French privateer had bounced a round shot off his head without doing him any permanent damage; as a rising young officer he had fought the Spaniards off Havana in the *Cornwall;* as captain of the sixty-gun *Dunkirk* he had fought and captured the French *Alcide,* which carried sixty-four guns; and finally, as captain of the *Magnanime,* he had led Hawke's line-of-battle ships at the magnificent victory of Quiberon. Here was an admiral who was no makeshift, but the realest of real things.

More than that, Jemmy Twitcher and thieving contractors notwithstanding, he had assembled in the waters around Rhode Island ships with guns enough to blow the Venerable Angel right out of the water and back into heaven, with hardly an effort.

And the Continental Congress had ordered Esek Hopkins to step right up and whip this fellow—"attack, take and destroy" Black Dick, whom all the navies of the world, at one time or another, had attempted to attack, take and destroy, but only to their lasting grief. All things considered, it is to the American's credit that he ventured within five hundred miles of this formidable adversary. But he did. Following his orders exactly, he made for Narragansett Bay, and off Block Island he had the luck to run into one of Howe's frigates detached from the rest of the fleet.

She was the *Glasgow*, carrying only twenty guns, but a fine new ship, well found and well manned, far beyond anything in the American fleet. In the darkness—the encounter occurred at one o'clock in the morning—Hopkins did not know exactly what he was facing. The terrible Lord Howe, as a matter of fact, was far, far away—perhaps ashore somewhere, trying to negotiate peace with his friend Benjamin Franklin, certainly nowhere in the vicinity of Block Island; but nobody on the American ships knew that. The *Glasgow* actually was carrying dispatches to southern ports and was quite alone; but a sizable squadron under Captain Wallace was lying in Newport Harbor, close by.

Nevertheless, the little *Cabot*, nearest American ship to the *Glasgow*, let go with a broadside and was promptly mauled so badly that she had to sheer away, unfortunately getting in the way of the *Andrew Doria*, which Nicholas Biddle was bringing up at all speed. But Dudley Saltonstall for once was not too drowsy, perhaps because this was one occasion on which the "antiquated figure" was swearing more than a little. He brought the *Alfred* within easy range and Lieutenant Jones, commanding the main battery on the gun deck, let the *Glasgow* have it.

Things looked bad for the Briton. Biddle, getting clear of the *Cabot*, was bringing the *Andrew Doria* into position to add the weight of his broadside, and Whipple, in the *Columbus*, whose twenty-eight guns carried a punch almost equal to the *Alfred*'s thirty, after stumbling over his own feet for a while, had things at last in hand and was swooping in. But at that moment a lucky shot from the *Glasgow* carried away the *Alfred*'s wheel block and ropes. Instantly she became unmanageable, and the *Glasgow* pounced. Before spare tackle could be rigged the American ship had been raked—that is to say, the enemy ship fired down the length of her deck—two or three times. Raking, in the days of sail, was fearful business, because a shot traveling down the length of the deck had many times as many chances of hitting a man as one flying across from side to side.

Worse still, the *Alfred*, lunging about out of control, all but crashed into the *Andrew Doria*. Biddle had to tack suddenly, thereby, of course, losing the range and his chance to land an effective blow.

Worst of all, Lieutenant Jones, down below earnestly working on the *Glasgow* with special attention to her spars and rigging, suddenly found his guns pointing at empty sea. There were no revolving turrets in those days. Cannon mounted on clumsy carriages pointed through open gun ports. They could be swiveled slightly to right or left, raised or depressed slightly; but in the main the gunner's chance of finding a target ahead of his sights depended on the helmsman up above. If he could bring the ship broadside on to the opponent, the gunner got a shot; not otherwise. Of course, when the steering gear was shot away, the helmsman was helpless and the gunner even more so. Lieutenant Jones and his gun crews could only stand and swear until others had repaired the steering gear and slowly brought the ship around again.

But the *Columbus* was coming in shooting. Far away, Hazard, in the *Providence*, had lost his head completely. He was merely wasting ammunition, popping away at a range too great for his shot to do any damage. But Whipple, in the *Columbus*, looked dangerous. His first broadsides were high and wild, but he was getting closer and the *Glasgow* had had enough. By the time the *Alfred* was under control again she was legging it for Newport, signaling wildly to Wallace's squadron for help. But Jones had brought his guns to bear again and was giving it to her heavily, and the *Columbus*, although too slow for the British ship, was hanging on grimly. Jones's hope was to get one of the masts, which would certainly have ended the fight, for speed was now the Briton's only hope. The clerk in charge of her dispatches, foreseeing capture, weighted the mailbag and heaved it overboard.

But at half past six that morning the vision of Admiral Howe became too much for the Venerable Angel. He could see three of Wallace's ships working their way out of Newport. He knew the British had mounted heavy shore batteries near the harbor entrance and he did not know at what moment he might come within their range. So he gave the signal to abandon the chase, came about, and made for New London. It was the end of the first cruise of the American navy.

IV.

And now poor Esek Hopkins learned about the gratitude of republics and had reason to believe that his parents had had a moment of prophetic insight when they gave him his bitter name. For now the Well of Strife fairly overflowed and washed his creditable record quite out of the memories of men.

The escape of the *Glasgow* ruined everything. The public could think, or chose to think, of nothing else. The truth is, she had escaped by a fluke. The shot that carried away the *Alfred's* steering gear was what did it, and that shot perhaps could not have been repeated in a hundred trials. Yet the fact remained that a British frigate of twenty guns had run squarely into an American squadron carrying a total of ninety guns and had come away. All Esek's explanations were countered with a single interjection, a "Bah!" that resounded from Massachusetts Bay to Georgia.

Yet it wasn't a battle that the British were anxious to repeat, or even to emphasize. All the higher officers were aware that the *Glasgow* had played the fool; she had been on a course that would have taken her well clear of the Americans, and she had deliberately veered from that course in order to investigate. She saw plainly enough that there were five sail present, but in her arrogance she assumed that one of His Majesty's ships ought to be able to take on five rebels.

She learned better. The whole fleet learned better, and for the rest of the war no British vessel ever tried that trick again.

The *Glasgow* really received a terrible mauling. There was no great exaggeration in the report of the enthusiastic war correspondent of the *Constitutional Gazette,* of New York, who was ashore near Newport when tremendous cannonading at sea just before dawn attracted attention; the correspondent wrote, "These things caused much speculation, but in a few hours the mystery was somewhat cleared up, for away came the poor *Glasgow*, under all the sail she could set, yelping from the mouths of her cannon like a broken legged dog, as a signal of her being sadly wounded. And though she settled away, and handed most of her sails just before she came into the harbor, it was plainly perceived by the holes she had in those standing, and by the hanging of her yards, that she had been treated in a very rough manner."

The state of the ship's rigging, had the correspondent but known it, was the sign manual of John P. Jones, Esq. Lieutenant Jones had no overweening respect for British tacticians, but he had an immense respect for British dockyards and ordnance makers. British hulls were built to absorb punishment, and British ships went into battle expecting to take it. Their method of fighting was to lay alongside the enemy and slug it out, battering him to pieces with broadsides and sending him to the bottom. Their guns were heavy enough to do it, and their sides were stout enough to take a terrific beating without caving in.

Whenever he met a British ship, therefore, Jones in the beginning of the fight went for the rigging. First kill the enemy's speed, was his theory, and then you might lie off and rake him at your pleasure, or choose your own point for coming in and boarding. His object always was not to sink but to capture the enemy vessel. In view of his position it was a sensible policy, but it may have been part of his nature, too. His position was that of an officer in a fleet that was desperately in need of ships. The British were in no great want of additional hulls, and it was hardly worth their while to take the trouble to run a battered and captured enemy into port. They might as well sink him and be rid of him. But to the Americans a capture was twice as great a victory as a sinking, for they needed the ships.

This unquestionably influenced John Paul Jones's policy as a raider; but it may have been the easier for him to bear in mind because he was born a Scot and warships cost money, a great deal of money. To send one to the bottom when it might be salvaged doubtless went against the grain, which was another reason for shooting at the rigging.

That he put his characteristic mark upon the *Glasgow* is attested by an American seaman, a certain Captain David Hawley, who was a prisoner aboard the British ship during the action and who took a careful look at her afterward. He reported, "The *Glasgow* was considerably damaged in her hull"—the *Columbus* may have done that—"had ten shot through her mainmast, fifty-two through her mizzen staysail, one hundred and ten through her mainsail, and eighty-eight through her foresail; had her spars carried away, and her rigging cut to pieces." That alone is strong evidence that John Paul Jones had been there; and it is also good and sufficient reason why lone British ships thereafter never ran recklessly into American squadrons.

Nevertheless, the *Glasgow* got away, admittedly because the American commander did not care to risk running into a stronger enemy force. Esek Hopkins was an eighteenth-century Jellicoe; but the criticism that followed the battle of Jutland was almost a eulogy by comparison with the storm of abuse touched off by the battle off Block Island.

It was too violent, but it was not altogether without foundation. Esek was not as bad as he was painted, but he was not very good, either. To abandon the chase when he did was prudent, certainly prudent enough, perhaps too prudent; but it did not justify his being denounced as a poltroon, if not worse, who should be instantly kicked out of the service. Not that the New Englander was the kind to shrink from controversy—on the contrary, he had two of his captains court-martialed: Whipple, of the *Columbus*, for his failure to come up faster, and Hazard, of the *Providence*, for cowardice in not coming up at all. Whipple proved that his offense at most was nothing worse than fumbling seamanship and was acquitted; but Hazard was found guilty and booted out of the Navy. Hopkins thereupon demonstrated beyond question his opinion of his first lieutenant by appointing Jones to command the *Providence* with the rank of captain. It was a promotion made on merit and made by the officer in best position to know what he was doing.

This should be noted carefully. It was, of course, a temporary promotion made on the authority of the squadron commander only, dated May 10, 1776, and giving the right to command the one ship specified and no other. But every navy in the world regards a promotion of this sort made by a commanding officer on active service on the basis of the promoted officer's proved ability in battle, as a very strong recommendation indeed. When the next vacancy occurs in the regular list, an officer so promoted should be passed over only if there is available another even better qualified. Since John Paul Jones was already the ranking lieutenant in the service, this promotion confirmed his position at the head of the list beyond any question. This should be remembered in view of what was to come.

Hopkins continued to give occasion for controversy. After a short stay at New London, the squadron slipped along the coast into Narragansett Bay and Howe promptly clapped the lid on. Off the mouth of the bay he posted a patrol force of cruisers that Hopkins dared not tackle, and for month after month the American navy was out of the war.

Naturally, the public criticism rose in a tremendous crescendo, and eventually Hopkins began to reply in kind. The privateers were getting all his men. Congress, immeasurably liberal with denunciation, was parsimonious with supplies. The courts-martial had filled the service with suspicion and bitterness. Even Jones, although nobody was attacking him specifically, turned sour and began to have delusions of persecution. He wrote a long letter to Joseph Hewes, explaining in elaborate detail what everybody knew, namely, that he was on the gun deck throughout the action, had no authority whatever over either the helm or the sails, and could not even see where the other ships were, let alone make tactical decisions.

Even fifteen years later he was sensitive on the subject. In an account of his career drawn up for the King of France, and written in the third person, he repeats that "as he had no direction whatever, either of the general disposition of the squadron, or the sails and helm of the *Alfred*, he can stand charged with no part of the disgrace of that night."

This illustrates the one definitely unpleasant characteristic of the man. He nursed grievances. He could magnify a passing slight until it took on the proportions of a monstrous insult. As he had never forgiven honest William Craik for being embarrassed by finding his protégé indicted for murder, so now he could not forgive the public for lumping all the squadron's officers together in a general derision. Of course, it wasn't just; but a man who expects to be treated with perfect justice in this world, and who is aggrieved when he isn't, is poorly equipped to play any part in public life. John Paul Jones was humorless, and it caused him great suffering. It also caused his friends great boredom.

But although the Commander in Chief of the Fleet dared not stick his nose out of Narragansett Bay, he did not hesitate to send Captain Jones out in the little, twelve-gun *Providence*. The first job was to return a detachment of soldiers Washington had sent from New York during the excitement over the first British raids. Loaded with troops, Paul Jones slipped out of the bay deftly. The British man-o'-war *Cerberus* was hanging around the entrance and made a dash for the *Providence*, but she was a lively sailer and the Briton could do no more than splash a few shots around her from extreme range.

The next mission was to slip up to Boston and convoy a number of ships loaded with coal thence to Philadelphia, but first he had to run a sloop laden with cannon into New York and to convoy back a number of vessels bound for Newport. On the return trip he had a brisk time with the *Cerberus* again; but since the Briton went for him, and not for the convoy, he was able to draw the enemy away from the merchantmen and then elude him.

Arrived at Boston, he found that the agent, as usual, had been slow in delivering the coal, and had to wait an interminable time before the convoy was ready. Coming down toward the Delaware he all but ran straight into the arms of Black Dick himself, who was at the moment assembling off Sandy Hook the mighty fleet that was to support his brother William's army in the assault on New York. Some elements of the fleet actually came in sight, but Jones was nimble enough to skip around them with his coal, which he delivered at Philadelphia August 1, 1776.

Something interesting happened during the next few days, but exactly what we shall never know, for those concerned chose to leave no record of it. It is a safe assumption, however, that the Captain, being in port, made a courtesy call on his personal friends, no doubt including Robert Morris, who was now on the maritime committee, and Joseph Hewes. It is equally safe to assume that he now told them in detail of his late adventures, for he had already kept them both fairly well posted by letter. Nor is it stretching credulity to assume that they were interested and impressed, for it was a record of smart work. What would be more natural, then, than for these two powerful members to join forces to see that proper recognition of this officer's services should be made?

All Jones says is that on August 8, 1776, he received his commission as captain in the United States Navy, signed by John Hancock as President of Congress. This was a general commission, not of the Continental Congress, but of the United States, giving the holder permanent rank and the right to command any United States ship to which he might be assigned. It did not, however, determine his rating among the captains. Congress had provided by statute that seniority should be determined, not by the dates of commissions, but by a special board appointed for the purpose. However, it was a commission that Esek Hopkins could not revoke—a commission, not an appointment.

Moreover, he was not ordered back to rejoin the squadron immediately. Morris unquestionably sounded him out on his ideas about the conduct of the naval war and perhaps determined on a test to see whether this captain's ideas were really as good in practice as they were logical in presentation. It was plain that nothing was to be expected of Esek Hopkins, for he was too busy battling with Congress to fight the British. In any event, the *Providence* was simply detached from Hopkins' command, apparently without anyone's troubling even to notify him, and ordered to sea under the authority of the maritime committee itself for a cruise in whatever direction her commander might choose to take.

V.

This was the first great moment of John Paul Jones's career. True, mid-August was very late in the season for commerce raiding, but what of that? At last he had an independent command, he was on his own, he could not be hampered by a doddering old incompetent of superior rank, he did not have to struggle with a lot of half-witted convoy captains, he did not have to be always on the alert lest an unreliable consort run afoul of him at a critical moment, he did not even have to make a given port on a given date on pain of being yanked up on the carpet by some irascible shore authority. With the whole Atlantic for his field of operations, at last he had a chance really to show what he could do.

His exuberant spirits are manifest in the dizziness of the campaign that followed within the next six weeks. As he had feared, mercantile traffic was thinning out rapidly as the summer waned. The first four ships turned out to be French, Spanish, and Danish, all homeward bound and not legitimate prize. He could not even obtain any useful information from them.

But if there were few British merchantmen about, there were

any number of warships, some of them heavy stuff, too. It must be remembered that, even in those days, to call a twelve-gun sloop a man-o'-war was ridiculous; by comparison with a first-class frigate, not to mention a line-of-battle ship, the *Providence* was a cockleshell, a bit of fluff to be brushed aside without serious effort. But when Paul Jones had run down as far as the latitude of Bermuda without finding anything but empty sea, and the aforesaid neutrals, he encountered a convoy under escort of the twenty-gun frigate *Solebay*. The correct procedure for a thoroughly sober, prudent officer was obvious; it was to stand not upon the order of his going, but to get out of that dangerous neighborhood as fast as the *Providence* and Providence would let him. Today, though, John Paul Jones was not entirely sober. It was not alcohol that exhilarated him, but the far headier wine of unlimited opportunity. Instead of instantly showing his heels, he charged straight in and fired on the *Solebay*, whipping away again before she could bring more than her bow guns to bear.

Perhaps sheer astonishment paralyzed the Briton for a moment, for the *Providence* slid away without a scratch; but then the wrathful foe went for her in earnest. However, she was by that time a small, dancing target, almost out of range, and all the Englishman did was waste a lot of ammunition. Without doubt, though, he talked about it when he got into port, and seafaring men took note and wondered.

The next day a prize was captured, the brigantine *Britannia*, and the day after another, the *Sea Nymph*. Paul Jones began to work northward, and a few days later picked up something really worth having, the brigantine *Favourite*, from Antigua for Liverpool, loaded with sugar. All these he sent in with letters to the maritime committee. The cruise was now beginning to be interesting, but his supplies of wood and water were running uncomfortably short. It would soon be necessary to touch somewhere.

But why run for Charleston or Norfolk merely to pick up wood and water? There was a spot where he could load both and at the same time annoy the British, doing them no military damage, perhaps, but pulling them off balance, irritating them, and adding to the area that their hard-driven frigates must patrol. This was the northern region where the fishing fleet in late summer prepared its catch for transportation to the home market. The fishermen had certain rendezvous on those lonely, rocky shores where they salted and dried the fish before packing them in barrels to take home; in September it should be easy to catch them at that work.

He did. In mid-September he burst like a bombshell upon the coast of Nova Scotia. On the nineteenth he ran in between Sable Island and the mainland and hove to so that the crew might do a little fishing, when suddenly around a point a mile or two away the British frigate *Milford* hove in sight, convoying a merchantman. Jones had plenty of time to get away, but he was still in high spirits—perhaps more so than ever, since he had sent in three prizes and already justified the cruise. Instead of running, he merely hoisted enough sail to get under way and engaged in one of the most curious actions recorded in naval warfare.

It must be borne in mind that the *Milford* far outclassed him. Let her once get within effective striking distance and that would be the end of the *Providence*, for a single well-placed broadside from the frigate could smash her. It was not even a duel between retiarius and secutor, for the light-armed gladiator had at least a trident with which he might dispatch his entangled foe, while the *Providence* had no chance to do anything more than tease her opponent.

But this she did for eight mortal hours, keeping always just within extreme range of the *Milford*'s big guns where it was possible for a lucky hit to stop her, thus inciting the Briton to keep blazing away frantically. "Finding I had the advantage," wrote Jones complacently, "I shortened sail to give him a wild goose chase and tempt him to throw away powder and shot."

After a full working day of this the Englishman lost his head altogether; when "he rounded to, to give his broadside" at more

than "twice the proper distance," Jones decided that it was no
longer amusing. Just to give it an artistic finish, when the broadside roared and the shot fell halfway between the two ships, he
had his marine officer stand by the rail, level a musket, and
solemnly pop at the warship. Then the *Providence* crowded on
sail and went away from there.

This wasn't war, this was mere persiflage, explicable only on
the theory that the American commander was feeling so good
that he couldn't resist the temptation to thumb his nose at an
enemy too big to whip. Yet, considering the general situation,
it may have had a strategic value not immediately apparent. It
must be remembered that the British up to this time were
utterly contemptuous of their opponents as war-makers. A good
many Englishmen thought and did not hesitate to say that the
colonists were politically and morally in the right; but practically nobody in England believed for a moment that they were
formidable from the military standpoint. Most Englishmen
thought that they lacked not only ships and guns but the will to
use them against the Mistress of the Seas. They might prey
upon unarmed merchantmen, yes, but any real show of British
sea power would send them scuttling for home. Nor is it to be
denied that experience thus far had justified the belief; the
Venerable Angel had scooted for his hole fast enough when Wallace came in sight with three ships during the Block Island fight.

Therefore the British were plunging ahead wide-open. Aside
from putting their frigates to running down privateers, they
worried little about communications, but concentrated on moving transports and sealing up harbors with blockading squadrons. Suddenly this complacency was jolted by the discovery
that there was a madman loose, who was not only snatching
prizes from under the very noses of the Navy, but was actually
going out of his way for no other purpose than to insult and
taunt first-class British ships, and he was so agile that they could
not touch him! They were not yet worried, but they were astonished and exasperated. Even thus early they must have begun to
wonder if their current naval policy was altogether wise; and to

make the enemy even slightly uncertain of his own plans is a strategic accomplishment exceedingly well worth while. The affair with the *Milford* was not altogether a joke; Black Dick could not have been amused at all.

But it was on the morning of the twenty-second that the bomb exploded. That day the *Providence* slid into Canso Harbor at the other end of Nova Scotia. There she found three English fishing vessels, which she seized; and there she took on the necessary wood and water. But Jones learned that the main fishing fleet was at Madame Island, across the bay, so he made for that place. Here he discovered no less than twelve craft and three hundred men, peacefully engaged in preparing the catch.

The surprise was complete. To this day Madame is no winter resort, and in the eighteenth century it must have been one of the bleakest, most desolate spots on earth. The horrified fishermen saw themselves condemned to spend the winter on that naked, storm-beaten rock unless the raider chose to be merciful, so Paul Jones struck a bargain with them. Most of the vessels were unrigged and he had not men enough to rig them swiftly; he therefore proposed to the three hundred fishermen that if they would rig nine of them in jigtime he would leave two schooners and a brig to carry them to their homes, mostly on the island of Jersey. Otherwise he would burn all twelve and leave the fishermen on Madame. They went to it with a will, but a furious storm wrecked two of the vessels and damaged another beyond repair. Still, Jones left the three he had promised, and after burning all the shore installations sailed away with an astonishing fleet.

But that put an end to the cruise. It was overwhelmed by its own success, for Jones by now had so many prizes that he had barely men enough to sail them and none to fight. There was a splendid opportunity to raid shipping in Louisburg Harbor, but he simply did not have force enough to manage it; so he turned toward Rhode Island, where he arrived six weeks and five days out from the Delaware capes.

How Robert Morris must have whooped with delight and

congratulated himself on his own shrewdness in picking this man to send to sea! Eight British ships burned or sunk and eight others brought in captive, a total of sixteen prizes in six weeks —it was colossal! The Canso fisheries destroyed and the whole British fishing industry thrown into a state of nervous apprehension. The haughty British navy filled with fury and chagrin by successive stings. It was more than colossal! Once more the Philadelphia gambler had played a hunch and won magnificently. More than that, he had found a sailor whose audacity passed his own, but who was yet a shrewd, canny man. From that time on Morris backed John Paul Jones to the limit.

Even the Well of Strife had to admit that it was pretty good, and Esek needed something good to show the country. He was now beginning to feel the retribution that usually overtakes a political admiral, for his political fences in Philadelphia were collapsing. The turnover in the Continental Congress was astonishing, what with deaths, resignations, and defeats. New men were popping up whom Stephen Hopkins could not handle.

Other political officers were shoving in, too. In the early days the Continental navy had looked too much like a suicide squad for gentlemen who valued their own skins to be much interested in it. But the United States Navy now began to look much more like a good thing, and the political boys began to scramble for commissions. Not a few of them had a fancy for Esek Hopkins' job, and they worked assiduously to build fires behind him.

It was not hard to do, for he presented an absurd picture, holed up in Narragansett Bay, with Howe grimly sitting on the lid. Yet it was not sheer poltroonery, as the political captains who wanted his job were saying. In large part it was due to the insane policy of Congress in making the privateer service as attractive as possible and the regular navy as odious as possible. Esek simply couldn't keep enough men to work his ships properly, let alone fight them, especially against such an antagonist as Richard, Earl Howe. Nor was he getting proper supplies. They sent him cannon too short for the bore, they sent him gunpowder that was practically fireproof, they sent him sailcloth that to the sailor's jaundiced eye looked more like mosquito netting. And with it all, time after time they sent him thundering orders to get out of there instantly and wipe Black Dick off the sea.

No wonder the harassed man on the spot began to snap back at Congress. It was bad business, of course; in fact, it was insubordination. But it was natural, and considering the immaturity of the service, it was perhaps inevitable. Therefore it must have been quite a relief to Esek when one of his officers, and one whom he had himself singled out for promotion, came in laden with prizes and covered with glory.

Captain Jones reported, however, that there was more work to be done in the region he had just left. There were other fisheries on Cape Breton Island still untouched. There was Louisburg Harbor still to be raided. Above all, it was reported that there were a hundred or more American citizens being held to slave labor—the Germans didn't invent that device after 1939—in the island's coal mines. A return trip was clearly indicated.

It suited Esek. Another spectacular raid would show the country that the Navy really was doing something, and perhaps would take the politicians off his neck, at least for a time. Yes, Captain Jones could return, by all means; but this time he must take something better than the coconut hull in which he had been sailing. What could he have? Why, anything. Take the flagship itself, take the *Alfred*. The *Providence* and the *Hampden*, a bit larger—fourteen guns—could go along as consorts to do the leg work, but the *Alfred*, with twenty-eight guns, could do something more than pop musket shots at any British frigate encountered. So Captain Jones was duly transferred from command of the *Providence* to command of the *Alfred* and proceeded to take over.

But the generosity of the Commodore was a Barmecide feast. When Jones went aboard his new ship, he found that she had 30 men, her full complement being 235. As for the *Hampden*, she had not a man. Indeed, she had less, for she was under the command of an incompetent, cowardly, and mutinous object named

Hacker whom it would be derogatory to the human race to call a man.

Although for many months Hopkins had been excusing his inaction on the ground that he could not get men in competition with the privateers, or had them enticed away as soon as he got them, somehow in that same place John Paul Jones got 110 within five days. He got his final orders on October 22, 1776; on October 27 he attempted to sail and the *Alfred* had a crew of 140. The time was growing so desperately short—he had to beat the ice to Cape Breton Island—that he decided to leave the *Providence,* transferring her crew to Hacker on the *Hampden;* but before they were clear of the harbor that officer demonstrated his quality as a seaman by running his ship on a reef and knocking off her keel.

Jones was fairly beside himself with rage, but there was nothing to do but turn back. He seems to have relieved his feelings in a letter to Hopkins demanding at least a half-competent navigator, and was promptly slapped down with an order to transfer Captain Hacker to the *Providence* and carry out his previous orders. He obeyed, but Esek Hopkins had made a mortal enemy at a time when he could ill afford to make new enemies.

On November 2 they got to sea at last, Hacker actually managing to sail around the islands, instead of trying to climb over them. But this time Jones was in anything but a buoyant mood. So much time had been wasted! The insolence and crookedness of the privateers, half of whose crews were deserters, as the captains well knew, the nasty temper of the bumbling old Commodore, the crass incompetence of the dimwit who was his junior officer—Jones had not yet discovered Hacker's worse qualities—had driven him into a silent, white-lipped rage.

Then as luck would have it, in Tarpawling Cove, off Nantucket, he stumbled upon one of those very privateers, the *Eagle,* commanded by one Field. His fury to get north was suddenly checked by his equal fury against the privateering gentry; he stopped, sent an officer to examine the *Eagle,* and sure enough, discovered four deserters aboard, so carefully concealed that it was necessary to break down a bulkhead to get at them—conclusive evidence that Captain Field knew perfectly well what they were. Jones bundled the four back on the *Alfred,* and then, to make the lesson stick, he lined up twenty of Field's own men and took them along. But then he erred. He proceeded on his way when he should have remained a few minutes longer in order to hang Field from his own yardarm for aiding deserters to escape. He had law enough; but he chose not to apply it.

As it was, he had lost too much time for his main purpose. When he arrived at Cape Breton Island the harbors were already choked with ice and there was no chance of releasing the poor devils in the coal mines. However, his time was not altogether lost. He wrecked the fisheries, burned a large tanker and the warehouses ashore, and picked up odds and ends of prizes, including a formidable letter of marque from Liverpool of sixteen guns. Perhaps the incident most soothing to his pride, though, was running into a convoy under the protection of the frigate *Flora* and cutting out four of its ships under cover of a fog, apparently without being perceived by the guardian.

A few days earlier Jones had made what was perhaps the most important single capture of his career. It was the *Mellish,* a large ship and a valuable prize in herself, the more notable in that she carried, in addition to her crew, a full company of British infantry, officers and men, who fell prisoners of war; but the great thing was her cargo, the main item of which was ten thousand heavy winter uniforms destined for Burgoyne's army. At this moment Washington was just finishing his grueling retreat across New Jersey and his army was in want of everything, but especially of warm clothing, so this was a prize indeed.

Jones had already sent in his first important capture, the *Active,* and in so doing has left vivid proof of how well he was served by the people under his command. In every deep-water port there was an official prize agent, who attended to the sale of prizes, collected and held the money for the captors, and received a commission for so doing. Jones ordered the prize master he put aboard to take the *Active* to Edenton, where Robert Smith, of Hewes & Smith, was prize agent. "I am happy in this opportunity of acknowledging the great obligation I owe to Mr. Hewes," he wrote Smith. But did the prize master obey orders? He did not. He took the *Active* into Dartmouth, where his own cousin was prize master. The Revolution resembled every other war in that it was a heaven-sent opportunity for grafters and scoundrels of all types.

Besides the *Active*, Jones now had on his hands the *Mellish* and five other prizes, and he was alone. As they had approached Cape Breton the weather had grown steadily nastier, with high seas and driving sleet day after day, and Captain Hacker got cold. Some of his sailors presented a round robin. They wanted to go back. As these were men many of whom had served cheerfully enough in the *Providence* with Jones in command, suspicion arises that the round robin may have been encouraged, if not instigated, by the Captain. He actually took the thing to Jones, and got for his pains a tongue-lashing that should have warmed him properly, had he been a man. But he was not; he was the true incarnation of John Randolph's "nameless, squat and noisome animal," for under cover of night he turned tail and deserted. Jones never saw him again.

It was too bad about the slaves in the coal mines, but the *Alfred* could do no more. Undermanned from the start, she now had six prizes, one of them extremely valuable, she was on a hostile and stormy coast in midwinter, and she was a long, long way from home with supplies running low. To linger would have been suicide, so Jones started for the nearest United States port, Boston.

Then a few days later the enemy he had insulted so outrageously, the frigate *Milford*, stumbled on him. Jones wasn't interested in fighting now. His one thought was to get that precious convoy home, above all those uniforms that Washington needed so badly. The *Milford* was sighted astern near the close of the short winter day. She was overhauling the convoy steadily, but

Jones saw that she would not come within range until after nightfall. Therefore the *Alfred* and the Liverpool letter of marque, in which he had placed Lieutenant Saunders, dropped back between the prizes and the frigate, and Jones signaled all other prize masters to douse their lights and hold their course, no matter what happened. He informed them that he might be signaling later, but they were to disregard his signals and hold their course, at all costs. It was so unusual for his orders to be obeyed that he must have been in despair, but it was all he could do.

He then hoisted a light to his masthead and held the course himself until night fell. As darkness came on he saw that the prize masters had obeyed orders at least to the extent of extinguishing all lights, for he could see nothing of them. The *Milford* when last seen was still far out of range. The *Alfred* continued to hold the course until midnight, then she and the letter of marque tacked, hoping the Briton would follow the masthead light. When it faded at last in the light of a cold dawn, Jones scanned the horizon anxiously. There was the *Milford*, getting close now; there was the letter of marque, exactly where she belonged; and there was nothing else in sight.

Vastly relieved, Jones now considered the possibility of a fight, but shorthanded as he was, he did not wish to take on too much, and as the *Milford* was coming bow-on he could not make out what she carried. Since the letter of marque was faster than either of the other ships, he signaled Saunders to drop back, determine the number of the frigate's guns, and signal him the information. While the lieutenant was doing so, a maneuver of the *Milford* disclosed her side to Jones, and the depressing number of gun ports he saw convinced him that to fight would be idiotic. Accordingly, he signaled Saunders to clear out immediately and prepared to do so himself; but to his astonishment and chagrin, the letter of marque bore straight down on the *Milford*, ran under her lee, and surrendered! Jones never knew what had happened, but rather than think Saunders had turned traitor he preferred to believe that the crew had mutinied and overpowered him.

In any event, the thing was done, so the *Alfred* crowded on sail and got away from there. In mid-December she dropped anchor in Boston Harbor with two days' water and provisions left. Here Jones learned that for once every prize master had obeyed orders exactly and that every prize had come safely to a United States port, the *Mellish* included. "This news reached the army," he wrote later, "in the critical minute before General Washington recrossed the Delaware and turned the tables upon the enemy."

The United States learned, too, in that critical minute, that it had at least two competent commanders, one by land and one by sea.

VI.

So Captain John Paul Jones was relieved of his command.

If the reader blinks and reads that sentence again, it is no wonder, for even yet it is hard to believe that anything so supremely idiotic could have been done by the nation that eventually won the war.

Yet it is the fact. It is on record, attested by official documents of whose authenticity there can be no doubt. John Paul Jones was kicked off the *Alfred* and the ship was turned over to some nincompoop that nobody had even heard of before and whose name would be utterly forgotten today except that, like the fly forever preserved in amber, by some accident he got into a place where he had no business to be.

It is a long, involved, and dismal story, showing up the American government and the American people in the worst possible light; yet there may be a certain profit in recalling it, because it shows that we have been infected from the very beginning with all the evils of democracy that Plato held must prove fatal. More than that, we have had every democratic disease in a virulent form; yet we have survived. We can certainly take no pride in the story of how John Paul Jones was treated by the United States of America, but we may be able to extract a degree of comfort from the reflection that if that sort of thing did not destroy us, we ought to be able to survive the pests that infest the country today.

While the Captain was on the high seas, fighting and raiding the enemy, on shore the Well of Strife began, not merely to overflow, but to spout like a geyser, drowning all common sense. Esek Hopkins may have been extremely pacific toward the British, but his war with Congress rose to tremendous heights and was mounting in fury every day. By the time the *Alfred* reached Boston, Hopkins had become the complete Ishmaelite, hating the human race, practically without exception. Jones had a hundred and fifty prisoners aboard, and when he asked what to do with them he was told snappishly to keep them.

At this he flared up, for the memory of the Hacker business still rankled, and the correspondence between the two officers grew heated to the point of scandal. It would be fatuous to pretend that Jones was altogether blameless in this business. He was still a young man, just turned thirty, and brilliantly successful. He was more than a little bumptious and arrogant in his exchanges with Hopkins; in truth, he came shockingly close to flat insubordination. There was always a streak of cockiness in his make-up, and it came out blatantly at this period.

But it is not to be denied that he had provocation enough to try the patience of a saint. For one thing, the privateer Field, far from being devoutly thankful to have escaped having his neck broken in a hangman's noose, had the impudence to sue Jones for ten thousand pounds. In removing those men from the *Eagle* the Captain was acting under orders, so if anyone were to be sued, it should have been the man who issued the orders, to wit, Hopkins. But when the papers were issued, Hopkins, instead of standing by his junior officer, quibbled and evaded, ducking his own responsibility. The courts threw the case out with a nonsuit, but now contempt was added to Jones's indignation against his commander.

In the meantime Jones, fuming at being made what he termed "a jail-keeper," nevertheless tried to improve the time by holding long conferences with brother officers in an effort to draw up a reasonable set of regulations for governing the Navy. It came to nothing, for these men had neither authority nor backing; but without doubt these discussions sharpened and clarified Jones's thinking on the subject, as appeared soon after.

Then, to cap the climax, up popped an individual named Hinman, with a commission as captain and orders to relieve Captain Jones of command of the *Alfred*. This blew the lid off. Hopkins sardonically offered him command once more of the little sloop *Providence,* but Jones posted to Philadelphia to find out what had happened.

Plenty had. So much had happened that it would take volumes to tell it all, but it may be summed up in the statement that the great Continental Congress had gone to pot. It had lost an appalling number of its best men and they had been replaced by peanut politicians. Franklin and John Adams were both abroad. So was Deane. Jefferson was down in Virginia, busy abolishing entails and the Established Church. Hewes, a sick man, had refused re-election. Some had died. Many others, including some of the ablest, were in the Army.

They had been replaced by a crew so nondescript that one can see some justice in the description of them attributed to the embittered Hopkins: "a pack of damned rascals, the best of them mere lawyers' clerks, who know nothing of their business." The Naval Affairs Committee had been replaced by a marine committee of thirteen, one from each state; and with Deane, Hewes, and Adams all missing, the committee had become principally Robert Morris and Hancock, chairman *ex officio*. But Morris was the whole Treasury Department, too, and Hancock was President of Congress, so they could not keep a very close eye on naval affairs.

Contracts had been let for thirteen new frigates, ranging up to thirty-two guns, which meant thirteen captains. For some strange reason the notion prevailed that the member for the state in which each ship was built ought to have the naming of the captain. None was built in North Carolina, and Hewes was absent anyhow, so there was nobody to back Jones. Morris was for him and so was John Hancock. "I admire the spirited conduct of little Jones," the latter had written after the *Alfred* came in, "pray push him out again . . . he is a fine fellow and shall meet with every notice of mine."

But the matter of determining seniority among the captains —it is to be remembered that this was not to follow the dates of commissions, but to be settled by special act—came up on October 10, 1776, when Congress was in a state of frenzy unusual even for it. The British were approaching Philadelphia, and Congress was on the eve of its precipitate flight to Baltimore.* Without doubt the attention of both Morris and Hancock was distracted and the political captains had a field day.

The result was a list so astounding that even the politicians could hardly believe their eyes. No officers higher than captain were commissioned, but on the list of captains the first man worth the powder and shot it would take to kill him was number five, Biddle, unless one grudgingly admits Sleepy Dudley Saltonstall, number four. Barry was number seven, Lambert Wickes number eleven, the indescribable Hacker number sixteen. The eighteenth place was given to John Paul Jones!

"If I be not ashamed of my soldiers, I am a soused gurnet," quoth Falstaff . . . "such as, indeed, were never soldiers, but discarded unjust serving-men, younger sons to younger brothers, revolted tapsters, and ostlers trade-fallen: the cankers of a calm world and a long peace."

Substitute "sailors" for "soldiers" and Congress might have quoted the rest of the passage verbatim had it possessed such remnants of a sense of propriety as remained to Sir John. But

---

* Incidentally, even after 170 years Baltimore still smarts under the memory of that invasion, especially the strong advice that Benjamin Harrison gave to Robert Morris, who had remained behind. "If you wish to please your friends, come soon to us," he wrote, "but if you desire to keep out of the damnedest hole in the world come not here."

there is no evidence that it did so; apparently it was highly pleased with its work.

If there is a choice among spoiled fish, the smelliest appointment of the lot was the first. The ranking captain in the United States Navy, that is to say, the highest line officer, was James Nicholson, no more a sailor than Falstaff was a soused gurnet, who owed his appointment to the fact that he was a heeler of the political boss of Baltimore, one Samuel Purviance, who had made a deal with Richard Henry Lee, one of a sinister pair of brothers who were to gall Jones bitterly, but their country worse, for years to come.

Yet Lee, far from being ashamed of his work, apparently regretted that he could not make Nicholson a commodore, instead of merely the ranking captain. Manley, number two, won his place by a skillful lobbying campaign, but in defense of the Congressmen it must be admitted that he had done some good small-boat raiding in the early days of the war; he was soon to prove his real quality, though, by losing his fine new frigate to the first Briton he encountered. For the rest there was no excuse.

But while there was no excuse, there was a reason—in fact, two reasons; nor do they include the one that will occur to any cynic, namely, that Jemmy Twitcher's agents had got to the members of the committee and bribed them, with an eye to ruining the American navy. There is no evidence that British gold played any part in the transaction, but the British caste system most certainly did. Appointments in the British navy went by personal favor and political influence, and all the members of Congress had been British in every sense up to a couple of years earlier, and even now were but doubtfully anything else. Even Richard Howe, although he was probably the best admiral afloat, owed his rapid rise in the service less to his demonstrated capacity than to the fact that his mother, the Countess of Darlington, had been the mistress of the present king's great-grandfather, old George I. It was natural, then, indeed it was almost inevitable, that most Congressmen should assume that commissions in the Navy should be awarded by favor. That was the method to which they were accustomed, and the method employed by every navy in the world.

If that were not enough, there was a second reason—one that did not disappear at the end of the Revolution, but survived to plague the development of American technical services for generations. This was simply the fact that the members of Congress were not merely Britons, but frontiersmen. At this period even Boston, Philadelphia, and Charleston, for all their citified airs, were in important respects still frontier towns. On the frontier the division of labor is but slightly developed because there are not enough hands available. On the frontier, every able-bodied man has to know how to do practically anything that must be done, simply because there is no one he can hire to do it for him. American frontiersmen had developed such versatility as their more specialized descendants can hardly imagine. Whether it was to "peg shoes or sing by note," the average American could do it, and usually do it fairly competently.

The result was that he was slow to admit the value of specialization. Indeed, nearly two centuries later he is still slow to admit it in many fields of endeavor; there is to this day an astonishingly widespread belief that any citizen not obviously half-witted can do at least three things—teach school, edit a newspaper, or govern a state. When the twentieth century was moving into its second third, great bitterness was aroused by a President who filled the technical jobs of the government with technicians—economists, linguists, psychologists, sociologists, mathematicians, and the like. He was giving us, said the disgruntled, a government of college professors; and they considered it unnecessary to say more. If this opinion was widely held as late as 1933, there is nothing astonishing in the fact that in 1777 many Congressmen regarded it as silly and rather effete to insist on filling the Navy with sailors. Oh, of course, a certain specialized skill was required for the actual handling of the sails and steering; professional sailors could be hired for that. When it came to the top command, any sound American citizen would do as well, certainly, as any younger son of a British nobleman.

In short, that astounding naval list was the product rather of ignorance and stupidity than of villainy—more evidence to support the theory that the damage this country has suffered at the hands of scoundrels in public office is as nothing to the damage inflicted on it by honest dullards.

All the same, it fell upon John Paul Jones as a crushing blow. Eighteenth captain in a list that was headed by James Nicholson—it was next thing to the disgrace of being dismissed from the service. More than that, it precluded all chance of doing creditable work, for anything he might attempt would certainly be bungled by some one of the seventeen above him. Heaven knew he had found it hard enough to do anything worth while under the Venerable Angel; suppose he had had not one, but seventeen of that type over him? The prospect filled him with despair.

But it was precisely at this moment of despair that he performed his greatest service for the United States Navy. This is the phase of John Paul Jones's life that we are prone to ignore, because it seems dull and in a way rather squalid. There are no roaring cannon in it, no flaming ships, no great slogan thundered through the din of battle. It is only a story of endless argument with fools and sometimes with knaves, endless running to and fro, endless writing and arguing, endless disappointment and frustration. It is dreary stuff.

All the same, there was greatness in it, for here was the first unmistakable appearance of the indomitable man. When that list of naval officers was officially published, John Paul Jones was sunk. That was apparent on the very face of things, and even his friends could not deny it. But the quality of the man that makes him unforgettable is the fact that it was just when he was sunk that he really began to fight. All the world learned it off Flamborough Head a few years later; but a few, who knew what was going on in the inner circle, learned it now. So even if it is rather dismal stuff, this crisis requires attention; since the way he carried himself through it explains a great deal of his influence upon the Navy.

VII.

Morris and Hancock were wise enough not to attempt to argue when the injured captain showed up in Philadelphia. They simply admitted that the political janizaries had swept the field; but they refused to admit that all was lost. They had been negligent, but they persuaded him that they had not deliberately sold him out. After all, Hewes was absent, the British were upon them, everything was in confusion. The truth is that for some months Robert Morris had been practically the whole United States government; he refused to join the stampede to Baltimore, and as the sole high-ranking officer left in Philadelphia had to attend to everything. Even Jones had to admit that Morris could not be greatly blamed for a moment of inattention.

Hancock, it is true, turned one nasty little trick. In an interview in which he poured forth the usual politician's stream of worthless reassurances, he asked to see Jones's original commission, that of August 1776, and requested that it be left with him a few days so that they might see what could be done. When Jones called for it again, he was handed a new commission, dated October 10, 1776, and numbered eighteen; when Jones asked for the old one, too, Hancock claimed that it had been misplaced among his papers, so the sailor was left without documentary evidence of his seniority. True, it did not establish his legal right to a higher place on the list, but it did support his moral right and it would have been embarrassing to Congress. So Hancock conveniently "lost" it.

Nevertheless, he promised Jones definitely that regardless of seniority he should have a command appropriate to his services and his demonstrated ability. This was the substance of what the sailor desired, and he did not choose to be a stickler for detail; he parted with Hancock on amicable terms, in spite of the "loss" of the original commission.

It was not merely the cruises of the *Providence* and the *Alfred* that made these two leaders so active in this officer's behalf; he had also written to Morris—and undoubtedly urged in conversation—an idea that appealed to that brilliant gambler. It was that of hitting the enemy as far from the coast of America as possible. "An expedition of importance may be effected this winter on the coast of Africa," wrote Jones. ". . . This expedition could be made with no great expense; besides the ship and vessels mentioned are unfit for service on a winter coast. . . . The small squadron for this service ought to sail early, that the prizes may reach our ports in March or April."

Here was something that Morris had hitherto been looking for in vain—the suggestion of a definite naval policy going beyond the tactics of privateers. Morris knew that Congress's notion of putting to sea and slugging it out with Black Dick Howe was utterly fantastic; the American fleet couldn't even make it interesting for that redoubtable person. Furthermore, while picking up individual merchantmen was important, both to annoy the enemy and to replenish American supplies, it did next to nothing toward relieving the pressure of British naval power on the American coast.

But here was something that seemed both feasible and strategically effective. While privateers and naval raiders operated in the Caribbean and the western Atlantic, Howe could employ his frigates against them without sending them inconveniently far from the main fleet. But let a squadron appear on the coast of Africa and the situation would be different. Howe would be compelled to detach a considerable number of frigates and send them so far they could not be easily recalled; for the appearance of a few raiders in those waters would set up a howl for convoys.

Indeed, it was an idea! British trade with America was interrupted in any case by the war itself; but her trade with the rest of the world was proceeding almost without interference. Let that be threatened, and even the resources of the British navy would be strained to protect it. Certainly it could no longer concentrate in the western Atlantic. This Captain Jones was obviously a man whose mind ranged beyond the problems of a single ship; and that sort of man was precisely what the American navy needed.

So Morris and Hancock between them worked out a beautiful *démarche* by which they hoped to make Jones useful and at the same time avoid a frontal assault on the politicians. Those new frigates were gone beyond recall, for each political captain by now had fastened onto his with a death grip, and if anyone tried to take it from him he would raise a political uproar that Morris and Hancock shuddered to contemplate. But nobody cared much about Esek Hopkins' original squadron—the *Alfred, Columbus, Hampden, Providence,* and *Cabot.* On the other hand, while Jones was justly indignant at not being given a new frigate, he would certainly be pacified by being given a squadron, even if it consisted of some of the old ships.

Accordingly, orders went to Hopkins to turn over the *Alfred, Columbus,* and *Hampden* to Captain Jones for use on detached service under orders of the marine committee; and the same day orders went to Jones, now back at Boston, to proceed to Rhode Island and assume command.

But they reckoned without the Well of Strife. When Jones presented his orders, Hopkins blandly asserted that they were forged and immediately sent one of the ships to sea. Then when it was proved that corresponding orders had been delivered to him, he regretted the impossibility of complying, because one ship was gone—and immediately sent out another.

This was, of course, rank insubordination, but it was more than that. Hopkins had refused to obey a legitimate order—insubordination—but in addition to that he had made it impossible for anyone else to carry out the order. This was outright sabotage. It can be argued plausibly that by making it impossible for the high command to execute its policies he was directly giving aid and comfort to the enemy, which is treason.

Today, any naval officer up to the rank of captain who would pursue such a course in time of war would almost certainly be court-martialed and shot. A rear admiral who would do it would be booted out of the service and perhaps imprisoned; and even a vice-admiral who would do it would probably be relieved of his command. In 1777 they were somewhat more tender, but even then they could not pass over this flat defiance. They had Hopkins up on charges, not indeed of treason, or even of mutiny, but of being a menace to the morals of young sailors because he swore at them. He was relieved of his command; and a year later, when Congress heard of that "pack of rascals" observation, he was dismissed from the service.

So much for him. He had done great disservice to the Navy, but he had given John Paul Jones a vivid impression of what a flag officer ought not to be, and he passed that information along to the civilian authorities, who have made use of it ever since. So perhaps Esek indirectly served us, after all.

But the *démarche* had failed. Captain Jones was still raging up and down the land, thanks to the politicos, instead of battering British ships at sea. Morris and Hancock picked their flints and tried again.

By order of Congress three ships were being fitted out in eastern ports for war service; and a special resolution was wangled through decreeing that Captain Jones should have his pick of the three for a special mission.

Before anything could be done, however, what looked like a brilliant opportunity presented itself. A fine French ship, the *Amphitrite,* arrived at Portsmouth, New Hampshire, loaded with supplies from Rodriguez, Hortalez & Co., and some officious fool sent word that the ship, as well as the cargo, was a gift to the colonists. Jones was ordered to take command of her, proceed to France, and there report to the American commissioners, who had an idea that they could get him a really first-rate ship.

The only trouble with this was that it wasn't true. The French captain had simply brought a cargo over under charter, and the idea of turning his ship over to anybody made no appeal at all to him. He readily agreed to take Captain Jones to France, but only as a passenger; and on that point he was adamant. So that scheme also blew up.

It is worth passing notice, however, for two reasons. First, it brought Jones into contact, indirectly, with one of the most curious figures of the Revolution; and, second, it illustrates the almost fabulous incompetence with which our foreign affairs were conducted.

At this time the most effective friend the United States had in Europe was no prince or statesman or diplomatist, or even a nobleman of high degree, although it had friends in all these ranks. The man who was really getting things done was a dubious character, a former clockmaker turned gag-writer named Pierre Augustin Caron, who, for no known reason except that he liked the sound of it, called himself Beaumarchais. In 1775 he had written a smash hit in the form of a farce entitled *The Barber of Seville,* the popularity of which it owed to the fact that it was full of cleverly disguised slaps at the government, the nobility, the rich, and the Church.

Beaumarchais apparently cherished a real enthusiasm for the colonists, which jibed perfectly with the widespread hatred of the British that made the French upper classes strong supporters of the Americans. But Beaumarchais, because he had no official or social position to lose, was well placed to do something about it. He proceeded to organize an entirely fictitious importing and exporting firm, and to dissociate it from anything French he gave it the spectacularly Spanish name of Rodriguez, Hortalez & Co. This company proceeded to act as purchasing agent for the colonies and delivered enormous amounts of munitions of war and other supplies. Theoretically, its shipments were to be balanced by return cargoes sent by the various colonies, and Virginia did send a load or two of tobacco; but actually Beaumarchais was getting the bulk of his funds from the French government, which employed this device to create trouble for its old enemy, England.

But the affair of the *Amphitrite* illustrates the principal difficulty that Beaumarchais faced throughout, and not he alone but everyone who tried to do anything for the colonists. He never could be certain with whom he was dealing. In his enthusiasm, when return cargoes did not arrive or funds from the French treasury were slow, he dipped into his own pocket to keep the supplies moving, and in the end he lost £140,000 sterling in this adventure—a sum that was paid by the United States to his heirs when Beaumarchais had been dead thirty-six years.

Who said that the ship was a gift? Certainly not Beaumarchais. Not anyone in position really to know. But streams of reports were constantly coming back from all sorts of dubious characters, and Congress chose to believe that one which best suited it.

Looking back through the haze of the years—well tinted by the efforts of sentimental historians—Americans frequently cherish the impression that the Founding Fathers were a band of loving brothers, all for one and one for all as they pursued right loyally their great enterprise. It would be nearer the truth to assert that each Founding Father cherished the sour but fixed conviction that every other Founding Father was a villain of such depravity that no sort of baseness was beyond him. None was to be trusted out of sight. Above all, when one entered the contaminating atmosphere of Europe the worst was normally to be expected.

For that reason Congress rarely sent abroad a single agent, and never permitted one to remain long alone. The usual procedure was to send a second agent to spy on the first, and a third to spy on the second. Sometimes a platoon of plain-clothes men went along to spy on the spy on the spy; but this was usually unnecessary, because there were always Americans in Europe unofficially who were only too happy to report to members of Congress all the dirt about their official representatives.

Not a man went to Europe at the behest of Congress during the Revolution without having his character torn to shreds by these night birds. Beaumarchais was accused of stealing half of all that the French king gave to the cause of America. Franklin was accused of treason, thieving, bribe-taking, and betrayal of trust in his official capacity, and of lechery, drunkenness, and toadying in his personal relations. Deane was actually ruined by such stories. John Adams was accused of being in the pay of the British. Jefferson was accused of practically every crime in Newgate calendar even after the war was over and suspicion should have begun to subside.

John Paul Jones was soon to learn all about this at firsthand, but his initial experience was with the *Amphitrite*. At the moment, though, it seemed merely another annoying delay, and he was irritated rather than dismayed.

He turned, then, to the three ships of which he was to have first choice and settled on the *Ranger,* a sloop of eighteen guns just being finished at Portsmouth by John Langdon, shipbuilder and member of Congress.

Langdon screamed. As builder of the ship, he thought he should have the naming of her master; but when it was pointed out to him that, after all, his ship had been given one of the most celebrated officers in the service, he subsided, stipulating only that if he consented to Jones as captain, he and William Whipple, his colleague on the New Hampshire committee, should have the naming of the subordinate officers. Jones did not contest the point and as a result got Thomas Simpson, Langdon's brother-in-law, and a relative of both Hancock and John Wendell, richest man in Portsmouth, as his first lieutenant.

This fellow was a fascinating type. His appointment was the old-style method with a vengeance, for he had never sailed in a warship in his life, yet he was to be first officer of the *Ranger.* Wendell wrote for him a letter of introduction to the American commissioners in Paris describing him as "a gentleman of most distinguished character as an officer and one whose abilities are known to be very great and universally respected among us. His promotion will be generally accepted of by every friend of America."

Yet Wendell was not consciously cynical when he wrote in that style about a man who had never, so far as is known, set foot on a man-o'-war. Wendell was simply accepting the prevailing theory that anybody could be a naval officer. He did not believe, and almost nobody in America believed, that a good naval officer must have special natural talents to begin with, and those talents must be developed by special training. Wendell would have admitted this as regards a doctor or a lawyer or a clergyman; those were recognized professions, requiring special aptitude and special education. But the navy was not a profession. The navy was merely an offshoot of the merchant marine, and its ships could be handled by any reasonably competent officer of the merchant service.

John Paul Jones knew better, but he was a minority of one. Nevertheless, he had set down his ideas on paper and sent them to Robert Morris, and Morris was impressed. He could not do much, but he could and he did read that report to his colleagues and put it on file in the committee records. Later, when its writer had been brilliantly successful, that report came to be regarded with much respect and the Navy came more and more to rely on it as an accurate outline of what a true naval officer should be. This was a greater contribution to the service than any battle John Paul Jones fought.

Incidentally, this Thomas Simpson proved to be a demonstration by contradiction that Jones was right. He had received his appointment in precisely the way in which Jones held that naval officers should not be selected. Under the test of war his qualifications proved to be really remarkable; he had the technical proficiency of Simple Simon, the courage of Miss Muffet, the integrity of Tom the Piper's Son, and the dignity of Humpty Dumpty. Afterward those who held that Jones was right had only to cite the record of Simpson to prove their point.

At the moment, however, Jones put up no fight. Without doubt one reason was his belief that he was only to take the *Ranger* across to France, where he would find a better ship waiting for him, and he doubtless assumed that Lieutenant Simpson would do for one voyage.

It is just possible that there was another reason for his acquiescence. Wendell was not only rich, but he had a remarkably pretty daughter who was a social leader of the younger set in Portsmouth. It is a known fact that while the ship was being fitted the Captain was very much in evidence at the Wendell house, and Simpson's pretty cousin may have influenced him to look with a more tolerant eye on Simpson. Lorenz, indeed, hints that if there had been fewer charming girls in Portsmouth, or if they had been less complaisant to the gallant captain, it might not have taken all summer to get the *Ranger* ready for sea;* but the same authority will not go so far as to admit the authenticity of the petticoat-flag story, which he considers one of Buell's ingenious fabrications.†

According to this tale, when the news came that on the same day the resolution appointing Jones to the command of the *Ranger* was passed, June 14, 1777, Congress had adopted another creating a new national ensign,‡ the young women of Portsmouth held a "quilting party" at which they cut up their best gowns to make a flag for the ship according to directions given them by the Captain. The story goes that Jones regarded this flag as his personal possession and broke it out only on special occasions, one being the day on which the Stars and Stripes was first saluted by the French fleet; and that finally, after the battle with the *Serapis,* when he saw that the *Bon Homme Richard* could not be saved, he nailed this flag to the broken staff of the old ship and sent it down with her to the bottom of the sea.

Years later—still according to Buell—he met one of the girls who had made the flag and apologized for not bringing it back. He said he had left his dead where they fell; and since he gave them a famous ship for their coffin, he gave them a glorious flag for their winding sheet. "If you had taken it and brought it back to us," said the girl, "we would hate you."

* See *John Paul Jones,* by Lincoln Lorenz, p. 119.
† See *Paul Jones,* by Augustus C. Buell, I, 245.
‡ It read as follows: "*Resolved,* That the Flag of the Thirteen United States of America be Thirteen Stripes, Alternate Red and White; that THE UNION be Thirteen Stars in a Blue Field: Representing a NEW Constellation."

In any event, it is certain that Captain Jones had an interesting summer, a very interesting summer. If the ladies of Portsmouth were amiable and charming, as much cannot be said of the gentlemen. On the contrary, the summer was characterized by one flaming row after another, most of them with Langdon, the shipbuilder, although there were some exchanges with Wendell, Esek Hopkins, now going down for the last time, but still capable of suggesting that Captain Jones be court-martialed for not having rescued Saunders from the *Milford*, and with others. But Langdon was the biggest thorn in the Captain's flesh.

There is no doubt whatever that John Langdon was as sincere a patriot as John Paul Jones himself. He has been sneered at because he profited handsomely by the war as a builder of privateers, and cynics have assumed therefore that he was one of those who followed for the loaves and fishes; but these cynics ignore the fact that at a moment of crisis he offered every cent he had in the world to the state of New Hampshire. Like Robert Morris, if he made a good thing out of it, he did so by taking appalling chances. An industrialist who risks ruin for his cause is entitled to credit even if he escapes disaster.

But if Langdon's patriotism is beyond debate, it is equally certain that he was an opinionated, arrogant old turkey cock. Nobody was going to tell him how to build and equip a ship, especially no young squirt of a naval officer, six years Langdon's junior, and who had never met a pay roll in his life. Navy men who had to do with procurement after 1941 will recognize the type and will have little difficulty in realizing what Jones was facing.

In this case, however, Langdon had run into an individualist every whit as rugged as he was. Nobody was going to tell Paul Jones how to equip a ship for a rigorous and unusual form of service, especially not some swab of an adz-wielder who had never fought a naval action in his life. Industrialists who had to deal with the Navy after 1941 will recognize that type, too, and probably will feel more than a twinge of sympathy for Langdon.

So the atmosphere of Portsmouth all that summer was filled with fury, and whatever amorous dalliance among the ladies it may have seen came in the intervals of furious quarreling and equally furious, but largely frustrated, labor. Jones wasn't going fishing. He proposed to put the *Ranger* through a tour of duty severe enough to strain the stoutest ship ever put together; therefore he deemed it vital that every item of her equipment should be of a quality capable of meeting not the usual but quite unreasonable tests. Langdon, on the other hand, was determined that she should be fitted out without bankrupting the United States. The sailor was thinking of quality, the agent of price. It was inevitable that they should end by hating each other violently.

Langdon put the cap on it by allowing one of Jones's drafts on him to go to protest; and just before his departure the Captain wrote his candid opinion of the agent to John Brown, secretary of the marine committee: "Instead of meeting with the necessary assistance of the agent, he thinks himself my master, and he, who was bred in a shop and hath been but a voyage or two at sea under a nurse, had once the assurance to tell me that he knew as well as myself how to fit out, govern, and fight a ship of war!"

No, things were far from peaceful around Portsmouth as the summer wore away; yet in spite of the uproars, little by little things got done. At last, on October 29, Jones could write to the marine committee that he was ready to sail, although he was still fuming. "I have not now a spare sail, nor materials to make one. Some of those I have are made of *Hessings* [a coarse thin stuff]," he growled. He was especially outraged because Langdon had not provided him with a proper boatswain's call, and was sending him to sea with only thirty gallons of rum for the crew—"this alone was enough to cause a mutiny."

But he was going and that was the point, after all. "I never before had so disagreeable a service to perform, as that which I have now accomplished," he told the marine committee, "and of which another will claim the credit as well as the profit. However, in doing my utmost, I am sensible that I have done no more than my duty."

In that last sentence suddenly shines out the officer who was an officer indeed. It is a truism that in the armed forces, naval or military, a man's rank is his all. A man who makes the navy his career need not expect success to bring him either wealth or ease; all that he can hope to attain by faithful and able performance of duty is the respect of his country, and rank is the outward, visible symbol of that respect. Thus an officer deprived of his rightful rank is a man hit where it hurts worst. He can stand up better under any other blow.

John Paul Jones had every right to rank not lower than fifth in the list of captains. For no reason other than swinish politics he had been reduced to eighteenth place. By comparison with that, the fact that he had been given a hard and disagreeable job in getting the *Ranger* to sea was nothing. Nevertheless, deprived of his rank and given the dirty work to do, he was still capable of saying, "In doing my utmost, I am sensible that I have done no more than my duty."

In other words, here was a man who acknowledged that nothing, not even insult added to injury, could release him from his obligation to do his full duty. To appreciate the excellence of this attitude, consider what was about to happen to another man who was also considered one of the ablest officers in the American service. Like Paul Jones, Benedict Arnold was kicked around by the politicians, deprived of his rightful rank, blamed for other people's errors, and forced to see the credit for his own good work given to an incompetent fool. But Arnold couldn't take it. For all his brilliance—and he was unquestionably a brilliant soldier—he was never an officer. He wore the uniform, he commanded troops, he fought battles; but at best he was but a pseudo officer, because the test of personal injury broke him and turned him into a traitor, and the true officer has a core of steel, a loyalty that nothing can break.

By November 1, 1777, everything was as well prepared as Paul Jones could hope it to be. Besides Simpson, the officers included Elijah Hall, second lieutenant, Samuel Wallingsford, third lieutenant, and Nathaniel Fanning, midshipman—the first two from Portsmouth, Fanning from Salem. The crew, scraped together in spite of the privateers, was a motley outfit, including men from Portsmouth, Nantucket, New Bedford, Boston, and Philadelphia. The cabin boys were two young Negroes, Cato and Scipio, formerly Jones's slaves whom he had set free in 1776 and who now called themselves Jones, after their former master. One of the seamen was an individual whom Phillips Russell calls the only unquestionably 100-per-cent American ever to serve in the Navy.* He was Anthony Jeremiah, a full-blooded Narragansett Indian from Martha's Vineyard, who had sailed on whalers and who was to prove a notable man. The crew called him "Red Jerry," later corrupted into "Red Cherry," and liked him for his unfailingly cheerful disposition.

So the Captain sat down and wrote his will, making Hewes and Smith his executors, and sending it to Hewes with a long letter of thanks and good wishes. One request he made of Hewes was to look into the matter of an estate that had been recommended to him in Virginia; if he survived, he might purchase it after the war and retire to a life of "calm contemplation and poetic ease." Yet even then he was counting on the commissioners' promise to give him a better ship as soon as he had brought the *Ranger* across; and a better ship meant more fighting.

At the last moment came a messenger in furious haste bearing splendid tidings. Burgoyne had surrendered! The captain of the *Ranger,* since he was ready to sail anyhow, was ordered to carry the news with all speed to the American commissioners in Paris, and accepted the mission with wild delight. So on November 1, the wind being fair at last, the sloop *Ranger* hauled up her anchor and stood out to sea exultantly; and Charley Hill, of Barnstable, the youngest midshipman, wrote the "Song of the *Ranger,*" which they bawled all across the Atlantic:

* See *John Paul Jones,* by Phillips Russell, p. 63.

So now we had him hard and fast,
Burgoyne laid down his arms at last,
And that is why we brave the blast,
  To carry the news to London!

Heigh-ho! Carry the news!
  Go! Carry the news to London.
  Tell old King George he's undone!
Heigh-ho! Car-r-r-y-y the news!

CHAPTER V.

I.

IT IS the common impression that when the *Ranger* left Portsmouth Harbor on November 1, 1777, John Paul Jones's real career, the historically important part of his career, was just opening.

But it can be argued plausibly that on the contrary it ended that day. Most of the spectacular, the dramatic, the legendary part was still to come; but it is by no means certain that this was the historically important part, except indirectly.

Before the *Ranger* sailed he had formulated and expressed to Robert Morris, Joseph Hewes, John Hancock, and others practically every one of the ideas that were to play a large part in the development of the United States Navy. From this time on he contributed nothing to the service except prestige.

Yet it is probably true that without that prestige his other work would have been of little avail. If he had died that morning, it is quite possible that his ideas would have remained buried forever in the archives; but when he demonstrated brilliantly that his theories would work, he attracted attention not to himself alone, but also to what he had said. Navy men studied his battles, and from his battles they proceeded to his ideas. He could not be dismissed as a mere theorist, because when he carried his own theories into practice he won; so men began to examine seriously even those theories that he had had no chance to put into practice. The more they were studied, the sounder they looked, and in the course of time they were embodied in American naval practice.

Needless to say, this does not apply to every idea he advocated. The mere passage of time invalidated many, for with the passage of time technology changed beyond recognition. His tactics, for example, became archaic with the introduction of steam and steel, and his strategy became obsolete as the political situation of the United States altered.

But the great central idea that he was the first to propound has not been affected at all, either by the passage of time or by the development of technology. This is the idea that the navy is a career, and that the naval officer is a professional man, neither owning nor needing any other claim to consideration than his competence in his profession.

"None other than a gentleman, as well as a seaman both in theory and practice," he had written the marine board the previous January, "is qualified to support the character of a commission officer in the navy; nor is any man fit to command a ship of war who is not also capable of communicating his ideas on paper, in language that becomes his rank."

That is to say, he demanded character and general intelligence, as well as technical skill, in officers; putting character ahead of skill, and general intelligence immediately after it. But these are precisely the qualities that distinguish a professional man from an artisan. A man who is capable of performing all the operations, manual and mental, required by his occupation is an artisan; if he can perform them rapidly and with a high degree of accuracy, he is a master craftsman; but it takes more than this to make him a professional man. A professional man must be able to cope successfully with ideas that do not pertain directly to the occupation by which he gains his livelihood.

In John Paul Jones's day "the professions" meant three only, law, medicine, and the church, so he did not use the word. But he understood clearly that, as a lawyer who knew nothing but the statutes, or a doctor acquainted only with therapeutics, or a clergyman whose mind never ranged beyond theology, was considered but a second-rate professional man, so a naval officer who knew nothing but ships and sailors could not be a first-rate naval officer.

His experience had taught him that a naval officer inevitably comes into contact with a wide variety of people, in all walks of life. To be a first-rate naval officer, he must be able to deal with them all; and to deal with them successfully, he must have some idea of how their minds work. This implies the development of a broad general culture, which is based on self-respect, which is based, in its turn, on character. Paul Jones summed it all up by saying that he must be "none other than a gentleman," but that word is now applied to any man whose manners are unobjectionable, and he meant a great deal more. His meaning is conveyed more precisely to the modern ear by saying that the naval officer should be a genuine professional man, rather than merely a technical expert.

Incidentally, it is a concept that applies to far more than naval officers. Within our own generation the professional schools themselves have sometimes forgotten the wisdom of this eighteenth-century sailor, and have turned out technical experts, rather than true professional men, to the general damage.

When it was first propounded, however, this was a completely new idea as applied to ships' officers. That an officer should be a gentleman was understood, provided the word "gentleman" was restricted to the meaning of a man of good family and some social position. But that he should be a gentleman and at the same time a thorough seaman in both theory and practice seemed fantastic. It was not believed that a gentleman could be a specialist. Thomas Simpson was a gentleman in the accepted sense; therefore the fact that he knew nothing about naval warfare was not regarded as disqualifying him to act as first officer of a warship. Even Paul Jones bowed and submitted.

Nevertheless, the idea was implanted; and although it was at first misunderstood and rejected, it remained; and the startling career of the man who generated it called attention to it in the strongest way. So in the end it prevailed and played no small part in making our navy great.

II.

John Paul Jones drove the *Ranger* like a man possessed. He chose the stormy northern route because it was shorter, and carried sail to the very limit that his ship would stand. As a result, vessel and crew took a terrific beating. Men were on duty eight hours and off four, but the Captain apparently never slept at all. They said afterward that he averaged about three hours in his bunk out of each twenty-four. He was everywhere, taking a hand in everything. More than once when sleet storms lashed the deck, and the crew, cold and miserable, were working furiously to keep the wind from taking the masts out of her, with so much sail on, the Captain himself went around serving hot grog to the men. Once when a sudden squall struck, it was the Captain who cut the fly sheets with a hatchet to keep her from capsizing.

In short, it was a terrible voyage, as far as physical conditions were concerned, one that tried both ship and men to the limit of endurance. Yet, curiously, all the way from Portsmouth to Nantes, thirty-one days of grueling labor, not a single man was punished, no one was even given a public reprimand. Yet perhaps it isn't strange at all. Every soul on board knew that they were carrying great news, knew that it was important, urgently important, to get that news to France without delay, and that this northern route, wicked as it was, was the shortest. That is to say, they all understood clearly that there was a reason, and a good one, for the beating they were taking; and when the American seaman knows there is a good reason for it, what he can take and will take cheerfully in physical punishment is beyond the belief of softer men.

Yet for all his haste as a bearer of dispatches, the Captain did not forget that his primary business was commerce raiding. He was not in too much of a hurry to intercept anything he encountered, but he found no English property until he was past Ushant, when he picked up a couple of brigantines loaded with fruit from Malaga to London and sent them in.

Then he encountered a convoy of ten sail and spent a day trying to cut out one or more. But they were guarded by the *Invincible,* nothing less than a line-of-battle ship of seventy-four guns. For the *Ranger,* with her eighteen six-pounders—too short for the bore, at that, and therefore reduced in hitting power— to come within reach of that giant would have been plain sui- cide. So, after trailing the convoy for hours enough to prove that the *Invincible* was very much on the alert, Paul Jones gave up the idea. At the same time, he took a sardonic delight in having chased a ship of the line with a sloop.

All this, however, while proper and necessary work under the circumstances, meant delay, and, as it proved, just enough delay to prevent his being first to Paris with the news of Bur- goyne's surrender. Another messenger, Jonathan Loring Austin, who had come as a passenger on a fast French ship, beat him to Paris by twelve hours.

III.

From Portsmouth to Nantes is something over three thousand miles, geographically, today just as it was in 1777. But when Paul Jones sailed the *Ranger* from America to France he traveled a distance incommensurable by any mathematical standards. He journeyed from one civilization to another, from one era to another, almost from one world to another. He stepped from a burgeoning society into one far gone in decay, which is the immeasurable distance between infancy and old age.

However, both were familiar to him and he was equally at home in either. This was true of one other American repre- sentative in Europe at the time, and only one; which goes far to explain why Paul Jones found in the Old World one man and only one who really understood what he was about and supported him intelligently as well as steadily. It also explains in part why both were misunderstood and suspected by their colleagues.

This other was the Industrious Philosopher of Philadelphia,

Benjamin Franklin, recognized head of the American delegation in Paris—recognized, that is, by everyone except his colleagues, who admitted nothing of the sort.

It was to Franklin that the Captain reported with his dispatches, outdated now by Austin's arrival half a day ahead. Nevertheless, he was received warmly, taken to Franklin's house at Passy, and presented to various persons of importance. It is interesting and significant that one of the first persons to whom Franklin commended the newcomer was one of the great ladies of the city, the Countess d'Houdetot, to whom he wrote, "When face to face with him, neither man, nor, so far as I can learn, woman, can resist the strange magnetism of his presence, the indescribable charm of his manner."

This is to be taken literally, not because old Ben was incapable of touching up a portrait with more regard to diplomacy than truth, but because the man described was shortly to be viewed by the Countess, who was as shrewd a judge of people as Franklin himself. To paint him in false colors therefore would have been silly. Unquestionably, this is Benjamin Franklin's true impression of John Paul Jones at their first meeting, or certainly the first at which Franklin had paid particular attention to the sailor. If they had encountered each other in Philadelphia it must have been briefly and when Franklin was too preoccupied to study the young man with care.

As for Jones, there is no possible doubt as to the effect of the meeting on him, for it is attested not only by dozens of letters in the years that followed, but by his entire course of action. He was captured, horse, foot, and dragoons. He was Franklin's man from that day. His judgment of people was not always good, but when he made up his mind promptly that in this man he had struck real greatness he was right. And as events proved that he was right, he governed himself accordingly. He was high-tempered, more than a bit arrogant, and too often looking for slights, which he resented haughtily; but not with Franklin. More than once, in days to come, old Ben was to rate him as severely as he himself would rate an incompetent bo'sun on his quarterdeck; once or twice he dressed him down more testily than justly. Yet the bristling, truculent Captain Jones, whom neither naval rank nor political influence awed in the least, and who was always ready to fight at the slightest aspersion upon his dignity, accepted meekly Franklin's harshest censure, took offense at nothing, and tried to follow the older man's advice.

This speaks volumes for both men. Popinjays resented Franklin's strictures furiously; and John Paul Jones furiously resented the strictures of popinjays. But because he was a big man himself, he could realize Franklin's size. To be corrected by a man who, in character and intellect, towered above him he considered no infringement upon his own dignity.

Here again was the officer who was made an officer not by a commission, but by nature and ability. Such an officer's real authority rests not on his rank, but on his genuine superiority in character and skill; logically, therefore, when he meets a man whom he recognizes as his own superior he admits the duty to obey as readily as in other circumstances he claims the right to command. "To be obeyed one must be esteemed" was the way Jones put it. Franklin was esteemed, therefore obeyed.

On his part Franklin made up his mind promptly that here was a man to be relied on; and the discovery of a single person to whom he could safely turn his back must have come as a huge relief to the Philadelphian, for he was surrounded by as slippery a group as can well be imagined.

Benjamin Franklin was himself no copybook hero. On the contrary, the pious who held him to be a cynical old reprobate had some foundation for their opinion. He believed that the lofty moral and ethical protestations uttered by men are largely tosh. He was a pretty thoroughgoing hedonist himself; he had a record with women that if not quite lurid, certainly was far from pale, and even at the age of seventy-one was looked upon somewhat dubiously by the austere. He laughed at the clergy, therefore was widely regarded as an atheist. He made no pretense of despising wealth, therefore was regarded as avaricious and materialistic. But withal he happened to be an honest man who, being sent to France to serve the country, served it with no regard for his own interest.

However, a completely honest man was incomprehensible to the sort of congress that sat in Philadelphia. It was not that they were all grafters or bribe-takers, although such characters were not lacking among them; but they were all very much on the defensive. They were revolutionists. They had overthrown the existing government by force and violence. They were in the distressing position of having to win or hang. Men in that position simply cannot be tolerant and confiding. This generation has observed the same phenomenon in the Russians since 1917 and has been astonished at the extreme suspicion with which they regard everyone and especially their own men. But they know themselves for revolutionists, and they assume, logically, that men who have overthrown one government are capable of overthrowing another. The very foundation of their policy, therefore, is to trust no man too far.

The Founding Fathers felt the same way. When the fighting developed into genuine war in 1776 they needed an agent at the French court, and Franklin was the obvious choice for diplomatic business; but they needed economic as well as military aid, and they deemed a businessman the best choice for that job, so they sent along Silas Deane. Had they been content with this, all might have gone well, but the inevitable suspicion of revolutionists rose in them, so they dispatched a third agent to keep an eye on the other two.

The whole thing had to be done more or less surreptitiously, as France was still neutral. Deane, in particular, had to cover his activities as well as he could, for he was running contraband and it was necessary to pretend that the French government knew nothing about it, or at least had no hand in it. Not only was he sending over supplies, but whenever he could he was sending volunteers also. The colonists had almost nobody trained in the art of European warfare, so a good officer was as valuable as gunpowder. Deane sent over a number of good ones and some brilliant ones—Lafayette, De Kalb, Pulaski, and Steuben, for instance. Unfortunately, he also sent over a swarm of incompetents and worse, including, notably, a certain Peter Landais, of whom we shall hear more, much too much more.

Deane joined forces with Beaumarchais, and together they had successfully run at least eight cargoes of munitions into American ports before Paul Jones reached France.

Silas Deane had been a successful Pennsylvania businessman, energetic, able, and bold. He was also an ardent patriot and had contributed much to the cause, notably in helping fit out the expedition that captured Ticonderoga. It is now known, too, that he was at least reasonably honest, and his operations in France did not include peculation.

But he was a businessman in government, which is to say a businessman out of place. Nothing in his training had taught him that the art of government is essentially a branch of dramaturgy, in which the way things look is, at least for the moment, more important than the way things are. Had Deane been required to do nothing but acquire the goods and get them transported, he would have been a decided, perhaps a brilliant, success. But he had also to make it clear to a suspicious Congress that he was acting honorably; and this was impossible for the simple reason that he was profiting by his transactions.

This was quite in order. It was in his contract that he should receive certain commissions; but in politics any man who puts anything in his pocket is instantly under suspicion and is fair game for every demagogue. Since Deane had to work somewhat under cover anyhow, he was unusually vulnerable; and his ruin was the result.

For Congress had also sent over and placed on equal terms with the others one of the most extraordinary characters in American history. Arthur Lee comes closer than any other man who has figured prominently in our public life to representing unadulterated malevolence. John Adams was a bitter man, and so was his son, John Quincy Adams; Calhoun and Sumner were bitter, and all four were far surpassed in that quality by John Randolph of Roanoke, who touched the summit—or the utmost depth—of bitterness. Yet in every one of these the tincture of aloes was adulterated by other elements, including brilliant ability and unquestionable patriotism. But in Arthur Lee it is difficult to discern anything but gall.

He was a member of the illustrious Virginia clan that has studded the history of the United States with great men. It is a singular fact that this same family produced a man with a strong claim to be called the noblest of all Americans. It would be foolish to claim that Robert Edward Lee was the greatest American, since he lacked the statesmanship of either Washington or Lincoln; but it may be argued plausibly that for sheer moral grandeur he topped them both. With equal plausibility it may be argued that "the least erected spirit" in the whole list was Arthur Lee; which would give the Lees of Virginia the questionable distinction of having presented America alike with her noblest and her ignoblest.

The Lees have all had brains, Arthur included. In his youth he went to Scotland and took the degree of Doctor of Medicine at Edinburgh, which at the time was the most difficult place in the world from which to secure a doctorate. He returned to Williamsburg and practiced there several years, not without success. But in the end he tired of his profession and coolly decided to adopt another. Already in his thirties, he proceeded to London and studied at Lincoln's Inn and the Temple—probably the most rigorous law course given anywhere in the world at the time. He practiced as a solicitor in London and eventually was called to the bar in 1775. No fool could possibly have passed in medicine at Edinburgh; none but an exceptionally intelligent man could have passed in medicine there and then in law at Lincoln's Inn and the Temple.

But if the Lees had brains, they were also, except for the greatest of them, cursed with a poisonous conceit that generated arrogance. This not only made them personally obnoxious,*

* One of the finest of the tribe, Henry, Washington's cavalry commander and known to fame as "Light-Horse Harry," ended by getting himself lynched in Baltimore by attempting to force his Federalist opinions on that violently Republican town; he did not die on the spot, but was left for dead by the mob, and

but reduced their Americanism somewhat below 100 per cent, because they never could cheerfully submit to majority rule. Arthur was one of four brothers, all able men, and one of them, Francis Lightfoot Lee, relatively free of the family vanity. Another, William, was a businessman in London who, if he did his country no great good, at least did it nothing more than financial harm. A third was that Richard Henry Lee who conspired with Purviance to make James Nicholson ranking captain in the Navy, and who had a resounding career in Virginia politics, half of it admirable, the other half detestable.

But Arthur was the prize packet in this basket. If he ever had a decent impulse or ever performed an honorable act it has escaped the record. It was not that he was thievish or venal. There is no evidence that he ever stole or accepted a bribe. Nor was he cowardly. He was never driven to villainy by fear. His was a natural affinity for villainy. He was a scoundrel as Raphael was a painter and Beethoven a musician, not by chance or circumstance, but by every impulse of his being. Careless writers have sometimes called him a Judas Iscariot, but he was not that sort of man at all. Judas had to be paid thirty pieces of silver to do a job of betrayal; Arthur Lee was never known to charge a cent.

No sooner had he arrived in France than he began to send back to this country the most venomous sort of accusations against both Franklin and Deane. It has frequently been assumed that this was due to the fact that before he got there the other two had the work pretty well organized, Deane handling commercial, Franklin diplomatic relations, and that because there was nothing much left for Lee to do he felt slighted. But this assumes that Lee was a normal man who had to have some reason for turning nasty, whereas the evidence available indicates that he needed no excuse at all. A little later John Adams, in similar circumstances, did feel affronted and did turn spiteful for that reason; but Arthur Lee apparently was born so.

never fully recovered from his injuries. Yet this was the father of Robert E. Lee, one of the least opinionated of men.

His amiable endeavor was to convince Congress that Franklin was a doddering old fool and Deane a crook. As regards Franklin, he got nowhere, because too many members had known the Industrious Philosopher for too many years; but as regards Deane the charges were more effective. The merchant was not nearly so well known to the country as Franklin, and it was a fact that he was drawing certain commissions. Congress began to demand investigations, and the Beaumarchais-Deane working agreement, by which supplies had been moving steadily, was hampered, if not disrupted by the malevolent Virginian's meddling.

Into this situation John Paul Jones stepped without any idea of what was going on. As far as we know, at this time he was utterly unknown to Lee. But that didn't matter. He was recommended by Franklin and that was enough to ensure Lee's enmity. In all probability even that was not strictly necessary. Paul Jones was an independent man and a decent one, and the Arthur Lees of this world are perpetually at war with all such.

But for the time being all this was hidden from him. His immediate job was to prepare the *Ranger* for active service as a commerce raider, and he was happy enough. He had plenty to do. Not only had she taken much battering in the passage across, but she was extremely crank to begin with—for landsmen, put it that she showed a tendency to tip over in a stiff breeze—on account of improper ballasting. In addition to that, her masts were too tall and there were a dozen other changes that her first trip had shown to be desirable.

Paul Jones expected to have a frigate shortly, as the commissioners had promised before he left America, but he hoped to command the *Ranger* as well, so he went briskly to work to get her into the best possible shape. So cheery was he that he was inspired to write a mock-poetic letter to Wendell, describing the voyage, of which these swelling periods were a part:

The *Ranger* was wafted by the pinions of the quietest and most friendly Gales along the surface of the Blue pro-

found of Neptune, and not the swelling bosom of a Friend's
or even an Enemy's sail appeared within our placid horizon
until after we had passed the Everlasting mountains of the
Sea (called Azores) whose tops are in the clouds, and whose
foundations are in the center. When lo! this halcyon season
was interrupted! The gathering fleets o'erspread the sea and
war alarms began, nor ceased by day or night until aided
by the mighty Boreas, we cast Anchor in this asylum the
2nd current, but since I am not certain that my poetry will
be understood, it may not be amiss to add, by way of mar-
ginal note, that after leaving Portsmouth nothing remarkable happened until I got to the eastward of the Westward
Islands.

Nor would Wendell only have been confused. All that stuff
about halcyon days would have been incomprehensible to the
seamen battered by that roaring passage. But it had ended well,
so from the Captain's standpoint, it was all well.

The ship that the commissioners—or Deane and Franklin, at
least—had in mind for Jones was a hush-hush job. An Amsterdam shipyard was just completing, ostensibly for the neutral
Dutch government, a fine, thirty-six-gun frigate called the
Indienne, with the intention of turning her over to the Americans when she was finished. If her real ownership had been
avowed the British would have lodged a protest, and, of course,
the Dutch government would have been compelled to step in
and forbid the transaction as a violation of neutrality. With
the Indienne as his flagship, with the Ranger, and perhaps with
a ship or two that Beaumarchais could abstract from the French
navy, Jones would have a squadron strong enough to play havoc
with shipping all around the British Isles.

Everything went well up to the last moment, and then suddenly the British Ambassador came raving to the Dutch Foreign Minister with complete, irrefutable proof that the frigate
belonged to the Americans. That upset the applecart. Not yet
ready to declare war, the Dutch government intervened. The

ship was sold to the French, still technically neutral, and by them transferred to the Duke of Luxemburg, whose need for a navy is unimaginable.

This was the work, directly or indirectly, of Arthur Lee. Historians have agreed that it is improbable—although by no means unthinkable—that he transmitted the information to the British himself, but someone in his entourage certainly did. His papers were rifled in Berlin, or so he said, and it may be true, for those confidential papers were a sacred trust, and he was incapable of keeping a trust. The charming Arthur, venomously suspicious of every honest man he met, with an unerring instinct clasped every rascal to his bosom, entrusting him with the most confidential information, especially with such official documents as belonged to his colleagues. Whenever he needed a confidential secretary he hired the chief British spy in Paris, and as often as one was exposed he hired another. This was probably not a consciously adopted policy. It is more likely that there was something imponderable in Arthur Lee, something analogous to a negative electric charge, that repelled loyal men and attracted the devious and the dubious.

However, the enemy's discovery of the plans ruined John Paul Jones's chances of securing the frigate. The attendant uproar and general embarrassment also delayed the entry of France and the Netherlands into the war and presumably cost American lives as well; but from the standpoint of the Captain the loss of the vessel was the immediate problem. As yet he had no suspicion of how it had come about, but he had a very sharp and gloomy idea of what was likely to follow. He expected any day to see one of the new American frigates in French waters commanded by one of the seventeen captains senior to him in rank, who would promptly assume authority over the *Ranger* as well and compel Jones to join in some idiotic and futile project that would disgrace both the officers and the flag.

His particular fear was that it might be the *Raleigh*, with Thomas Thompson (number six) in command, for he had heard a rumor that Thompson was heading for Europe. "He may be a good carpenter," was his summing up of that officer; and he meant it when he wrote to Morris, "Guard me against such connections, which would be worse than death." The loss of the *Indienne* naturally redoubled these fears.

The commissioners, or at least Franklin and Deane, were also deeply chagrined. For one thing, they had brought the man over from America on the definite promise that he should have a good ship. For another, they liked his plan of employing a squadron to raid commerce in British waters. For a third, they liked the man himself, when they came to know him, and believed more strongly every day that he could perform what he promised.

So, since the *Indienne* was gone, they did the next best thing. On January 16, 1778, they gave him a free hand. Their letter read:

> As it is not now in our power to procure you such a ship as you expected, we advise you, after equipping the *Ranger* in the best manner for the cruise you propose, that you proceed with her in the manner you shall judge best for distressing the enemies of the United States, by sea or otherwise, consistent with the laws of war, and the terms of your commission. . . .
>
> We rely on your ability, as well as your zeal to serve the United States, and therefore do not give you particular instructions as to your operations. We must caution you against giving any cause of complaint to the subjects of France or Spain, or of other neutral powers; and recommend it to you to show them every proper mark of respect, and real civility, which may be in your power.

Arthur Lee refused to sign this letter. It contained, in addition to the orders above, detailed instructions as to sending prizes into various ports, naming agents regarded as reliable. Among these was the firm of Gourlade & Moylan, American merchants at Nantes. Lee said these people were incompetent, or worse, but his real reason was that he wanted Brother William to handle all prizes and draw the commissions thereon. However, the others, knowing nothing against the firm, overruled him and dispatched the letter.

It relieved Jones's worst fears, for not even Carpenter Thompson could override direct orders from the American commissioners. He went happily and vigorously to work refitting his sloop, since he couldn't have a frigate. He was fortunate, too, in having at hand an energetic and able agent in Jonathan Williams, whose fatal defect had not yet come conspicuously to light. All Jones saw in him at this time was a first-rate businessman, honest, intelligent, and resourceful about finding scarce items of equipment. It was some months before he learned that these qualities counted for nothing against the crime of being Franklin's nephew; for when John Adams arrived to succeed Deane, he promptly discharged Williams.

Before that happened, however, much progress had been made in various directions. Putting the *Ranger* in shape involved the slow and laborious task of changing the ballast as well as shortening the masts and taking one out completely to move it a little farther forward. Once the work had been laid out, the boss carpenters could oversee its execution better than Jones could, so he spent the greater part of his time dickering and dealing with the American commissioners, the French government, and the French naval authorities.

Jones was bursting with ideas. It was a certainty now that France would intervene on the side of the Americans, and the only question was that of choosing the right moment. The news of Saratoga seemed to indicate the moment, and Jones had the plan, which he proceeded to urge upon everyone in authority.

He knew that Howe was tremendously extended, covering well over a thousand miles of coast line, from Boston to Charleston. That didn't matter as against the microscopic naval strength of the United States, but if a fleet of any real size caught him in that position, even Black Dick would be seriously embarrassed.

Jones proposed, therefore, that the French fleet under Admiral Count d'Estaing, whom Jones regarded as a highly competent officer, should strike at the Delaware capes, the point of Howe's principal concentration at about the center of his long line. A successful blow there would leave nothing more than mopping-up operations to the north and the south.

As for himself, he would like to command one of D'Estaing's ships; but he would be equally content to be given a squadron of small, fast commerce raiders with which to create a diversion in British waters. He believed that while D'Estaing was crossing the Atlantic a squadron of that sort, skillfully commanded, could set up such a fanfare in the Irish Sea and the Channel itself that Jemmy Twitcher would blow up and in his panic would recall every available British ship to the defense of the home islands, thereby ensuring that Howe would not be reinforced.

D'Estaing approved the idea. Franklin liked it. It appealed to De Sartine, French Minister of Marine, or, as we should say, Secretary of the Navy. Vergennes, the Foreign Minister, had no objection. In short, everybody in authority agreed that it was obviously the thing to do, and nobody doubted that D'Estaing and Jones were the men to do it. But it was not done.

In the implications of that four-word statement, "it was not done," lies the whole history of the American Revolution and much of that of the French Revolution to follow. The authorities on all sides knew what to do, were willing to do it, and had sufficient means. But they could not act.

The same situation existed across the Channel. Little has been said about it in these pages, because this story is concerned with the other side, but there had not been a moment for the past three years when the British officers in the field had not known how to whip the rebellious colonists into line, and during a good part of the time they had had the necessary means. But their hands were tied by the fact that the home government did not know how to govern.

Burgoyne, for example, was not the rash fool that is presented, or used to be presented, in American school histories. On the contrary, he was a reasonably good general carrying out an excellent strategic plan. That plan was simply to split the United States along the line of the Hudson and then conquer it in detail. To effect this, Burgoyne was to move down from the north and Howe—Sir William, the general, not Lord Howe, the admiral—was to advance to meet him from the south. It failed simply because an incredibly incompetent general headquarters ordered Burgoyne to march without explaining the plan to Sir William Howe. Howe did not refuse to move. He had no orders to move. He heard from American sources that Burgoyne was on the march, but why he had not the faintest idea; and when his orders did arrive it was a month too late.

Comparable things were constantly happening to the fleet. Where William Howe, the general, got no orders at all, Richard, the admiral, got too many—confused, contradictory, and frequently incomprehensible orders. His supplies were of like kind —round shot too large or too small for the bore of his guns, shipments of gunpowder in which half the casks were filled with sand, sailcloth so old and rotten that it ripped in the first stiff breeze, and provisions so far gone in decay that not even eighteenth-century sailors could eat them.

It was, in fact, a moment when there was no government in the world. In England, as in France, absolutism was dying, while in America democracy was struggling to be born. In the interval, ignorance and inexperience rendered the one impotent, folly and corruption the other. At such a moment real ability is likely to be a trial rather than a blessing to its possessor, for the man of ability, seeing what is to be done but restrained by fools and incompetents from doing it, suffers; while the man too stupid to see what needs to be done is tranquil.

No doubt Paul Jones was happy in not being philosopher enough to perceive the real hopelessness of the French system as it existed in 1778. Having no doubt that the tremendous potency that France had exhibited a generation earlier could again be aroused, he did not lose hope. It may be, indeed, that he rather enjoyed the battle of wits as he tried to overcome the lethargy into which absolutism was sinking, never suspecting that it was soon to deteriorate into the coma preceding death.

IV.

As a matter of fact, the Paris in which John Paul Jones lived in 1778 was something of a wonder. The modification is important; this applies to the Paris in which he lived, which was not everybody's Paris. It emphatically was not the Paris of the common people. That still remained in important respects a medieval city. Even the royal palaces of the Louvre and the Tuileries would be described today as drafty old barns, rather than as residences fit for human occupancy. The court, indeed, had practically abandoned the city in favor of Versailles, fourteen miles away.

There were even then some marvelous houses in France, but only their stony façades were known to the generality of the inhabitants. They belonged to great nobles or to rich bankers, or sometimes to those curious characters that seem to materialize as if out of the air when a civilization reaches a certain stage of decay—creatures defying classification and not infrequently almost fabulous in their manners and customs. Even in this century we have seen specimens in Rasputin, in the Russia of 1917, and in certain of those unbelievable beings that surrounded Hitler, some of whom we hanged at Nuremberg.

When John Paul Jones arrived there, Paris was swarming with improbable persons, had been for many years. John Law had created the Mississippi Bubble half a century earlier, and not for a moment since had he lacked successors, who tended to grow ever more fantastic. The individual who called himself Count Alessandro di Cagliostro was at the moment rising toward the apex of his singular grandeur, the Countess de la Motte was perhaps already turning over in her mind ideas connected with a diamond necklace. There was a warrant out for the sometime director of the French state lotteries, one Giovanni Jacopo Casanova. The city swarmed with soothsayers and fortunetellers, some of whom were mulcting great businessmen and the high nobility of enormous sums.

These frequently lived sumptuously for long periods, although many of them ended in a great, square, tower-like building that loomed up in the midst of the town, the fortress-prison called the Bastille. In view of its size and its prominent situation, it is unlikely that John Paul Jones could have missed seeing the Bastille, but he paid no attention to it. Why should he? It was not part of his Paris.

Neither were the swarming, noisome streets in what were still called the *faubourgs*, that is, suburbs, although they had long since become an integral part of Paris. Another decade was to reveal that they were the most important part of Paris, for a few unforgettable months the only part of Paris that counted. Here in sunless, fetid alleys the poison was distilling that was to destroy the Paris of John Paul Jones and Franklin, the Paris of Cagliostro and the Paris of the King.

In St.-Antoine, in the Marais, in a dozen other places ancient stone structures more like rabbit warrens than human habitations leaned until their upper stories almost touched each other over what were less streets than shallow, cobblestoned troughs, each an open sewer. In these structures spawned a race that spectators a few years later were to call hardly more than half human, reduced by savage taxation, by governmental corruption, by an ironbound social system that afforded no hope, to a condition not far removed from that of the beasts. A few years later they were to be fit tools in the hands of one who in 1778 was a most respectable lawyer over in Arras, a lawyer who was becoming more respectable by the minute and who bore the name, as yet unknown outside of his provincial city, of Maximilien Robespierre.

But Paul Jones did not see this Paris at all. He was engaged in an enterprise that was to play a large part in releasing the desperate energies of these creatures, but apparently he was unaware of their existence. So, it would seem, was Franklin. So was the Duc de Chartres. So was the King. So, as far as any real understanding of their nature is concerned, were most of the people who considered themselves liberals—Lafayette, Necker the sedulous bookkeeper, Mirabeau, and the amiable, chatter-ing scatterbrain who was destined to give his name to an empire unrecognized by any prince or potentate but nevertheless potent enough to challenge comparison with that of any Louis de Bourbon—the disciple of Quesnay, friend of Franklin, and, as he stoutly maintained, friend of mankind, Pierre-Samuel du Pont de Nemours.

From the modern standpoint it seems incredible that John Paul Jones, an intelligent man, should have overlooked this Paris. But he did, and if he is to be condemned for it, all other Americans save one stand in the same condemnation. Franklin was as blind as Jones. So were Silas Deane and John Adams, not to mention Arthur Lee. So were nearly all other Americans in France during these years with the exception of that strange, inquisitive genius whom Jones had encountered years earlier in Philadelphia. Thomas Jefferson saw, and was half horrified, half exalted. But Thomas Jefferson believed that Kentucky Long Hunters, Mississippi flatboatmen, and Virginia hill farm-ers were men, a theory accepted only in principle by half his colleagues among the founders of the American republic.

Paul Jones, first, last, and always a seafaring man, not a states-man, worried his head not at all about such matters. There was a Paris ready to accept him, and with it he was content. If it was not the Paris of the common people, neither was it the Paris of the merchants and other businessmen. Arthur Lee never lived in it, nor did John Adams enter it, except occasionally. Silas Deane knew little of it, and the King himself knew of it more by hearsay than by experience.

But it was a city that Benjamin Franklin not only inhabited, but to an astonishing extent actually dominated. The Romulus of this city—too old now to be its effective ruler, but still its Grand Old Man and the embodiment of its spirit—was Denis Diderot, nicknamed Pantophile, which may be roughly defined as "lover of everybody," the Encyclopedist. Diderot and Franklin really came into contact at one point only. Each was consumed by an insatiable curiosity concerning everything under heaven, and believed that the application of intelligence supported by diligence could unravel most of the mysteries of the universe.

Diderot was actually a product of the preceding reign, when the classes in France that possessed leisure, having pursued frivolity to the extreme limit of satiation and boredom, turned to the cultivation of the mind, with extraordinary results. It was the age of Voltaire, Rousseau, Montesquieu, and other members of the most brilliant galaxy that French intelligence has produced. Better representative of the reign of Louis XVI than Diderot was a man who had died two years earlier, but whose memory was still a profound influence. This was François Quesnay, the King's physician and an associate of Diderot, but better known as the founder of physiocracy, an economic theory that had a tremendous vogue.

Apparently Dr. Quesnay is not ill described when he is referred to as a Dr. Benjamin Rush magnified by ten, or a Dr. John Read magnified by a hundred diameters. Louis XVI was healthy enough to render Quesnay's professional duties easy; so his apartment on the mezzanine floor of the royal palace became the resort of everybody who liked to discuss ideas, rather than court scandal, and before Quesnay's life ended these *réunions de l'entresol,* or "mezzanine meetings," became famous throughout France. One need only name some of those who used to frequent the doctor's apartment—Diderot, Condorcet, Mirabeau, Turgot, De Gournay, Du Pont de Nemours, Lafayette, even Adam Smith—to realize that attendance there was likely to be a memorable experience.

Louis smilingly declared that Quesnay was not in fact "the King's physician," he was in reality "the King's thinker," and perhaps he was; but if so it only goes to show that thinking in France was already on the decline, for François Quesnay's true supremacy was not as a thinker, but as a talker. The ineradicable impression he made upon the group surrounding him, a group that included many of the best talkers France ever produced, is evidence that this must have been one of the finest conversationalists of his, or any other, time.

That was the trouble, or, rather that was the last, conclusive symptom of the deep-lying trouble—the intelligence of France was spending itself in talk. The system was dying, and it is so frequently the case as to be almost normal for a social system that is on its last legs to flare up in a burst of brilliant talking and writing, sometimes of expression in all the arts, surpassing anything it produced when it was in health and vigor. What John Paul Jones saw was the hectic flush of dying absolutism. Nevertheless, it was worth seeing, and it is no wonder that he was fascinated.

As the protégé of Franklin he was introduced into the heart of this society that touched the courtly world on one side, the scholarly world on the other, and that was permeated with politics all through. But he needed no more than an introduction; thereafter he could make his own way, for he understood it—not profoundly, to be sure, but well enough to appreciate its merits.

John Adams, with a mentality that dwarfed Jones's, was introduced, too, but he never proceeded far in this particular Paris. He was contemptuous of it. He had the penetration to perceive its hollowness, but not the taste to appreciate its grace. Indeed, merely to mention Honest John and grace in the same sentence is somewhat incongruous; at least it is as applied to this period of his life. Many long years were to pass and he was to be an old man before there was to spring from the stony soil of his New England mind one of the most graceful garlands of American letters, his share of the wonderful correspondence with Jefferson.

The brisk young captain, though, was a thorough cosmopolitan who would have been baffled by Jonathan Edwards as completely as John Adams by Balthasar Gracian. From Franklin he went to Madame d'Houdetot, and from her into half the great houses of Paris—indeed, into practically all where the prevailing fashion of intellectual curiosity held sway. He had everything. He had personal charm, he was an American, at least politically, he was a warrior and a poet, and as time passed and British propagandists vilified him more and more recklessly, he acquired, through the efforts of his enemies, the last touch necessary to ensure his success in the world of wit and fashion—the reputation of being, perhaps, a bit of a rakehell. Nothing was proved—of course, nothing could be proved—but it gave fashionable ladies a not unpleasant thrill to know that about this charming, witty, and delightfully courteous gentleman dark stories were told, of massacres, of pillaging by land and sea, of slave trading, piracy, and every other crime that hardworking manufacturers of atrocity stories could imagine. Socially, Captain Jones strode from triumph to triumph.

Among others whom he encountered and whom he charmed was that ornament and scandal of the age, Louis Philippe Joseph, Duke of Chartres, and his duchess, who had been Louise Marie Adelaide de Bourbon-Penthièvre, daughter of the Grand Admiral of France and one of the greatest heiresses in the country. Chartres, who was later to become Duke of Orléans, and still later Philippe Egalité, and in that quality to die on the guillotine during the Terror, has been roughly handled by history, but he epitomized the virtues as well as the vices of his age.

For one thing, he was a sailor, and when Paul Jones first encountered him he was fresh from creditable service with the fleet at the battle of Ushant. For another, he was openhanded, magnanimous, and free of the petty cruelty that blackened many of the French nobility. His house had a sort of literary tradition going back to Charles of Orléans, the poet who had fought at Agincourt, and it pleased the present duke to cultivate writers and scholars. He was intelligent enough to perceive the worthlessness of the Queen, and she hated him with a remorseless hatred, which he delighted in exacerbating by making witty and stinging epigrams about her.

Chartres understood clearly that the old order was dying, but his ideas of what to do about it were anything but clear. He had spent much time in England, where he found a kindred spirit in the Prince of Wales, who was later to be George IV, and who solved the problem, at least as far as he personally was concerned. They were both roisterers, both sniffed at by posterity on account of their dissipated habits, yet both were intelligent enough to despise the stupidity, if not the real vices, of the old regime. George was fortunate in that the representative of absolutism in his country eventually went mad, affording him an opportunity to effect the transition to a more workable system without a social cataclysm; so he lived to be sixty-eight and died in bed. Philippe had no such luck. Absolutism in France went to its logical conclusion, with the result that he, by that time Duke of Orléans, died on the scaffold at forty-six.

But in 1778 he was still flourishing and still trying to introduce something of the English system into France. Unfortunately, he could appreciate only the superficialities of the English system. He could popularize jockeys and riding coats and fashionable patronage of the French equivalents of Sheridan and Fox; but he could not inculcate English realization of the fact that the nation is, after all, the people, whose welfare is the king's first responsibility.

As Bourbons went, Philippe Egalité was not below but distinctly above the average; one thinks of him in connection with Gracian's observation that "some men have deserved a better century," for he might have shone had he not been born in one of those eras of transition when only really great men shine.

For the old order was dying and the new was not yet born. In such times civilization is carried across the intervening chaos between the two orders, not by brilliant men or learned men or good men, but by unbeatable men, men who fight on when all is lost, men who fight without success, without weapons, without hope. In such times the incomparable Erasmus, for all his intellectual power, is futile, and the bullheaded Luther counts for ten times as much. In such times the brilliant Arnold and the sparkling Chartres eventually are lost, while George Washington, the general who fought without an army, and Paul Jones, the admiral who fought without a fleet, survive to gather brighter and brighter luster as the centuries pass.

Nevertheless, write it down to the everlasting credit of Chartres that he knew a first-rate man when he saw one. The American sailor appealed to him—amused him, no doubt, and lightened his boredom, but commanded his genuine admiration as well. He readily gave the man countenance and, when he could, more substantial aid.

But in the year 1778 and for some time thereafter, His Grace of Chartres was not in position to be of much help to anyone. He had made the mistake of acting creditably enough in battle to stir up some public acclaim. That would have been all very well in a commoner, but Chartres was a great prince; and any member of the high nobility who was cheered by the populace instantly felt the spite of the venomous little viper from Austria. The Queen demanded Chartres's removal from the fleet and his transfer to an innocuous command of hussars. She succeeded also in having him virtually banished from the court and confined to his country estates. Marie Antoinette was God's bitter jest at the expense of France. He had made her vicious and stupid, which was nothing unprecedented in queens of France; but in addition, He had given her extraordinary beauty, and this made her not merely unprecedented, but also ruinous. Yet the joke, in the end, was on the woman. Fifteen years later, in her moment of deadly peril, this same man, now Orléans, came with an offer of help and might have brought her to safety; but her viciousness and stupidity now recoiled upon her. She rejected his aid and went to her death.

But although the Duke was out of favor, his wife remained in Paris and retained her influence. She was the Duchesse de Chartres, to be sure, but she was also Louise de Bourbon, daughter of the Duke of Penthièvre, granddaughter of the Count of Toulouse. There were limits even to the Queen's stupidity. To attack the Duchess for her husband's sake would have been to raise all the nobility of France to her defense.

Besides, the whole world knew that the alliance was one of convenience and that the woman least likely to have any responsibility for the doings of Chartres was his wife. In addition to that, she was singularly invulnerable; essentially a goodhearted creature, she was famous for her charities and for more than that—she had a ready sympathy and sufficient understanding to make it gracious sympathy, and so harmless was she that even the ravening Jacobins could not suspect her of evil intent, and she lived in Paris undisturbed through the Terror.

This woman, even more than her husband, was enchanted by Paul Jones, and she was in position to do a great deal for him. In return he gave her a filial devotion really extraordinary.

"In all my checkered life," wrote her son, who was to be Louis Philippe, King of the French, "I have never known so beautiful a relation between woman and man as that of my mother and Paul Jones."

Sherburne* has a story that on one occasion when the Duchess at a dinner party announced one of her many favors the grateful sailor exclaimed, "Madame, I shall lay an English frigate at your feet!" Lorenz is inclined to scout this as a fable, and it is not mentioned by Jones in any extant document; but there is no doubt about the favors, and the exclamation is quite in character. Nor would the promise have seemed to him extravagant or inappropriate. If he sent—or tried to send—a captured prize to the firm of Hewes & Smith out of gratitude for what Hewes had done for him, the even larger generosity of the Duchess must have seemed worth a frigate. Perhaps it never happened; but it was the sort of thing that could have happened, for in the brilliant and gay, if essentially empty, social world of Paris in the reign of Louis XVI, Paul Jones knew how to conduct himself perfectly and was a smashing success.

* *The Life of Paul Jones,* from Original Documents in the Possession of John Henry Sherburne, published in 1825 and said to have been written by Benjamin Disraeli.

V.

But his social activities did not prevent work on the *Ranger* from going forward steadily, and when on February 6, 1778, France took the decisive step of signing a virtual treaty of alliance with the United States, Jones's hopes flared high. He envisaged a really powerful blow at British maritime strength, both naval, in the western Atlantic, and mercantile, in European waters. However, France was not·yet formally at war, and although it was Jones's hope at some time to command a fine French squadron under the American flag, his immediate purpose was to get to sea with what he had and do as much damage as he could with his sloop.

One consideration that spurred him on was the fact that other Americans were beating him to that goal. Lambert Wickes, in particular, was playing havoc with British shipping. He had brought Franklin over in his fast, eighteen-gun *Reprisal*, and had then assembled a squadron, including Henry Johnson's *Lexington* and Samuel Nicholson's *Dolphin*, with which he was harrying commerce off the French and Spanish coasts. Gustavus Conyngham, too, while he had done less damage than Wickes, had achieved even more spectacular diplomatic results by darting into the North Sea with the *Surprise* and picking off the Harwich packet *Prince of Orange*. Plainly it was time for Paul Jones to get to sea if he were not to be outclassed. He could not afford to wait either for a frigate or for a French declaration of war.

Before he put out for a regular cruise, however, there was one matter he could attend to that to a civilian of the twentieth century may seem trivial but that to a naval officer of the eighteenth was highly important. It was to exchange official salutes with a French warship. By the treaty of February 6 the civilian government at Paris had formally recognized the independence of the United States, but the French navy had not as yet made any sign that it knew anything of the treaty or of the United States as a nation. A formal exchange of salutes would be such a recognition, and Jones intended to have it as soon as possible.

The opportunity came when he was ordered to convoy a merchant ship from Nantes to Quiberon. In Quiberon Bay lay a French squadron commanded by an admiral. A salute from a mere captain would not have served the purpose from Paul Jones's standpoint, but from an admiral it would count. On arrival, therefore, after sending his convoy in he hove to in the offing and dispatched his longboat with a message saying that he proposed to salute the French flag over the fort with the heaviest salute allowed by American naval regulations, to wit, thirteen guns, and asked shot for shot in exchange. Admiral La Motte Picquet replied that he would certainly return the salute, but French regulations forbade him to return shot for shot. He would, however, since Captain Jones was the ranking American naval officer then in French waters, consider him entitled to the salute due to a Dutch admiral, or to any republic, namely, four guns less.

A spirited argument followed, but at length Jones was convinced that La Motte Picquet was not trying to deceive him, but was really quoting the law; so the *Ranger* approached the fort, gave it thirteen guns, and received nine in reply, to the satisfaction of all concerned. But the next morning the American added the touch that proved how well he knew Europe; he asked permission to run his ship through the French squadron and salute the Admiral personally. The Frenchman, gratified by this recognition of his rank, saw to it that as the little sloop ran down the line, she got her nine guns from his ships as she had from the fort.

That, as poker players say, put a lock on it. The Stars and Stripes had been saluted by a French fort and by a French fleet at the command of an admiral and with the full approval of the home government. Never again could it be denied that it was one among the flags of the nations. It had been saluted before by a Dutch governor of an island in the West Indies, but the Dutch government had disavowed the salute and recalled the governor. It had been saluted again by a Danish captain, but the Danish government ignored the incident. The salute on February 14, 1778, at Quiberon, however, was not only official, but rendered by one of the great powers. It was definitive.

At Brest a few weeks later the *Ranger* received her third salute, this time from no less an officer than D'Orvilliers, ranking admiral in the French service commanding the main battle fleet. Incidentally, the American captain's visit of courtesy to the flagship turned into something quite different from the ordinary official call. Admiral d'Orvilliers took an instant liking to him and became, and remained, his warm personal friend.

But all this, while important in its way, was incidental to the main business for which the *Ranger* was now ready, and that business deserves careful examination for it was at once highly professional and at the same time one of the most fantastic projects in the history of naval warfare.

This project was to deliver a psychological shock to the British Empire.

The mere conception of the idea is enough to acquit John Paul Jones forever of the charge that he was a mere corsair. Lambert Wickes might have been called a corsair with much more justice, or Conyngham, because they were both primarily commerce raiders who avoided battle whenever they could and planned no large operation that did not afford at least the promise of yielding valuable prizes.

On this occasion Paul Jones was so well aware that the operation could not be expected to yield any great amount of prize money that he appealed to Franklin for something to pacify the crew, and the commissioners accordingly promised the men in writing that in view of their important services they would be recommended to Congress for special recognition.

It must be remembered that the vast majority of the enlisted men in the American service had not gone to sea for the purpose of winning a war, but for the purpose of winning prize money. Most of the officers, if they did not share this view, at least acquiesced in it, which is to say they adopted the view of true corsairs. The possibility of having to fight was always recognized, of course, but the feeling of the crew was that time spent in fighting was time wasted from the real business, which was running down prizes.

The conspicuous exception to this rule was Captain John Paul Jones. "I propose to go in the way of danger," he said, which was exactly contrary to the policy of a corsair. The truth is that he was the one commander who was most emphatically not a corsair. The difference between the true naval officer and the corsair in the eighteenth century was merely one of emphasis; the officer was intent on winning the war, with prizes as an incidental; the corsair was intent on winning prizes with victory as an incidental.

Yet for a hundred years it was precisely Jones who was singled out for denunciation, in England as a pirate, in other countries, including the one for which he fought, by the politer term of corsair.

The reason, no doubt, is a matter of semantics. What does the word "pirate" connote to the mind of the average man? Lawyers apart, few could give a definition acceptable to a court of admiralty; what they mean by "pirate" is not a man who commits a particular sort of crime carefully defined by statutes, but simply a terrible fellow connected with the sea. Well, there is no doubt at all that within a few months John Paul Jones had become the most terrible fellow connected with the sea known to the populace of the British Isles. The rest of them, although they took more ships than he, were merely expensive annoyances, but this one was a direct menace who prevented honest burgesses from sleeping soundly o' nights in their English beds in English towns. Any man who did that was obviously a pirate, regardless of statutes and lawyers' quibblings.

In truth, the British cannot be much blamed for holding that this sailor was worse than Rollo the Norseman, Blackbeard, and Captain Kidd rolled into one, for it was their sleep that he disturbed; but others should have known better, and above all, his own countrymen should have known better. If we did not, it was only in part because we remained in intellectual bondage to the British long after the political bonds were riven, and our historians, even Theodore Roosevelt in 1888, were given to parroting British views; in great measure it was another difficulty, namely, that we did not know exactly what to call him. He was plainly different from most ship captains, but he was in a class to himself; for at that time the professional naval officer did not exist as a class. He was the only specimen in our service, and it was many years before the category was recognized.

There was never a more completely professional idea than that of administering a psychological shock to the British. It was the sort of thing that would contribute to the winning of the war and to nothing else. It was conspicuously the idea of a professional officer, and just as conspicuously not the idea of a corsair.

At the same time it was fantastic, and this perhaps may be too much for followers of Mahan and other such strategists. Nothing fantastic on the face of it, they will aver, can possibly be professional.

But there they err. Strategy is scientific and science has its limits, which genius transcends. Strategy calculates probability, and when an event is improbable beyond a certain point it is regarded as strategically impossible. Mahan would have dismissed Paul Jones's idea instantly. Indeed, he has criticized it as violating all the canons of strategy, which, indeed, it did. Yet the very title of Mahan's classic, *The Influence of Sea Power upon History,* is enough to show that his general argument is irrelevant to this case. The strategist assumed the existence of sea power and Paul Jones had none; hence the strategist's arguments simply do not apply.

To appreciate what was proposed, it is essential to make a rough translation into modern terms. The factors are so numerous that anything like precision is impossible, but it is not altogether wild to say that a sloop of eighteen guns was to the British navy of 1778 as a single destroyer is to the modern British fleet, disregarding modern air power. A naval officer who would propose today to attack Great Britain with a single destroyer would certainly be commended to the attention of the ship's surgeon as a lunatic.

But in Paul Jones's day there was a factor in the situation not listed in any navy roster or tables of organization, yet all-important. This was Jemmy Twitcher. John Montagu, fourth earl of Sandwich, had indeed made his name immortal by refusing to leave a card game to go to lunch, having, instead, his servant bring him a piece of meat between two slices of bread, but that is the only efficient thing he was ever known to do. As First Lord of the Admiralty he made as obscene a mockery of running his department as he had formerly made of the rites of the Roman Church as a member of the Hellfire Club. He had plenty of force at his disposal, and not a few good men, Howe for a conspicuous example; but under his management the force was never intelligently disposed and the men were for all practical purposes handcuffed, so Britain was really wide open to any seaman of skill and daring.

This was, if you please, an insane situation, but it existed. Paul Jones knew it existed; and he had the extraordinary wit to perceive that in an insane situation, lunacy may be the only good sense. This was where genius overleaped strategy and made the seeming madman an immortal.

So in April the little *Ranger* stood out from L'Orient Harbor and vanished over the western horizon; and presently such a pandemonium of yells and curses arose from Britain as the tight little isle had not emitted for two hundred years, not since Medina-Sidonia bore down upon it with the Invincible Armada under his command.

VI.

This cruise of the *Ranger*, as one looks back on it now, was certainly among the weirdest voyages since Sinbad the Sailor retired from the sea.

Nothing happened until the sloop was halfway between the Scilly Islands and Cape Clear, headed straight for St. George's

Channel and the Irish Sea, when she took a brigantine bound for Ostend with a cargo of flaxseed from Ireland. She was promptly sunk—no percentage in that for the crew, and they did not like it.

Then straight into the Lion's den she went, through St. George's Channel, and almost in sight of Dublin overtook the *Lord Chatham*, from London, loaded with porter and general merchandise. There were some things that even the audacity of John Paul Jones could not compass, and to sink a shipload of beer in the presence of an American crew was one of them, so he put a prize crew on this ship and sent her in. The next day he made for Whitehaven, intending to raid the harbor, but the wind increased to such an extent that a landing was impossible, so he stood off again and shot up a revenue wherry, but she was too fast for the *Ranger* and got away. The next morning he fell in with a Scotch schooner loaded with barley and sank her; no percentage for the crew, and they liked it less than ever. He heard of a fleet of ten or twelve sail at anchor in Lochryan and made for it, but it came on to blow again, so he had to turn away. He discovered a sloop from Dublin and sank her to prevent her giving intelligence of his presence. No percentage for the crew.

The next day, the twenty-first, off Carrickfergus an Irish fishing boat came off, which he seized. He saw a ship at anchor in the road, which the fisherman told him was the British ship of war *Drake*, twenty guns, which was Jemmy Twitcher's idea of a sufficient guardian for that coast, and the *Ranger* went for her. All this time the *Ranger* was disguised, her warlike equipment kept out of sight, and the *Drake* suspected nothing. It was Jones's purpose to come down on her as if blunderingly, crash into her, and board before she knew what was happening; but some prize idiot failed to let go the anchor the moment the order was given and the delay spoiled the maneuver; and wind and tide prevented another trial. In fact, the gale increased to such an extent that Jones had to get out of there and take shelter under the south shore of Scotland.

But the twenty-second dawned fair, "though the three king-doms were, as far as the eye could reach, covered with snow," as Jones reported later. He was in a position where he could see Ireland, Scotland, and England. He now decided to try White-haven again, but as usual everything went wrong. The wind was so light that the ship sailed all day and most of the night before she came into position.

All this time the crew had been getting more and more dis-contented. A devil of a cruise this was! The only thing the Cap-tain seemed really enthusiastic about was piling into an enemy warship, which meant hard blows and very little booty. When he did seize a prize he sank her; besides, getting one out of the confinement of the Irish Sea, presumably patrolled by British warships—although they had seen none but the *Drake*—would be ticklish business. Now he was bent upon stirring up the hor-nets' nest by raiding an English town. He wasn't even expect-ing to carry off anything worth while. He was simply going to burn the shipping and perhaps the town. This might be war, but there was no percentage in it for sailormen, who wanted something more than victory to take home with them.

More than that, Whitehaven was English soil. It was all very well to talk about Norfolk, Virginia, and Falmouth, Massa-chusetts, which had been burned by the British, as affording ample reason for this raid. But this was England, and nobody had successfully invaded the soil of England since William the Conqueror in 1066. Raiding England was defying the lightning and the crew didn't like it, not even a little bit.

However, the vengeance of the Lion was a theory and the Captain was a very present fact; nobody durst stand up to him when he was in a fighting mood, so thirty-one of them piled sullenly into two boats and started rowing ashore shortly before dawn.

What they might have felt had they suspected that one among them was a spy is unimaginable, but it was so. A seaman who had shipped as David Smith was in fact one Freeman, an Eng-lishman who was only awaiting an opportunity to desert. Naturally he was prompt to volunteer as a member of the landing party, and as the boats pulled through the darkness he was meditating plans to slip away and warn the town.

Simpson had not volunteered for the expedition, nor had Hall, the second officer, so the Captain led it himself. No more need be said of the two officers. Lorenz remarks that they "feigned illness" when the moment came, but perhaps there was no feigning about it. A yellow-livered specimen confronted with danger does not have to pretend to be sick; he actually is sick. For that matter, sometimes a brave man is, too, but the brave man goes on anyhow, while the coward drops out. But Wallingsford, a lieutenant of marines, and Hill, a midshipman —but Benjamin, not Charles, who wrote the "Song of the *Ranger*"—stepped up when the ship's officers quit, and a Swedish volunteer named Edward Meyer, an old army man, offered to go. Jones accordingly gave one boat to Wallingsford and Hill, taking the other himself with Meyer as second in command.

Whitehaven Harbor was crowded. There were more than two hundred ships there, and at low tide most of them were aground, some entirely out of the water. It was a perfect setup for an incendiary raid. Jones ordered Wallingsford's boat to the north side, where some seventy ships lay, while he took the south side, with a hundred and fifty. The first objectives, however, were the two forts at the harbor mouth, and these Jones's party took with ridiculous ease. Just as dawn began to break they approached the first; lacking ladders, they climbed on each other's shoulders and scrambled through the embrasures. Jones leading. Since the weather was cold, the sentinels had been withdrawn and the entire garrison was in the guardroom when the invaders swarmed in. Not a shot was fired.

Jones then ordered his boat to proceed with the firing of the ships. They were provided with pine torches and other combustibles, and each boat carried a lighted lantern to touch them off. Jones and one man, Green by name, proceeded to spike the fort's guns, walked to the other fort, found nobody there, and spiked its guns also, putting, all told, thirty-six cannon out of commission. Coming back, he expected to see smoke rising from the harbor, but none was in sight. Arrived at the harbor he found Wallingsford's party returned, explaining that their lantern had gone out so they could set no fires, and besides they had heard noises; so they fled. Meyer, too, was raving, for when he tried to set a fire he found that his lantern, too, was out. Cowardice seemed to have defeated the whole project.

In the meantime, although nobody knew it yet, Freeman, alias Smith, had slipped away in the darkness and was now running through Whitehaven, hammering on doors and spreading the alarm.

But John Paul Jones always shone in the moment of defeat. Furiously damning the blundering incompetents, he sent Meyer and Green to the nearest house to procure a light, and those two had spirit enough to obey. Then he chose the largest ship near by, which was deserted, compelled the men to pile up inflammable matter in her steerage, and himself put the fire to it. Most of the men he ordered to fall back to the boats, under the command of Meyer, while he looked about for something to speed the fire. He discovered a barrel of tar, which was poured on the flames with a prompt and gratifying effect.

By this time the inhabitants were pouring down to the harbor "in great numbers," said Jones. The Captain ordered the rest of the men back, but he stepped between the crowd and the burning ship, drew a pistol, and ordered the civilians to draw back, which they did with great promptness.

In the meantime the boats' crews had fallen into abject terror, and only the lurid language and menacing gestures of Meyer kept them from actually deserting their commander and pulling away.

Then John Paul Jones made one of the great theatrical gestures of American history. When the crowd had recoiled before his pistol, leisurely he strolled out upon the mole alongside which the boats were lying, but instead of stepping in he stopped, turned his back upon them, and stood for some minutes contemplating the scene. The fire by this time had caught the rigging and was shooting up the mainmast and the ship was transformed into a mighty pillar of smoke and flame standing against the rising sun. Beyond it, the muttering crowd still held back and John Paul Jones looked on.

It had not happened before for seven hundred and twelve years. It was not to happen again for at least a hundred and seventy years. In the mighty expanse of nine centuries this figure stands solitary, unrivaled, uncompanioned, an armed enemy upon the sacred soil of England with none to strike him down.

At last after minutes that seemed like hours to the spellbound sailors, he turned and stepped into his boat, the first man since William the Conqueror to invade England and come away unharmed. Even the Norman's feat was less spectacular, for William came backed by a great army composed of some of the finest fighting men on earth; while Paul Jones invaded England with two men, Meyer and Green, twenty-eight poltroons, and a spy!

VII.

But this incredible cruise was as yet only begun. Upon the colossal it was to pile the fantastic and follow that with the fabulous. The fantastic began to creep in before the boats were fifty yards offshore. There was racing and chasing in Whitehaven the moment that threatening pistol was removed. Running alongshore the populace swarmed to the forts, easily outpacing the boats. Frantically they swiveled the guns around to command the channel through which the boats must pass—but the guns were spiked. Furiously they worked to bring up other guns from the ships, or perhaps to get into place some that had been lying dismounted about the forts. In the meantime the boats swung jauntily past, and when at last the forts did open fire they were so far out that the shots fell short and splashed harmlessly into the sea. The crew, tremendously brave now that the danger was past, responded with derisive pistol shots and taunting yells. Presently they were aboard and heaving up the anchor while the smoke of the burning ship still hung over Whitehaven.

While the crew was thinking of prize money, the Captain had in mind two objects. One was to convince the British people that the British naval policy of burning American coastal towns might have unpleasant repercussions and therefore was worse than dubious. The destruction of two hundred ships in Whitehaven Harbor and, if the wind carried the fire in the right direction, possibly the destruction of the town itself would have proved that point with a vengeance. But as the *Ranger* drew away, he had to reflect bleakly that a combination of cowardice and treason had largely defeated that object.

The other thing he had in mind was to obtain a better bargaining position for the Americans with regard to American seamen held prisoner by the British. British policy, based on what logic no man can tell, was to recognize a captured American soldier as a prisoner of war, but to hold that a captured American sailor was either a deserter or a pirate. Captured seamen, therefore, were treated as criminals, and the eighteenth century was not tenderhearted in its treatment of criminals.

The Americans by this time had rounded up a considerable number of British seamen, but the vast majority of them were foremast hands and none was of any considerable importance. The British, therefore, haughtily rejected all proposals for an exchange and the Americans held in England were in a very bad way. Jones conceived the idea, and he was probably right, that one really important Englishman in his hands would be worth a thousand ordinary seamen in bringing the British naval authorities to see reason.

Now it seemed to him that he had a chance to pick up one. Almost directly across from the Solway lay Kirkcudbright, and off the port St. Mary's Isle, seat of the Earl of Selkirk. Why not seize the Earl, and for his ransom demand the release, or at least the exchange, of the American prisoners? The fact that Selkirk was a noncombatant was a detail; he was an important Briton, reputed to be influential in London, and as for the laws of war, the British were violating them flagrantly every day in their treatment of American seamen.

Toward the mouth of the Dee, then, the *Ranger* headed, and now her crew was jubilant. Raiding a peaceful country estate, and in Scotland, at that, was more to their taste than raiding a fortified harbor in England itself. The short run was made speedily, but when the *Ranger* dropped anchor in the estuary Jones did not ask Simpson or anyone else to volunteer. A job of this delicacy he would handle himself.

But his hopes were soon dashed. A boatman encountered near the landing told him, with patent honesty, that the Earl of Selkirk was in London. So that was that. The Captain ordered a retreat, but now he encountered a real revolt among his men. Why all this delicacy? they demanded. When the British landed in Virginia they did not retire if the master of the estate happened to be away. On the contrary, they carried off everything movable, down to the very pigs and cattle of the tenants. They emptied the smokehouses and corncribs, they shot the draft animals, they burned the barns with the wagons and farm implements. Above all they went for such valuables as might be readily turned into money, and they weren't in the least delicate about it.

The men were telling the truth and Paul Jones couldn't deny it. More than that, everyone knew that this was his old home and these were people whom he had known from his youth up. If he were adamant, he could be accused with some color of plausibility, if not of truth, of sacrificing the interests of his men to protect the property of his personal friends. The situation was out of hand, and he realized it.

Accordingly, he agreed to send a detail to the house to demand the Earl's silverware. He sent along two officers with strict orders that they alone were to enter the house, posting their men around it, that they were to offer no discourtesy to Lady Selkirk or to anyone else in the place, and that they were to accept the plate given them without undertaking a search of the premises. One of the officers was Wallingsford, and as the other appeared to be his superior in rank he must have been either Simpson or Hall, the gentry who were too sick to raid Whitehaven. The only identification we have is Lady Selkirk's declaration that he "seemed by nature very disagreeable . . . had a vile blackguard look" and was remonstrated with by his junior when he began to be offensive.

However, they followed their instructions, took the plate as it was offered them, and gave Lady Selkirk a receipt for it. They did not trouble even to empty the silver teapot of the tea leaves that were still in it. They then removed their men and departed without offering molestation to anyone. A very civil raid it was indeed, by comparison with what had been going on in Virginia.

Not that that did anything to appease the chatelaine. It is said, indeed, that she was so relieved at the moment that she offered the officers a glass of wine and sent a courteous message to the Captain; but she was wrathful enough the next day when she wrote her husband, "It was immediately known that this Paul Jones is one John Paul, born at Arbigland, who once commanded a Kirkcudbright vessel belonging to Mr. Muir and others, a great villain as ever was born, guilty of many crimes and several murders by ill usage, was tried and condemned for one, escaped and followed a piratical life till he engaged with the Americans. He seems to delight in that still, as robbing a house is below the dignity of the States of America."

But not below that of the British Empire? Well, she was doubtless convinced that what was told of the British in America was all propaganda. We always believe that of tales told against our side.

It must be admitted, however, that this did look like a crazy adventure from her ladyship's standpoint, and probably from that of Paul Jones, too, as the *Ranger* stood away from the Solway. The fates seemed to be dead against him. He had had two good ideas and both had gone wrong. His descent upon Whitehaven had resulted in the burning of one wretched ship, and his plan to assist the imprisoned American seamen had resulted only in annoying a lady. He must have been in a pretty grim mood as the Scottish shore receded.

Then as if to add to the jollity of the occasion Edward Meyer, the Swedish soldier, came to him with a tale that he had been told by a compatriot, a Swede who had enlisted as a seaman. According to this yarn, the American members of the crew were completely fed up. They were making no money under this captain and they were constantly taking fearful chances. They had already been away from home longer than most of them had expected and they wanted to go back. They had just about made up their minds to mutiny, clap the Captain in irons, or heave him overboard if necessary, put Simpson in command, and head back for America. Meyer thought they had sounded Simpson out and found him agreeable, if, indeed, he had not instigated the plot.

So, having in hand a small, lightly armed ship, with a mutinous crew and a certainly cowardly and probably traitorous first officer, Jones decided that he was in position to give battle.

VIII.

All this part of the coast was supposed to be guarded by the *Drake*, the twenty-gun ship that Jones had tried to reach but couldn't. Since the *Drake* was never around during the raiding operations, the *Ranger* now went out looking for her; she found her the next day in Belfast Lough, lying off Carrickfergus.

Jones proposed to bore right in and blast her out, but at this the crew rose in open rebellion. The officers sided with the men. They declared roundly that they were poor men, out for gain, not for honor. They did not want to fight a British warship in any circumstances, and as for fighting one under the guns of British shore batteries, they weren't going to do it and that was flat. The Captain might order until he was blue in the face, but they simply would not take the *Ranger* in. It was a tense moment. "The mutiny," wrote Jones later, "almost reduced me to the necessity of putting some of them to death."

That is an interesting remark. Meyer, a volunteer, not a ship's officer, and therefore in this crisis a bystander, thought it was the Captain who was in imminent danger, seeing that the odds were 123 to 1. Apparently that did not occur to Jones at all; to him it seemed that it was the foolish sailors who were risking sudden, violent death. Arithmetic certainly supports Meyer's view, but if anything is certain about this man's career it is that it cannot be measured by arithmetic. True, there were 123 in the crew and there was only one captain; but the captain was John Paul Jones, so perhaps the odds really were against the crew and it was they who were in peril.

In any event, just as an explosion seemed inevitable, everyone's attention was diverted by the *Drake*. She sent out one of her boats to investigate. Jones ordered the crew to their quarters below, where they could not be seen, and they sullenly obeyed. The gun ports, of course, were closed, the tops were empty, and superficially there was nothing warlike in the appearance of the *Ranger*. British colors drooped from her mast.

Then the crew, peeping through interstices, began to be interested in the way the Captain was decoying the scout. The Briton wanted a look at her sides, but the *Ranger* kept her stern directly toward the boat. Again and again the latter swerved to one side or the other, but always at the same moment the *Ranger* swerved, too, and the boat could see nothing but the stern. Yet it was done with such casualness that the British officer could not be sure it was intentional, and not simply the work of a clumsy helmsman. The *Ranger*'s crew began to be amused —"it tickled their caprice," said Jones—to see the enemy so neatly deluded; and when the boat at last shot alongside and the officer in command stepped aboard to find himself a prisoner, the sullen muttering of an hour before was transformed into cheers and laughter.

The mood did not change when the *Drake* began firing signal guns to call her tender back. The delighted sailors had only taunts for the ship they had been dreading, and when the *Drake* made sail and began to work her way out of the harbor to come after her boat, interest and excitement, but no panic, mounted. Jones had been tacking back and forth, and now as the *Drake*

approached he edged farther and farther out, not intending
to engage until he had plenty of sea room.

Excitement was mounting ashore, too. Smoke from signal
fires was spreading the alarm up and down the coast as far as the
eye could see, and a small fleet of pleasure boats followed the
Drake to see the fun, but as the *Ranger* drew her antagonist well
out into the North Channel these prudently put back, decid-
ing that it might not be much fun, after all. Slowly the distance
between the two vessels narrowed, and late in the afternoon
the *Drake* drew within pistol shot, almost astern. Jones had
hauled down his British colors some time earlier, and now,
when the *Drake* ran up hers, he broke out the Stars and Stripes
and flung it to the breeze, expecting to be fired upon immediately. Instead he was hailed and his identity demanded. Jones
gave his master instructions to make a long reply to hold the
British captain's attention a few seconds more, and at the same
time ordered the helm up; that is, he turned his ship at right
angles so that she would be dead ahead of the *Drake* and broadside on.

So the master bawled through his speaking trumpet, "This
is the American Continental ship *Ranger;* we are waiting for
you and desire that you come on; the sun is now little more than
an hour from setting, it is therefore time to begin."

Whether his attention was distracted by the master's gab-
bling, or for some other reason, the Briton did not perceive
the significance of the deadly maneuver in time to counter it,
and the *Ranger,* in perfect position, raked him from stem to
stern with her first broadside, and then spun about so neatly
that in this first exchange she did not receive a shot. Furthermore, since she was within pistol shot, the *Drake*'s deck received
a hail of musket balls from the *Ranger*'s fighting tops.

But the battle was far from being finished. The *Drake* was
not a British man-o'-war with all the traditions of the British
navy behind her for nothing. She was tough. Burdon, her captain, was a good man, and when the *Ranger* was first sighted a

Lieutenant Dobbs, who was in Carrickfergus on leave from a ship of the line, volunteered to go with him as second in command. With two such officers and a well-disciplined crew of 175, the ship was well handled and well fought. The *Ranger* had won the first round, but that only made her antagonist settle down to work.

The unfortunate Burdon, however, was pitted against something like a miracle. The sullen, mutinous crew, the pack that had acted like whipped curs at Whitehaven the previous morning and like jackals at St. Mary's Isle in the afternoon, the crowd whose mutiny at noon that day had branded them as the world's prize lot of seagoing riffraff, now at dusk turned into a compact, machine-like organization of fighting devils.

Paul Jones was one of the hardest men in the world to satisfy on anything touching naval affairs, but he said afterward that he had never seen guns served so magnificently, or such a steady drumming of musketry from the fighting tops, or had his orders to helm and men at the ropes executed so promptly and with such hairbreadth precision.

The *Ranger* was not a good ship. Ordinarily she was crank and slow and her helmsman never knew exactly what was going to happen when he undertook to change course; but now the wills of all the 123 men in her were compressed and absorbed into one will, the powerful, cold, and steely will of the greatest seaman of his time, and she became a thing possessed. She spun and pirouetted around the astounded Englishman like a mad ballet dancer around a stolid policeman; her yelling guns never ceased their clamor for an instant while the waspish musket balls flailed every exposed foot of her deck.

The *Drake* was tough. For an hour and four minutes she took it, landing only occasionally, and then never solidly, on her dancing foe. But the toughest fighter has his limit, and the limit eventually was reached. Captain Burdon was dead. Lieutenant Dobbs was dying. The bo'sun was dead. Forty-two of the crew were laid out, dead or disabled. The rigging was a tangled mess and the ship was unmanageable. She struck her colors and asked for quarter.

John Paul Jones had written his characteristic signature all over His Majesty's ship. Let it be told in the words of his official report: "her fore and main-topsail yards being both cut away, and down on the cap; the top-gallant yard and mizzen-gaff both hanging up and down along the mast; the second ensign which they had hoisted shot away, and hanging on the quarter gallery in the water; the jib shot away and hanging in the water; her sails and rigging entirely cut to pieces; her masts and yards all wounded, and her hull also very much galled."

Get the rigging first, cripple her speed, and then pound her at leisure—it was unmistakably the Jones formula.

The *Ranger's* losses were two killed and six wounded, one fatally. One of the two who got it was Lieutenant Wallingsford, commanding the marines, and therefore largely responsible for the excellent small-arms fire that swept the enemy's deck.

So now it is necessary to go back and erase something from the previous record. This officer had shown up badly at Whitehaven. He let his lantern go out, or be put out, he let his men get completely out of hand, he fumbled his mission and accomplished nothing, and had it not been for the resolute Meyer he might have been involved in the disgrace of deserting his captain. Rather a messy record, that. But at least he went when his superior officers cravenly refused to go. That is something. Then when the test of real battle came, he stood up, fought well, and died at his post of duty. That is everything.

We can forget the rest. Indeed, we cannot remember the rest, not honorably, not we who profited by his death, we who today enjoy life and liberty because the country has always found men like him at its hour of greatest need. Let it be written, then, that there was a man named Wallingsford who sailed with John Paul Jones; and all that we can remember of him is that he died like a man, he died like an officer of the United States Marines.

The *Ranger* had a prize indeed in a British ship of war, but what she was going to do with that prize was something of a problem. Obviously, both ships had to get away and get away fast, for the Irish Sea was really a British lake and as soon as word of the battle spread half the British navy would be converging on the spot, boiling with wrath and desire to wipe out the humiliation. It was an extremely hot spot and getting hotter by the minute.

Fortunately, the night was mild and the sea smooth, so Jones ordered Simpson to get aboard the wreck, clean up the mess, and put her in shape to move by morning. But the first lieutenant, instead of obeying, impudently replied that it wasn't humanly possible to do the job in one night and he wouldn't even try. Jones must have wondered, as history has wondered ever since, if there was anything, any one solitary thing on God's green footstool, that Mr. Simpson was good for. If there was, it has escaped the record.

So the Captain turned to Hall, the second lieutenant, who took forty men aboard the *Drake,* and although it was an unholy mess indeed, went at it with a will. By the time the sun rose he had cleared away the wreckage and had rigged up something that would carry her through the water. It had been Jones's purpose to go south and out through St. George's Channel, right through the British frigates that by now must be swarming like angry hornets. But the wind was in the wrong direction and above all else he had to move, so he steered north, to pass around the west coast of Ireland.

Now Paul Jones did a thing for which his biographers have never been able to find an adequate excuse. Once the ships were under way Simpson demanded command of the prize and Jones let him have it. This act was bound to be regarded as in some measure condoning that officer's flagrantly bad conduct, and to condone bad conduct is a serious fault indeed in a commander. Perhaps the most charitable assumption is that by this time it made him sick even to look at Simpson; and on the prize he would at least be out of sight.

By keeping well out in the Atlantic they avoided any hostile encounter, the *Drake* limping along with such difficulty that she had to be towed part of the time. Off Ushant, though, they ran into the traffic lanes and presently sighted a big ship that Jones thought might be a valuable prize. He had the *Drake* in tow at the time, so he signaled what he was about to do and ordered her to cast off. They promptly cut the hawser and Jones took after the stranger. It took some time to run her down, and then she turned out to be a neutral Swede.

He had ordered the *Drake* to trail along, but when he had found that his chase was fruitless and looked about for her, he found her, to his astonishment, legging it for the far horizon. There were ships all about and he was sure that some were British, therefore lawful prize, but first he had to find out what possessed Simpson. Night was coming on before he got close enough to make sure his signals could be read, and then he ordered her to heave to, but she paid not the slightest attention and as darkness came on disappeared from view.

Morning discovered an empty sea except for one sail very far away to the south-southwest, that is to say, directly in the wrong direction for Brest, whither the ships were supposed to be bound. The *Ranger* gave chase and after hours of hard driving ran her down. The ship was the *Drake*. Simpson was making off with it for purposes known to him alone.

This was too much even for the unduly tolerant Paul Jones. He did now what he should have done a week earlier—he slapped Simpson under arrest. Then both ships put about and retraced their way to the French port.

They arrived at Brest at night, and when they were challenged by the first ship of the harbor patrol, Jones muffed his reply signals, undoubtedly with intent. Of course this suspicious act promptly brought two big frigates tearing down upon him, snapping, "What ship is that? What is your convoy?" Having thus secured an appropriate audience, Jones replied, this time very clearly indeed:

"The American Continental ship *Ranger,* of eighteen guns. The prize is His Britannic Majesty's late ship the *Drake,* of twenty guns."

Well, Captain John Paul Jones had won another battle, so, in accordance with the American custom in dealing with him, there was nothing to do except take his ship away from him.

So they did.

CHAPTER VI.

I.

Paul Jones returned to a situation materially altered, although he did not know it at the moment. Silas Deane had been recalled and John Adams had taken his place, which meant that for a time Arthur Lee had two votes in the commission instead of one.

But the Captain's first thought, on dropping anchor in Brest Harbor, was of a matter only indirectly bearing upon politics. It was of Lord Selkirk's plate. The booty was not, as a matter of fact, of any overwhelming value. The design was old-fashioned and of an English type never popular in France, and the service had been in use for a long time. Jones negotiated with the crew and finally purchased their interest in it for £140, which he paid out of his own pocket. Then he sat down and wrote Lady Selkirk a letter that became famous at the time and that has astonished and greatly interested historians and biographers ever since.

Exactly what he meant nobody has quite made out to this day. He was returning the silverware, of course, but that could have been done with a covering note of a few lines, instead of the pages he wrote. He was clearing himself of the accusation of piracy, but the act was enough to do that; indeed, the act was all that had any bearing on that accusation. He was calling attention—for he intended the letter to be made public—to the lamentable condition of the American seamen in British prisons, but that did not call for the folderol with which he loaded the letter.

Some have expressed astonishment that he wrote to Lady

Selkirk, but that seems to explain itself. The whole point of the letter was its denial that John Paul Jones made war upon women. He was admittedly making war upon Selkirk. The primary purpose of the raid was to seize the Earl and hold him to ransom, not in money, but in an exchange of American prisoners for British. He had no apologies to make to Selkirk; it was the lady to whom he felt he owed amends. So it was Lady Selkirk whom he addressed in the following rather booming terms:

Ranger, Brest, May 8th, 1778

Madam,

It cannot be too much lamented, that in the profession of arms, the officer of fine feeling and of real sensibility should be under the necessity of winking at any action of persons under his command, which his heart cannot approve; but the reflection is doubly severe, when he finds himself obliged, in appearance, to countenance such actions by his authority.

This hard case was mine when, on the 23rd of April last, I landed on St. Mary's Isle. Knowing Lord Selkirk's interest with his king, and esteeming, as I do, his private character, I wished to make him the happy instrument of alleviating the horrors of hopeless captivity, when the brave are overpowered and made prisoners of war.

It was, perhaps, fortunate for you, Madam, that he was from home; for it was my intention to have taken him on board the *Ranger,* and to have detained him until, through his means, a general and fair exchange of prisoners, as well in Europe as in America, had been effected.

When I was informed, by some men whom I met at landing, that his lordship was absent, I walked back to my boat, determined to leave the island. By the way, however, some officers, who were with me, could not forbear expressing their discontent; observing that, in America, no delicacy was shown by the English, who took away all sorts of moveable property—setting fire, not only to towns and houses of the rich, without distinction, but not even sparing the wretched hamlets and milch-cows of the poor and helpless, at the approach of an inclement winter. That party had been with me, the same morning, at Whitehaven; some complaisance, therefore, was their due. I had but a moment to think how I might gratify them, and at the same time do your ladyship the least injury. I charged the two officers to permit none of the seamen to enter the house, or to hurt any thing about it—to treat you, Madam, with the utmost respect—to accept of the plate which was offered— and to come away without making a search, or demanding any thing else.

I am induced to believe that I was punctually obeyed; since I am informed, that the plate which they brought away is far short of the quantity expressed in the inventory which accompanied it. I have gratified my men; and when the plate is sold I shall become the purchaser, and will gratify my own feelings by restoring it to you, by such conveyance as you shall please to direct.

Had the earl been on the *Ranger* the following evening, he would have seen the awful pomp and dreadful carnage of a sea engagement; both affording ample subject for the pencil, as well as melancholy reflection to the contemplative mind. Humanity starts back from such scenes of horror, and cannot sufficiently execrate the vile promoters of this detestable war.

"For *they*, 'twas *they* unsheath'd the ruthless blade,
And Heaven shall ask the havoc that it made."

The British ship of war *Drake*, mounting twenty guns, with more than her full complement of officers and men, was our opponent. The ships met, and the advantage was disputed with great fortitude on each side, for an hour and four minutes, when the gallant commander of the *Drake* fell, and victory declared in favor of the *Ranger*. The amiable lieutenant lay mortally wounded, besides near forty of the inferior officers and crew killed and wounded; a melancholy demonstration of the uncertainty of human prospects, and of the sad reverse of fortune which an hour can produce. I buried them in a spacious grave with the honours due to the memory of the brave.

Though I have drawn my sword in the present generous struggle for the rights of men, yet I am not in arms as an American, nor am I in pursuit of riches. My fortune is liberal enough, having no wife nor family, and having lived long enough to know that riches cannot ensure happiness. I profess myself a citizen of the world, totally unfettered by the little, mean distinctions of climate or of country, which diminish the benevolence of the heart and set bounds to philanthropy. Before this war was begun, I had, at an early time of life, withdrawn from sea service, in favour of "calm contemplation and poetic ease." I have sacrificed not only my favourite mode of life, but the softer affections of the heart, and my prospects of domestic happiness, and I am ready to sacrifice my life also, with cheerfulness, if that forfeiture could restore peace and good will among mankind.

As the feelings of your gentle bosom cannot but be congenial with mine, let me entreat you, Madam, to use your persuasive art, with your husband's, to endeavor to stop this cruel and destructive war, in which Britain never can succeed. Heaven can never countenance the barbarous and unmanly practice of the Britons in America, which savages would blush at, and which, if not discontinued, will soon be retaliated on Britain by a justly enraged people. Should you fail in this, (for I am persuaded that you will attempt it, and who can resist the power of such an advocate?) your endeavours to effect a general exchange of prisoners will be an act of humanity which will afford you golden feelings on a deathbed.

I hope this cruel contest will soon be closed; but should it continue, I wage no war with the fair. I acknowledge their force, and bend before it with submission. Let not, therefore, the amiable Countess of Selkirk regard me as an enemy; I am ambitious of her esteem and friendship, and would do any thing, consistent with my duty, to merit it.

The honour of a line from your hand in answer to this, will lay me under a singular obligation; and if I can render you any acceptable service in France or elsewhere, I hope you see into my character so far as to command me without the least grain of reserve.

I wish to know exactly the behaviour of my people, as I am determined to punish them if they have exceeded their liberty. I have the honour to be, with much esteem and profound respect, Madame, & c. & c.

John Paul Jones

Perhaps it is as well to anticipate the story somewhat to dispose of the effects of this remarkable effusion as it concerned the private lives of those involved. The letter got through with reasonable promptitude, for wartime, and Selkirk was at first inclined to be a bit stuffy about it. He is hardly to be blamed for being somewhat nonplused, inasmuch as the labor of the whole faculty of history for a century and a half has not resulted in any general agreement on just what that letter meant.

Yet he had to do something. After all, the fellow was returning the plate, at considerable expense to himself, and the Earl could not permit it to be said that a pirate had outdone him in politeness. At the same time, it was out of the question for the Countess to enter into communication with an enemy, especially such an enemy. So the Earl, never overburdened with brains anyhow, sat down and replied to the letter with a proposition as preposterous as anything the sailor had suggested. He wrote that he would be willing to receive the plate only if Congress ordered its return, not at the hands of Jones.

Apparently it did not occur to him that Congress could not order the stuff returned without repudiating its own officer; whereas Jones was quite at liberty, having paid for it, to send it back without repudiating the government. Lord Selkirk's counterproposal, however, did not come to Jones's attention, because the general post office in London held up the letter for some months and then returned it to the writer with the statement that it was deemed improper to forward any communication to John Paul Jones.

The French, on the other hand, were enchanted by the whole business. They considered Jones's letter a very gallant gesture, and some months later, when he got the silver together—he had been pretty busy with other matters in the meantime—the French government not only ordered it to be passed through all French ports free of duty, or even examination, but also gave it special priority on post roads so that it might reach a neutral ship and be transported to London without delay.

By this time Selkirk, too, had come down off his high horse. He wrote a stiff but altogether courteous letter of acknowledgment to Captain Jones, disavowing any personal animosity toward him and assuring him that the conduct of his men during the raid had been quite correct.

When the silverware eventually reached St. Mary's Isle the tea leaves were still in the teapot. The Selkirks never used it again, and for generations it was kept on exhibition as a museum piece, with the tea leaves undisturbed.

II.

Quite aside from the writer's intent, the Selkirk letter reveals a mystery that has puzzled biographers ever since. That letter is completely, utterly, fatally humorless. The mystery is how a man without humor survived what John Paul Jones was put through by the people and the governments with whom he had to deal. Perhaps the true answer is, he didn't. After all, he died at forty-five, while Ben Franklin, who had to deal with the same people, but who knew how to laugh, lived to eighty-four.

For instance, Jones's first official reward for his raid, up to that time the most brilliant episode in American naval history, was to have his sailors' pay stopped.

This is a long and complicated story, obscured by so much plain and fancy lying that the whole truth about it can never be known. But the undisputed facts—about the only ones that are undisputed—are that in order to enlist men for the cruise Jones had promised that they might draw half their pay in Europe, instead of waiting until the end of the voyage; that the men, knowing too much about the financial responsibility of the United States at that time, were not content until the Captain promised to be personally responsible for the amount; that on arrival at Brest he drew on the commissioners for 24,000 livres, something less than $5,000; and that the commissioners refused to honor the draft.

Jones said he had explained his personal responsibility to Lee. Lee said he hadn't. Adams and Franklin certainly knew nothing of that phase of the matter, and if Deane did that was no help, for Deane was gone. All this is as it may be, but it is a certainty that Jones was stuck for a matter of nearly $5,000 which he had promised a crew that was already mutinous, but that had nevertheless fought well against the *Drake*.

The *Ranger* had sent in a ship loaded with beer that was worth much more than the amount due the seamen; and she had brought in the *Drake*, worth several times as much. Half of this prize money would go to the government; which is to say, the sailors had actually turned in to the government property worth far more than their pay. Nevertheless, that government would not pay them a cent. How could any captain hope to maintain discipline under such conditions?

The fly in the ointment, of course, was Arthur Lee; but at this juncture he was receiving able assistance from the new commissioner, John Adams, who had replaced Deane. Lee's stream of venomous reports had at last induced Congress to recall Deane, ostensibly to report on conditions in France, but really to face a savage investigation. Deane accepted the order to report in good faith, and left in such a hurry that he did not take along the vouchers and account books necessary to prove his honesty; so when the investigating committee put him on the grill they had him right where they wanted him. After they had leisurely torn his reputation to shreds and tatters and damned him utterly before the public, they permitted him to return to France for the papers in 1780; years later they were subjected to a proper audit and no serious discrepancies were found in them. But by that time Deane had completed his own ruin. Harried, harassed, and bankrupt, he had fallen into black pessimism, and had written people at home that the colonies might as well give up the struggle and make the best peace they could with their king. After that, he could never return, and he died miserably in England in 1789. Score one for Arthur Lee.

John Adams went to France never doubting that Lee's reports were true. This was easy for Honest John, who was not yet a great man. He was not one of those who are born great. He acquired greatness, and he acquired it by painfully slow degrees. At this time it was still far from him. At this time he was merely an epitome of Boston at its most objectionable. Already he was beginning to fancy himself something of a liberal in theology, but in reality he was permeated, soaked, saturated in at least one of the doctrines of Calvinism and that the deadliest of all— the doctrine of original sin.

In the mind of John Calvin himself it is possible that this doctrine was basically a mystical concept of the continuity of experience involving the indefinite transmission of evil; but the practical New Englanders had drawn it from the realm of abstraction and employed it to give moral sanction to their natural human conceit. If all men are worms, which is sound New England Calvinism, then it is easy to believe that the wormiest are those outside our own clan.

John Adams came to France charged with a philosophy that was at least beautiful in its simplicity. It was a profound conviction that all men are scoundrels save those born in Massachusetts, and even of them most are suspect. Since depravity increased in direct ratio with distance from the center of morality, it followed that Virginians were to be reckoned as worse than Pennsylvanians, and foreigners as worse than Virginians.

The Lees, however, were in political alliance with Samuel Adams, therefore they could not be classed with ordinary Virginians and were probably better than the Pennsylvanian Deane. As for this sea captain Jones, he had been inducted into the Navy from North Carolina, farther from Massachusetts than Virginia, which was suspicious enough; but to add to that, he had been born in Scotland. John Adams was ready to believe anything of such a person.

Arthur Lee told him plenty. He said that this Jones had never exhibited much confidence in any of the commissioners except Franklin—in which Lee for once was telling the truth. He said that Jones was hand in glove with Franklin's nephew, Williams, agent at Nantes, and together they had fitted out the *Ranger* pretty much as they chose, referring nothing to the commissioners except the bills, and Mr. Adams could imagine for himself what went with government money under such conditions. Mr. Adams could, seeing that the men involved were a Pennsylvanian and a North Carolina immigrant, neither of whom had ever breathed the morally stimulating air of Massachusetts. Lee said that he had tried repeatedly to stop this fellow's extravagance and teach him a lesson, but had been overruled by Franklin and Deane. Now, however, the time had come to call a halt, and with Mr. Adams' assistance it could be done.

It was done. Mr. Adams went happily about the business of introducing some sound, Massachusetts decency into this sink of iniquity. He himself promptly discharged Williams, the American, as agent at Nantes, so that Brother William Lee could take over; but Brother William, having a dozen other offices—with commissions—chose not to take charge himself, and appointed a German, one Schweighauser—described by Paul Jones as "that pig of a Schweighauser"—to act for him. Mr. Adams joined with Lee in voting to dishonor the draft. Thus Mr. Adams cleaned up the situation by firing an honest man to make room for a thief and humiliating an American officer in order to prevent American sailors from getting their pay.

Bear in mind, though, that this was John Adams in 1778. He had, although it was not yet apparent, one quality in common with the great John Adams of 1798. That quality was honesty. Lee could, and did, fool him for a while; but the time came when Adams began to see what was what, and then Honest John, like the man he was, ate his own words and paid tribute to the Scotch immigrant.

But that didn't help Jones out of the jam he was in. The Pig had the ships he had taken as prizes and was taking his time about selling them; nor was Jones hopeful of getting the money when they were sold. The sailors were getting in a more and more dangerous mood, nor could the Captain altogether blame them. His situation was desperate, but only once did he give outward evidence of his inner tension.

Through Edward Meyer and others he had a pretty good idea of what the men were saying. Among other things he knew that Simpson was not the only agitator who was stirring them up. Arthur Lee's agents had been busy, too, particularly a fat man named Hezekiah Ford. Lee had been warned against this man by a resolution of the Virginia Legislature, but obstinately refused to part with him; so Ford was in position to furnish a steady stream of information to his British paymasters. Jones did not know this, but he knew what Ford had been doing among the crew.

One morning he encountered Ford in the courtyard of an inn at Brest, where the spy was about to step into the diligence for Paris, and at sight of him the Captain blew up. Ford was a six-footer, weighing two hundred pounds, and Jones was five feet seven and not heavily built, but that had no effect whatever on the proceedings. The thrashing that Ford took was the talk of Brest tavern loungers for months. One straight right to the jaw sent the big man down like a poled ox. Jones whirled upon the stupefied diligence driver, snatched the whip out of his hand, and laid it on the prostrate Ford with fury that mounted with every blow until suddenly he flung away the whip and snatched a pistol from his belt. But by that time the spectators had recovered the power of movement and some of them seized his arm while the fat man, blubbering like a baby, scrambled into the diligence and the driver caught up his whip and got out of there.

Ford never filed a complaint with the police, and the bystanders, having prevented a shooting, let it go at that. They didn't know what it was all about, but they probably decided that a man who fought like that had a good reason for fighting.

III.

But while he was struggling in the toils of politics and finance, proof of his accuracy as a strategist was pouring in. The actual damage his raid had done was inconsiderable. Jones, indeed, regarded it as a failure in every important particular. He had not burned the shipping in Whitehaven Harbor, much less the town. He had not captured Lord Selkirk, or any other important hostage. He had not effected the release of a single American prisoner. In every detail that he had planned in advance, the cruise had proved abortive.

All these, however, were intended to be contributory to his main objective, which was to deliver a psychological shock to the British Empire; and within a week after his arrival at Brest it began to appear that he might have accomplished something toward this. Within a month it was plain that he had achieved it brilliantly.

The *Drake*, for example, was no great loss to the British navy. Hurricanes or tidal waves or even errors of navigation might have wrecked a dozen such ships without dangerously impairing British sea power. But she was a twenty-gun ship that had been beaten in open battle by an eighteen-gun enemy. More than that, she hadn't made the mistake, which the best of ships sometimes made, of running down an antagonist who proved to be unexpectedly strong. She had herself been sought out by a weaker antagonist, challenged, taunted, and really forced into battle. Worst of all, she had been lying in a British port, not even facing the high seas but looking out upon narrow waters with British territory on either side. Far from protecting the area she was supposed to patrol, she had not been able to protect herself. It was as if the burglar, not content with looting the premises, had gone hunting for the policeman on the beat, knocked him out, and carried him off.

To say that this was a shock to the British navy is an understatement. It was that, indeed, but it was also a shattering blow at British prestige all over the seven seas. Every seaman in the world understood at once that it wasn't a question of power, it was a question of wits. To the Dutch, in particular, it was plain that the only possible explanation of Jones's success was carelessness and slow thinking on the part of the British giant. But if the British navy was in fact careless and dull-witted, then the Dutch might have a chance against it, if they joined the Americans and the French. There is no doubt that Whitehaven and the *Drake*, small successes though they were, helped draw the Dutch into the war.

But it was not the navy only that was jarred. England had been invaded! True, it was by a handful of men only, and for no more than a few hours, but the fact remained that invaders had landed, had captured an English fort garrisoned by English soldiers, had destroyed English property, and had withdrawn at their own chosen moment without having received a scratch.

To the rest of the world this may have been incidental, but to the English it was the very heart and center of the whole business. It proved that their fancied security behind their "wooden walls" was illusory. What had happened to Whitehaven might happen to any coastal town, and the next raider might not, almost certainly would not, be handicapped by an incompetent and insubordinate crew.

The response to this stimulus was confused, contradictory, illogical, and typically English, but it was prompt and strong.

The reaction first apparent to the outside world was one characteristic of any nation suddenly confronted with unexpected danger, but at which the British and the Turks seem to be more adept and more reckless than any other peoples of modern times. It was an attempt to prove the moral delinquency of the attacker, thereby converting the struggle against him into a crusade. Things may have altered somewhat in this century, but in the eighteenth Briton and Turk alike seemed to think it somehow indecorous to fight for the Union Jack or the Horsetails; it had to be a fight in defense of the Faith, if they were to do their best, which meant that it was necessary to prove that the enemy was not merely an armed foe, but also an infidel.

To this end the British press went to work on John Paul Jones, and it is not to be denied that it did one of the most complete and uninhibited jobs in the history of journalism. Americans whose memories go back to the post-1929 days of Herbert Hoover and the pre-1941 days of Franklin D. Roosevelt may think they know something about "smear" campaigns; but those efforts at their most venomous seem the work of bungling tyros compared to what the British newspapers did in 1779 and 1780.

They began with "pirate," but that was only the beginning. From that they worked up, and some of their efforts deserve immortality as masterpieces of misrepresentation. A particularly flagrant one* appeared in the London *Morning Post,* whose research staff apparently had dug up something about the Mungo Maxwell incident. As presented to London newspaper readers it runs:

"As the carpenter was, in one of the hot days of summer, laying fast asleep upon the deck, Paul anointed his hair plentifully with turpentine, after which he led a train of gunpowder at some distance, which setting fire to the carpenter, he instantly bounded up, and in the confusion . . . jumped overboard and was never more heard of."

Every other incident in his early career received similar treatment. He was originally gardener to the Earl of Selkirk; discharged for insolence, he ran away to sea and turned pirate; during a murderous career he never ceased to cherish a grudge against the nobleman; it was to vent this spite and not for any

---

* It impressed Sietz and Russell, both of whom quote it in their studies of John Paul Jones.

military purpose that he descended upon St. Mary's Isle, completely sacked the place, insulted her ladyship, and subjected her people to gross abuse; and so on, with anything the atrocity-mongers could think up.

Paul Jones, being humorless—he had a certain wit, but that is a different quality—was incapable of perceiving that this was, in a fashion, quite impersonal. It was merely the customary British procedure with regard to any unusually dangerous enemy, and its object was less to destroy the man's character and reputation than to spur the British to fight the more valiantly against him.

On the contrary, it seemed to Jones that he had been singled out for a persecution unique in history, and instead of taking it philosophically, as part of the game, he waxed indignant in the extreme. It was this assault that provoked him to his furious and famous outburst to the Baron van der Capellan: "I was indeed born in Britain; but I do not inherit the degenerate spirit of that fallen nation, which I at once lament and despise. It is far beneath me to reply to their hireling invectives. They are strangers to the inward approbation that greatly animates and rewards the man who draws his sword only in support of the dignity of freedom."

This sort of thing justifies the comment that Sands* found in the London papers of February 22, 1778: "His letters in foreign Gazettes show he can fight with the pen as well as the sword."

But the smear campaign, although it maddened Jones, was not important historically, and some of the other effects of the cruise were. For one thing, although he burned a single ship and carried away nothing but silverware worth $700, his descent upon the English coast was enormously expensive to English business. Immediately after the raid war-risk insurance, which of course was carried by private underwriters, not by the government, shot to unprecedented heights. Underwriters hitherto had figured that their real risk began only when an insured ship

* *Life and Correspondence of John Paul Jones* (sometimes called the Janette Taylor Life), 1830 edition, p. 87, note.

emerged from home waters and ended when she got back into them; the appalling discovery that ships were in danger even lying at the wharves in British ports made them hastily revise all their rates sharply upward. The premium on a cargo to Ireland, for example, jumped from 1½ to 5 per cent. This alone probably cost British merchants every day more than the value of what Jones had destroyed.

In addition to this there was some interruption of business and a very considerable expenditure of public funds in every coastal town in the three kingdoms following the raid. There was a furious rebuilding and strengthening of coast defenses everywhere. If Jones and Green between them could spike thirty-six cannon at Whitehaven, it was time for every town that faced the sea to look to its defenses, even if it had to devote to that purpose no small sums of money and a great many laborers that it could have used otherwise.

Finally, there was an annoying disruption of ordinary life all along the coast. Nervous old women, of both sexes, hastily departed for the interior, and even coolheaded businessmen who would not themselves leave their countinghouses sent their wives and children on long visits to inland relatives, while countless wagonloads of plate, jewelry, and other valuables moved out of the coastal towns, all involving trouble and expense. The movement grew so general that the press began turning it to ridicule, and Whitehaven in particular became the shining mark of all the satirists. A favorite jape was that the faculty of the famous medical school in Edinburgh was moving en masse to the town to try to restore the inhabitants to sanity. Nevertheless, people kept moving. If a noble lord's teapot wasn't safe on his own table, it was time for common people to look out for themselves.

Historically, though, the really important effect was the sudden increase in the respect paid thereafter to the arguments of Pitt, Burke, Fox, and other liberals who had been contending all along that the war was unjustified and senseless. Nobody had ever answered these men effectively because they were unanswerable. Logic, precedent, tradition, and the very spirit of the British constitution were all on their side. But if they had not been answered, they had been placidly ignored.

Now, however, it began to appear to the average Englishman that not logic, only, but interest also might be on their side. If the war had been unjust from the beginning, it was now threatening to turn very nasty indeed. The average Englishman was of the opinion that any injustice is bad; but injustice that threatened to bring down unpleasant reprisals on his own head was more than bad, it was intolerable.

To be fair it must be added that respectable numbers of the population of England were moved by another consideration, to wit, the sporting instinct. The more they learned about this raid, the more astonishing it became. Say what you would about the pirate, he had the nerve of the devil himself, and his skill, too. It simply is not in the English to hate thoroughly a fighter who is fast on his feet, takes hair-raising risks, and hits hard. They are too capable themselves not to appreciate and admire warlike ability wherever they see it; and when they see it in an enemy it interferes somewhat with their detestation of him.

Thus the main object of the expedition was achieved in spite of its failure in detail. A psychological shock had been administered to the British Empire, and when it was repeated the next year the total effect became tremendous. The damage that Paul Jones inflicted upon the British navy was trifling by comparison with the damage he inflicted upon the British will to fight. But reducing the enemy's will to fight contributes as effectively to winning a war as reducing his armed forces.

But it takes a strategist to understand this. A mere tactician can grasp the importance of sinking or capturing the enemy's ships. A tactician in the grand manner, one fit for the rank of admiral, may understand immensely complicated movements, involving synchronized operations by fleets striking at widely separated points, and yet be no more than a tactician, albeit a great one. But a man who can calculate the political effect of naval operations with the accuracy of a gunner figuring the trajectory of a shell, a man who can devise naval operations that will, with a minimum of effort, inflict maximum damage upon civilian morale, is a true strategist. Such a man should rarely, if ever, go to sea in time of war; his place is at headquarters ashore, where the war is being planned as a whole.

The concept of attacking the British mind, rather than the British navy, was a gigantic one. It is what sets John Paul Jones apart from and above such captains as Lambert Wickes, Conyingham, and Barry. As seamen they were his peers; as fighters they were his close rivals; as commerce raiders they were perhaps his superiors; but as strategists not a man of them was in his class. If the United States Navy is to be regarded merely as a striking force, they are among its distinguished ancestors; but when it is viewed in the wider aspect as a means of achieving the nation's purposes, that is, not merely as a combat unit but as sea power, then the man from Kirkcudbright is its "onlie begetter."

IV.

The effectiveness of the raid became apparent, however, only by degrees, and the real greatness of its commander only by very slow degrees—never, in fact, to his generation.

On the other hand, the impotence of John Paul Jones became painfully apparent as soon as the *Ranger* dropped anchor at Brest. The Pig at first refused to do anything, and never furnished supplies, but finally he took charge of the prizes as agent of William Lee, successor to Jonathan Williams. The Pig actually impounded Lady Selkirk's silverware and Jones had to get a special order from the commissioners before he would release it.

In Brest the French local authorities scratched their heads and wondered what to do. France was not yet officially at war, and here was Captain Jones with a badly smashed British warship and a couple of hundred prisoners. The French did not wish to embarrass the Captain, but they positively could not permit him to land those prisoners on French soil even long enough to repair his ships. They told him flatly that if the prisoners landed, they would have to go free.

In Paris Arthur Lee had managed to get his draft protested. The sailors of the *Ranger* were dead broke to a man, and some of them half naked; they had been sullen before and Lee's agents were moving among them saying, in effect, "Well, what did you expect with this Kiltie in command? Under Simpson, a true American, you would have been halfway home by now, but the foreigner puts Simpson under arrest and here you are." Their mood from being ugly became dangerous, and to pacify them Jones borrowed every sou he could raise on his personal credit to make good his promise to see that they got half their pay.

"By his personal credit with Count D'Orvilliers, the Duke de Chartres, and the Intendant of Brest, he fed his people and prisoners, cured his wounded, and refitted both the *Ranger* and *Drake* for sea," he wrote years later in the journal he prepared for the King of France. It was still a bitter memory; but, after all, he got things done. He clung to his prisoners, not because of any animosity against them, but because he was determined to have an equal number of Americans out of British jails in exchange for them.

Simpson, although under arrest, was still a thorn in his flesh, for he was stirring up insubordination in the crew. Admiral d'Orvilliers gave Jones a quiet bit of help on that. Simpson was not a prisoner of war, therefore for the French to hold him was not a breach of neutrality; he was accordingly removed from the *Drake* to a French prison ship, and when he tried to escape Orvilliers popped him into the city jail—where, by the way, Jones paid for his board out of his own pocket to save any expense to the city of Brest.

As for the prisoners, he removed them to another ship lying in the harbor, the *Patience*, while the *Drake* was being refitted for sea, intending to send them in her to America, since he could not land them in France. Hearing that they were being mistreated by the man he had put in charge, one Riou who "does not deny that he is a scoundrel," he arranged with Orvilliers to permit his chaplain, Father John, who spoke English, to act as liaison officer to transmit any complaints. But when he learned that there was a chance that the English would consent to an exchange in Europe, he let the *Drake* go without them when it was ready for sea.

Immediately on his arrival Jones had demanded that the commissioners order a court-martial to try Simpson for insubordination and refusal to obey orders. But John Adams was against trying any New England man on the word of an immigrant from the South. Arthur Lee was against trying any man who had such politically powerful relatives as Langdon and Wendell. Both of them were against doing anything that would please that man Jones. They found an excuse in the difficulty of assembling enough officers of sufficiently high rank to try a first lieutenant. No court was ordered and Lee sent encouraging messages to Simpson, who was now out of jail, for Jones had accepted his parole.

Franklin deplored all this imbecility, but what could he do? They were two to his one. Adams, it is true, was growing more than a little uneasy. Close association with Lee was teaching the New Englander more than he liked to learn about the Virginian's true character. Honest John was cherishing a growing suspicion that he had made a fool of himself in taking Lee's word instead of Franklin's; but he was not yet quite convinced, and until he was he was sure to remain as stubborn as ever.

Franklin, in the meantime, had a quiet word with Sartine, French Minister of Marine. Slippery as an eel was this curious character, but not without ability; with a strong and able government behind him he might have given the French navy an excellent administration, but like every other intelligent man in Paris, he was aware that the rottenness of the monarchy had proceeded so far that it was beyond the power of any one man to do much about it. His policy, therefore, like that of practically all other public officials of the time, was merely to get by without precipitating a crash.

Yet he was convinced that John Paul Jones was one of the best naval officers in Europe, and in view of the impending war with England he was unwilling to let any good naval officer get away. He had, moreover, great confidence in Franklin and none whatever in the other two commissioners. He was sympathetic, therefore, when Franklin asked if something couldn't be done for Jones.

Sartine thought it possible, provided the thing were worked quietly. Prejudice against foreigners ran almost as high in France as it did in America, and to assign a first-class ship to a Scotchman would precipitate a political uproar the very thought of which made Sartine shudder. However, there was the *Indienne*, still technically in possession of the French, although everyone knew it had been intended originally for the Americans. It might be feasible to ease that ship over to Captain Jones before the French political captains got wind of it; or if that failed, there were several frigates nearing completion but which had not yet been assigned to French officers, and Captain Jones might have one of them. Sartine was positive that he could use him somewhere.

But there was one condition. Sartine had heard detailed reports of the conduct of Simpson and the crew of the *Ranger*, and he did not want that collection of riffraff at any price. They would give Jones not only a good ship, but a stouthearted French crew; let Dr. Franklin summon the Captain to Paris without any publicity. They would talk it over and fix up something.

Jones's hopes soared again when Franklin wrote him a confidential letter with this information. As soon as he could arrange affairs at Brest he rushed to Paris, where Sartine confirmed what Franklin had said. However, there was one complication. The *Ranger* had to go back to America, and with Simpson under arrest, who was to take her? Would Captain Jones consider releasing Simpson from his parole for that purpose?

Certainly he would. He thought Simpson should be tried for the good of the service, but if the commissioners thought the

Navy would be better served by sending him back, Jones would bow to their judgment cheerfully. He promptly gave Franklin a letter releasing Simpson.

All this required a great deal of negotiating and it was not finally settled until the *Ranger* was practically ready to sail, in August; and no one knew anything of it save Sartine, Franklin, and Jones. But when Franklin at last informed Lee and Adams that Sartine had use for Jones, therefore Simpson had been released to take the ship, they were furious, and, being two to one, issued peremptory orders that Captain Jones and no other was to return in command of the *Ranger*. Jones prepared to obey, being privately assured by Franklin that he could return to France immediately and find things prepared.

But at that Sartine took a hand. He informed Lee and Adams in no uncertain terms that he wanted this officer. He pointed out that the Americans had not used him for months, and were even now preparing to send him across the Atlantic for nothing more important than to carry dispatches, whereas he could use him for fighting. He intimated that the French would consider it discourteous, if not unfriendly, for the Americans to deny his request.

At that, Adams and Lee backed down. Of course, if the French really wanted the man, they could have him. They had thought it was all a put-up job on the part of Franklin and Jones. The orders were canceled and Simpson took command of the *Ranger*, telling the crew, in his pleasant way, that Jones had been raked over the coals in Paris, compelled to admit that he was in the wrong, removed from his command, and practically booted out of the service.

That was Jones's reward for being reasonable about the parole. If the Captain had been blessed with humor, he would have seen in it nothing but proof of the old adage—he had lain down with a dog, so of course he got up with fleas.

There were twenty-seven men in the *Ranger*, however, who couldn't quite swallow that stuff. Informed that if they chose they might remain in France and sail with Jones in his next ship, they remained. One of the group was Red Cherry, the Indian, which greatly pleased the Captain.

"My little red Indian is not homesick," he wrote. "Maybe he had no home to yearn for. But I prefer to explain his choice to stay with me on other grounds."

So he let the *Ranger* go without regrets, except, of course, a keen regret that he had not been able to give that fellow Simpson the booting that he had richly earned. Ever optimistic, he was sure now that he would have a better ship almost immediately; he could not foresee that for eleven tedious months he was to spend his time kicking his heels ashore while the war raged and far less competent officers were losing men and ships right and left. But so it was. His reward for raiding England, capturing the *Drake*, and jarring the Empire was to be deprived of any command whatever.

V.

He went up to Paris, and Franklin, thoroughly interested now, invited him to share the quarters at Passy that Le Ray de Chaumont had put at the disposal of the Americans. Chaumont had a big place in the suburb called Valentinois, one wing of which he had turned over to Franklin and Deane when they first came to Paris, rent free as far as they were concerned, although it was generally understood that the court saw to it that the owner lost nothing by his generosity. It suited Franklin and Deane admirably, because at the time they were still operating more or less under cover and Passy was semirural, therefore people, including high officials, could drop in without attracting undesirable attention. Franklin remained there even after Deane had left, but Arthur Lee and Adams, whether through chronic suspicion or because they never were invited to Valentinois, found quarters elsewhere.

Chaumont offered more than a house. He was a businessman of real competence, although rather inclined to take in too much territory if left to himself, and he seems to have developed a genuine liking for Franklin. He shared, too, the fashionable enthusiasm for Americans. He put his business connections at Franklin's disposal and made himself useful in many ways. Being a thrifty Frenchman, he did not fail to collect his commission, of course, and thereby incurred the suspicion of John Adams. In fact, it is not beyond belief that he may have padded his expense accounts a bit in dealing with the French treasury; if he did not, he was a rare exception in those days. But it is certain that he performed valuable, if not unprofitable, services for the Americans, and Franklin depended on him for many things.

He interested himself in the cause of Captain Jones, too, when the latter came to Paris. The Captain, indeed, was quite a hit with the Chaumonts. In the sequel it proved that he was rather too much of a hit, for Madame de Chaumont was charming, the Captain was impressionable, and toward the end of his stay there was talk. In fact, there was more than talk. Certain of his letters to the lady have survived, and they are a good deal warmer in tone than the customary note of thanks from a guest, even one who has been entertained for months. A distinct coolness developed between Chaumont and Jones, but there never was anything approaching an open scandal.

Perhaps a coolness would have developed anyhow, for Chaumont became the principal business agent of the Americans and Jones never got along well with his business agents. Indeed, have shipmaster and ship chandler ever seen eye to eye, except, of course, when they have joined forces to swindle the shipowner?

More than that, it is certain that any affair that may have developed with La Chaumont was not very serious or long enduring, for it was not suffered to interfere in the least with his incessant effort to get to sea. Lorenz, indeed, makes the deplorable suggestion that the Captain may have courted the lady more in the hope of winning a ship than of winning her favors.

The story of that effort is long, complicated, and dismal.

Word had come from Amsterdam that, apart from the involved question of ownership, the frigate *Indienne* was far from complete, and neither Jones nor anyone else could expect to take charge of her for a long time to come. This was the report of the agent sent to inspect her, a curious character whom Jones was to know better, to his sorrow, in later years, but who impressed him mightily at this time.

Charles Henri Nicholas Othon, Prince de Nassau-Siegen, one of those German princelings without a principality that infested Europe at this time, was appropriately a countryman of Munchausen, for a fancier liar has rarely appeared in the chronicles of the race. They are not to be bracketed together, though, for the Baron is presented as pursuing the art of lying in a disinterested fashion, art for art's sake, whereas the Prince lied only for profit or for malice. He was a swine in every aspect; but he was a prince, and in the eighteenth century noble birth was sufficient cover for every form of everything contemptible that a naturally villainous mind could conceive. He was essentially a yellow-livered poltroon, but he had something of the bravado of the born thug. He had sailed with Bougainville around the world. He had never won a fair fight—it is doubtful that he had ever engaged in one—but he had exhibited prowess in barroom brawls on every continent, so he was currently accepted in the decaying world of absolutism as a mighty man of valor.

This sweet-scented specimen was just the man to appeal to Arthur Lee, of course, and even Franklin and Paul Jones were taken in by him at the beginning. Nassau-Siegen remarked to Sartine that he would like to sail in the *Indienne* with Captain Jones, and the gardener's son was so overcome by the honor that he wrote to Nassau-Siegen the one letter in all his voluminous correspondence that cannot be described by any other term than sycophantic. Many of his letters are filled with extravagant flattery, but this is usually no more than a concession to the manners and customs of the time; but the prospect of having a real, live prince under his command reduced him to a pitiable state.

To salute this German hog as "My Prince" was doubtless to adopt the customary form of salutation; but to repeat it four times in the body of the letter was not necessary, and to refer to "prospects I have voluntarily laid aside, that I may pursue glory in your company," was going too far. He had done nothing of the kind, for he had never heard of Nassau-Siegen when he made his choice. In this letter Jones demeaned himself.

However, he was by this time so desperate for a ship that he would have done almost anything to secure one. Sartine promised and promised, but never made good. "The minister," wrote Jones wrathfully to his good friend the Duc de Rouchefoucault, "has treated me like a child five times successively, by leading me from great to little and from little to less." In addition to that, Sartine had written to Orvilliers "proposing to send me home in *'une bonne voiture.'* This is absolutely adding insult to injury, and it is the proposition of a man whose *veracity* I have not experienced in former cases."

Sartine was slippery; that is not to be denied. But Paul Jones's assumption that the minister deliberately set out to make a monkey of him was probably wrong. He was a representative of absolutism, and absolutism was dying. The power of intelligent and energetic action had departed from it. It is characteristic of a dying system that toward the end its own agents lose confidence in it and every man looks out for himself.

In the matter of this ship, for example, Sartine, according to Jones's own account, had made five proposals, and it is probable that he made them in good faith; but always there was someone with better political backing than the American, and he got the ship. This was bad for the service, but it was better for Sartine; for if he had tried to fight the political system he would have lost his own job. That is the way things were going in France. The monarchy was headed down the road to ruin and a ruinous policy was the only one it could adopt.

In the end—but not until after nine exasperating months of letter writing, interviews, pleadings, and running to and fro, all in vain—Jones stumbled upon the only procedure that could get results in such a situation. He decided to employ political pressure himself, and discovered, doubtless to his own surprise, that he had it. He wrote a letter directly to the King.

Louis XVI was a feeble monarch, but monarch he was, and all those whose personal fortunes were inseparably bound up with monarchy were under the necessity of propping him up to make him seem stronger than he was; for, as the event abundantly proved, if he were to go down they would all go down together. Therefore on those rare occasions when the King issued a command it was obeyed.

This presented no great difficulty, since Louis was much more interested in lockmaking than he was in statecraft, and ordinarily had but the vaguest notion of what was going on. However, this man Jones had been the talk of the court for months, and the King had not only heard the gossip, but had evinced an interest in it quite unusual for him. He also liked Franklin. So if the Doctor came in his official capacity and presented a letter to the King, it was a certainty that the King would read it; and it was highly probable that the result would be a royal command to get something done with perhaps a royal investigation into why nothing had been done for so long, which would be embarrassing for everybody. So, when Franklin dropped a discreet hint that he had such a letter in hand, the political pressure, which had all been against the Captain, was suddenly in his favor, and things happened with remarkable speed.

For one thing, the Captain was ready as soon as he got some real backing in Paris. Nassau-Siegen, the prince, couldn't find a ship, Sartine, the Minister of Marine, couldn't find a ship, Chaumont, the commercial agent, couldn't find a ship, so Paul Jones turned from the nobility and officialdom and put his problem up to an American businessman, James Moylan, the merchant, and junior partner of the firm of Gourlade & Moylan, which Arthur Lee had said was no good; and Moylan found a ship promptly.

True, she wasn't much of a ship by comparison with a first-rate man-o'-war. She was the *Duc de Duras*, an East Indiaman, twenty-three years old and battered by the typhoons of those years, somewhat waterlogged and with a disconcerting fashion, unless deftly managed, of making nearly as much leeway as headway—that is, of going sideways nearly as fast as she went forward. But the timbers of her frame, although somewhat rotted, were still stout in the opinion of the American captain, and as she had been built to take the ponderous seas around Cape Comorin, they were heavy enough to sustain a battery of eighteen-pounders. It seemed possible to convert her into a warship; if not of the first class, still of a pretty good second class.

At that they almost lost her through Paris's delay. The first ten-day option ran out and Jones had to do some ardent pleading with her owner to get it extended; but he managed it, and the order arrived just before the extension ended. Once more the Captain had a ship.

His exuberance swept away in a moment all his animosities against everybody. For the moment he was almost in love even with Sartine, to whom he wrote rapturously, "It shall be my duty to represent in the strongest terms to Congress the generous and voluntary resolution which their great ally, the protector of the rights of human nature, and the best of kings, has taken to promote the honor of their flag." Then followed a passage of honorable acknowledgment of a great debt he owed: "Your having permitted me to alter the name of the ship has given me a pleasing opportunity of paying a well-merited compliment to a great and good man to whom I am under obligations and who honors me with his friendship."

This compliment he paid delicately and delightfully. A heavy-footed blunderer would have named the ship directly for the man, thereby precipitating an avalanche of jealous and malicious criticism. But Paul Jones was a diplomat. The aphorisms in *Poor Richard's Almanac* had been collected and published in a French translation, and the book was all the rage in Paris; but the translator had followed the spirit, rather than the letter, in turning the first word into "goodman," *bon homme,* or as modern French has it, *bonhomme.* Thus the former *Duc de Duras* became the *Bon Homme Richard,* and all France laughed and cheered, while even in America they could not very well take offense. Nay, even John Adams realized that to give public expression to his disgust would be undignified and let the thing pass; nor could Arthur Lee himself twist this into additional evidence that Franklin was stealing everything that came into his hands and probably conspiring to betray his country to the British king.

John Paul Jones has more than one clever stroke of diplomacy in his record, but his way of naming his ship was the most masterly of them all.

VI.

But at this juncture into French waters and into the life of John Paul Jones came breezing the worst mistake of Silas Deane, bringing strife, trouble, and dishonor in his train.

Pierre Landais was a character so improbable that no writer of fiction would have dared invent him. In the eighteenth century, when psychopathology was not even a budding science, they simply called him as mad as a hatter, and let it go at that. But he wasn't insane in the legal sense. Certainly he talked rationally enough and in ordinary circumstances acted rationally; but there was an emotional imbalance in the man that showed up under any unusual stress. He was a perfect example of the sort of man who should under no circumstances be allowed to become a naval officer.

They had discovered that in the French navy long before. If Deane had been wise enough to investigate he might easily have discovered that Landais had been eased out of the service as temperamentally unfit for command. But in 1777 Deane had yet a great deal to learn, and when Lieutenant Landais offered his services to the new American navy Deane took him at his own valuation, promised him a captain's commission, and sent him to Congress with the warmest sort of recommendation.

In Philadelphia they were even more credulous. It is not merely embarrassing, it is bewildering to learn with what infallible precision Congress singled out every mountebank for adulation and every first-rate man for injustice and abuse. How did we ever win that war? From the beginning Washington was reviled and attacked while Gates was adored. From the beginning Paul Jones was subjected to insult and injury, but Pierre Landais was given everything he asked for.

Voluble, picturesque, and plausible, Landais not only persuaded Congress to confirm the promise of Deane and issue him a captain's commission, but he also was assigned the finest warship as yet built in the United States, a frigate named, in deference to the French, the *Alliance*.

Yet Congress, no less than Deane, might have known better. The Frenchman had come over in command of a merchant ship, the *Flamand*, and before he reached Portsmouth he had a mutiny on his hands. Von Steuben was a passenger and doubtless could have given plenty of information on the subject to an investigating committee had anyone ever thought of investigating. But no. They were quick enough to investigate Robert Morris and Silas Deane, against whom no charges could be sustained. A dozen times motions were made to investigate Franklin, Washington, John Paul Jones, and Lafayette; but nobody thought to investigate the real fraud Landais. On the contrary, they voted him a commission, a frigate, special pay, special privileges, a bonus. Paul Jones couldn't get even a proper bo'sun's call and went to sea with only one barrel of rum. But Pierre—or, as contemporary letters and documents usually call him, Peter—Landais was lavishly equipped.

So he set out for France in the splendid *Alliance* and arrived with half the crew in irons—another mutiny. But this time there was a competent witness. Lafayette, coming home on leave, was a passenger. Publicly he did not seek to contravene the Captain's voluminous explanation that it was all due to the presence of British deserters among the crew; but privately he advised Franklin to watch out for that fellow. The mutiny seems to have been real enough, but Lafayette was of the opinion that it had been provoked by Landais's outrageous conduct.

In addition to that, the subordinate officers—sound Americans, all of them—sent a letter to the minister registering their protest against serving under Landais. But what could Franklin do? At that time we had not progressed so far as to have a naval attaché in attendance on the envoy, and Franklin had to attend to everything himself. His knowledge of naval affairs was of the slightest, but if he had been a very Mahan he would not have had time to explore the business thoroughly, in view of the fact that he was now solely responsible for all diplomatic, commercial, naval, and military interests of the United States in France.

For we had progressed far enough to perceive the nonsense of dividing authority, and Franklin was now no longer a commissioner, but the minister of the United States at the French court, and the only one. The credit for that belongs largely to John Adams. He still held a low opinion of Franklin's morals and a still lower one of his manners; but he perceived that they were morals and manners that were highly esteemed in the city of Paris, and he perceived that he and Arthur Lee were merely in the way and were doing more harm than good. Once the idea percolated into his brain, Honest John told Congress just that, and recommended that Dr. Franklin be given complete and sole authority, even though the recommendation involved a certain embarrassment to himself. Honest John was achieving greatness.

That disposed of Adams and he went home, but unfortunately it did not clear the scene of Arthur Lee, for he also held the post of commissioner to Spain, which he regarded as excuse enough to continue to hang around Paris creating trouble. His power for mischief was considerably reduced, however.

The chief mischief-maker from Paul Jones's standpoint was now Le Ray de Chaumont. Sartine, Minister of Marine, had had an assistant named Garnier to whom he delegated the task of helping Jones to prepare his ship for war duty; but hardly had the work begun when he was offered the post of Minister to the United States, and Sartine replaced him with Chaumont. The two men had already begun to dislike each other, whether over Madame de Chaumont or not, and their relations were strained from the beginning.

Chaumont almost lost the *Duras* by suddenly making a lot of impossible demands after the deal was complete, but on Jones's frantic plea Sartine overruled him. Then when it came to the job of equipping the ship he was of very little help. It was not altogether his fault, to be sure. France was now at war, and every available scrap of war material had become priceless. Ordnance, in particular, was impossible to find. Week after week Jones scoured the country for guns, but could find nothing except prehistoric relics vastly more dangerous to the gunner than to the target. He was reduced at last to placing an order with the royal foundry and was cheerfully assured that it would be many months before it could be filled.

Yet at the moment that he was reduced to utter despair he found something—not what he wanted, but something he could make do. It included a battery of six eighteen-pounders, which he proposed to place on the lower gun deck, which had six ports on each side so that all the guns could be used at once. These ports were so near the water line that they could be opened only when the sea was calm, but Jones was doubtful of those old guns anyhow, so he would not clutter up his main gun deck with them.

The battery on which he really relied consisted of twenty-eight twelve-pounders, mounted on the gun deck, and eight nine-pounders for the forecastle, quarterdeck, and gangways. This is the armament as it is given in Jones's reports at the time, yet Lorenz points out that later reports state that the *Bon Homme Richard* actually sailed with forty guns instead of forty-two. In any event, all of it was secondhand and none of it had been too good to begin with, but it was all that was available; and if he could not get what he wanted, Jones was always the man to fight with whatever he had.

Orders were for Jones to command a squadron consisting of his flagship and the *Alliance*, American, with whatever French ships Chaumont could find. As possible landings were contemplated, Lafayette made application to sail with him in command of four or five hundred French soldiers; and to transport these, as well as to assist the American ships, Chaumont furnished the *Pallas*, captain Cottineau, a converted merchantman of thirty to thirty-two guns, the *Cerf*, captain Varage, a cutter of eighteen guns, and the *Vengeance*, captain Ricot, a tender of twelve guns. The *Cerf* alone was fast and efficient, but they were all ships, and to this extent Chaumont had done his part.

But Lafayette gave over the idea, and as he did Chaumont began to exceed his proper authority. Like the crew of the *Ranger*, Chaumont's idea was money. Like the Congress in Philadelphia, he had a natural affinity for frauds. He now began to do everything his ingenuity could suggest to send Landais out alone in the *Alliance* to raid commerce. Probably his real wish was to make Landais commander of the squadron; certainly he did not wish the squadron to waste its time fighting when vastly more profit would accrue to Monsieur de Chaumont if it devoted its time exclusively to capturing prizes for the agent to sell on commission.

Since he could not have Jones superseded, he began to irritate him with a series of petty demands, reinforcing them with reminders that as the King of France was supplying the money, he had a right to say how it should be expended. The fact that the King of France had ordered Jones to proceed at his own discretion, waiting for no "ulterior orders," did not affect Chaumont in the least. He told Sartine that Jones was incapable of maintaining discipline on his own ship, therefore the French captains must not be subjected to his command. He intimated

that Jones was unfit to command the squadron anyhow. Jones
already had too great a reputation for Sartine to swallow this;
but he did allow Chaumont to tie the American's hands by com-
pelling him to sign a preposterous "concordat" just before sailing, which had the effect of canceling all discipline in the squadron and permitting each captain to do as he wished.

Chaumont was, of course, merely another symptom of the
disease that one short decade later was to precipitate the French
monarchy into the convulsions of its hideous death agony. When
the great offices of state are filled by chiseling pettifoggers,
innocent of the slightest taint of patriotism, each intent solely
upon what he can grab for himself, the nation is doomed. Or,
if you prefer, a nation whose doom is sealed finds its offices
filled with men of that type.

It is an old story, incessantly repeated in the pages of history.
It was true of the Greece of Alcibiades, of the Rome of the
Oligarchy, of the Byzantium of Constantine Palaeologus, of the
Russia of Nicholas II, and of France again just before the Third
Republic went down in 1940. Le Ray de Chaumont was an early
precursor of Pierre Laval, except that he had not a tenth of
Laval's brains. Under such auspices John Paul Jones struggled
to equip his squadron and get to sea.

VII.

Arthur Lee was out, yet information kept slipping over to
England. Things were not quite as bad as in the days of the
cruise of the *Ranger*, when all Jones's plans except those he
mentioned to nobody were promptly revealed to the British,
but they were bad enough.

Jones could not understand it. Franklin could not understand
it. Nobody understood it, indeed, for a hundred years—to be
exact, until 1889, when B. F. Stevens began to publish his fac-
similes of documents in European archives respecting America
during the revolutionary period, and Paul Leicester Ford read
them. Then it was revealed that both Jones and Franklin had

been dupes of the ablest spy in the lot, none other than Edward Bancroft, whom both had honored with their friendship and whom Franklin had employed in much confidential business.

This, unquestionably one of the vilest characters in American history, yet has certain touches that makes him not quite such a dreary villain as Arthur Lee. For one thing, his scientific attainments were decidedly respectable, and his title of doctor was far from meaningless. He had published a *Natural History of New Guinea* that was of value; in the Netherlands his experiments with dyes had been turned to commercial account; in England he was a respected contributor to the *Monthly Review* and was regarded as an authority on American affairs. Here, in fact, was where Franklin fell into his trap; he met Bancroft in England before the war began, and after the outbreak of hostilities it never occurred to him to doubt the loyalty of this son of Massachusetts.

For another thing, he was adroit. So cleverly did he cover his tracks that suspicion never touched him except by a process of elimination, and when it did both Franklin and Jones rose to his defense and whitewashed him with great success.

For a third thing, and for a spy the most remarkable thing of all, he was not insatiable. His advance knowledge of the treaty of alliance enabled him to make a killing in the stock market; and once he had acquired a fortune large enough to keep him comfortably for the rest of his days, he allowed his activities to taper off. By the time the highly efficient French secret police began to go after British spies with real vigor, Bancroft was out of the game, and welcomed their investigations with unction. Naturally, they found nothing, so for the next forty years he lived "in calm contemplation and poetic ease" on blood money and died in the odor of sanctity. A villain so thoroughpaced and yet so canny forces a reluctant admiration; it is doubtful that Dr. Edward Bancroft ever had a peer.

His prestige at this moment is evidenced by the fact that he was one of the two men to whom Paul Jones entrusted the secret of that affair at Tobago. The other was Franklin. For Franklin he wrote a detailed account of the business and sent a copy to Bancroft. He stated it as a hypothetical case, but with no doubt that both men would identify the principal, which both did. But since this was not a military secret and therefore had no monetary value, Bancroft kept it honorably.

As for Franklin, he wrote immediately that if the sailor had been killed under the circumstances described by Captain Jones, then it was a clear case of self-defense and the officer should not allow it to burden his conscience. It is possible that Franklin did not welcome this confession. It had been precipitated by a reference in one of his letters to some scandal connected with Jones; and it is significant of the way the thing had preyed upon the Captain's mind through all the years that he at once assumed that any scandal involving his name must be based upon this incident. It is evidence, too, that his conscience was clear as far as any financial or political misbehavior was concerned.

Franklin attempted to turn it off by asserting that what he had in mind was a somewhat Rabelaisian invention about a servant who had borrowed one of Jones's uniforms to wear while making improper advances to a hideous old woman who worked about the garden at Valentinois. It may have been true, but it sounds rather like a bit of Franklin's jocosity, which was sometimes pretty heavy-handed.

In any event, it was probably a relief to the Captain to know that his friend was in possession of the facts, and he went briskly about the job of rounding up a crew for the *Bon Homme Richard*. After Chaumont's insinuations to Sartine that he could not maintain discipline, he discharged most of the Englishmen he had signed on, and he might have been hard put to it to find men had not a consignment of American prisoners just then arrived from England for exchange.

He had one midshipman, Nathaniel Fanning, who had sailed in the *Ranger*, and twenty-seven men, including Red Cherry, the Indian. He had collected a motley array of Portuguese, Spaniards, Malays, and what not to supplement these, and now,

among the released Americans, he recruited enough to fill up
the crew, at least to the point at which he might hope to sail
and fight the ship.

Originally, his first lieutenant was Robert Robinson. The
second was Richard Dale, who had sailed with Lambert Wickes,
twice been captured by the English and twice escaped, and who
was to prove a tower of strength in days to come. Others were
Henry Lunt, Edward Stack, and Eugene Macarty. Master—what
is now called navigating officer—was Cutting Lunt; surgeon,
Laurens Brooke; and purser, Matthew Mease, a Philadelphia
merchant who volunteered for the cruise. Fanning was among
the midshipmen, as was John Mayrant, who was later to be an
acting lieutenant. Paul de Chamillard was captain of the French
marines, who were drawn in part from the royal dockyard at
Lorient and in part were French soldiers who volunteered for
this service.

At last things were ready, or as nearly ready as they could be
made, and Paul Jones stood prepared to strike a blow at Great
Britain that should be a real blow and no mere annoyance. He
meant first to scatter and if possible to capture or destroy a considerable fleet of West Indiamen that would presently be standing in for the west coast of Ireland; then he would whip past
Cape Clear and smash at Liverpool. Relying upon these two
blows to draw every available British frigate to the neighborhood of the Irish Sea, he would run through the North Channel,
wheel around the northern end of Scotland, and smash at Leith,
port of Edinburgh, on the opposite side of the island from
Liverpool. Hoping by this time to have the patrolling British
cruisers utterly confused, he proposed to lie in wait for the
Baltic fleet, a convoy of merchantmen bringing naval stores
from Sweden and Russia, capture it, and run the whole business
into the Texel, that is to say, into the anchorage in the Zuider
Zee behind that island.

It was a brilliant but hair-raising scheme, and its success
would have had a prodigious effect. If the Indiamen on one side
and the Baltic fleet on the other were both struck, England

would be left gasping, but that was a minor matter. If Liverpool on the west and Leith on the east were both smashed, England would be stunned; that was the great objective. Finally, the choice of the Texel as the goal had a double objective, first, if the squadron had collected a huge fleet of prizes it could hardly hope to run them through the English Channel in the teeth of the whole British navy, but it might make the Texel, straight across the North Sea, and by sweeping an immense number of prizes into a Dutch port the raid would almost certainly force Britain to exert pressure upon the Netherlands, and a little more pressure on the Dutch would bring them into the war on the side of the French and Americans.

But the whole operation depended for success upon surprise, and surprise depended upon three factors—perfect timing, extremely skillful seamanship, and desperate courage. None of these did Paul Jones command. To begin with, every important detail of his plan was promptly reported to the British. Apparently this was done, not by Bancroft, but by Arthur Lee's platoon of spies; yet the damage was not irremediable, for the British simply didn't believe the information they were given. The scheme looked so fantastic that they considered it a hoax and took no effective measures to combat it.

As for the timing, at the moment they were ready to sail Chaumont intervened with an order that the squadron first convoy a fleet of merchantmen to Spain, and Jones could do nothing but obey. He had his own orders from the King, of course, but the other captains did not, and under the concordat they were free to abandon him if he did not conform, and they frankly said they would abandon him.

As for seamanship, the squadron had barely started toward Spain when the Bon Homme Richard fouled the Alliance, doing considerable damage to both ships. Jones was in his cabin when it happened, and Robinson, the first lieutenant, had the deck. Jones promptly court-martialed Robinson, broke him, and made Dale first lieutenant, but the damage was done.

As for courage, when the Richard suddenly bore down on the

Alliance and a collision was seen to be inevitable, Landais, who was on the quarterdeck of the *Alliance*, instead of doing what he could to minimize the damage, gave no orders at all but bolted down to his cabin to secure a pair of pistols. What he intended to do with the pistols no mortal has ever been able to imagine; but the incident showed what sort of officer he was in a pinch.

The ships were not rendered unseaworthy by the accident and were able to complete their mission; but on their return extensive repairs were essential and more time was lost. Furthermore, the test cruise had showed that the *Bon Homme Richard* was the slowest ship in the squadron, sluggish in answering the helm and badly trimmed on account of the alterations made in her hull to accommodate troops.

Under such conditions, then, at four o'clock on the morning of August 14, 1779, Jones moved from where he was lying before the island of Groix and set out to invade the den of the Lion— with a decrepit old ship, a green, untried crew, with one captain already proved cowardly and with no real authority over the others, and with his secret plans already reported to the enemy by traitors.

By all the rules of logic he didn't have a chance. He was whipped before he began to fight. But that is precisely where he stands out from the ruck of sea captains—it was just when he was hopelessly beaten that he really began to fight. It was by that characteristic that succeeding ages have remembered him.

VIII.

At the last moment the squadron was joined by two more ships, the *Monsieur*, of forty guns, and the *Granville*, of fourteen, both privateers. Here was more evidence of disunity in the high command. Jones didn't want privateers. What he was most anxious to avoid was giving the impression that his was a piratical expedition, out for money. Such an impression, he felt sure, would reduce the effectiveness of the cruise by half. A raid by corsairs would prove nothing, because corsairs would fight under any flag as long as there was a chance of profit; as soon as the fighting was over they would go back to their home ports, and when the next war broke out they were as likely as not to appear again fighting on the other side. In short, privateers were no proof of sea power.

John Paul Jones was first, last, and always a naval officer, not a corsair. He was anxious above all else to demonstrate that regularly commissioned ships of the regularly constituted United States Navy could strike at the very heart of the British Empire, in spite of all the British navy could do to stop them. This would establish the United States as a sea power, and once the British realized that they must fight by sea as well as by land they would have more reason than ever to bring the war to an end. To accomplish this, Jones was willing to pass up prizes altogether.

Le Ray de Chaumont, on the other hand, was neither a naval officer nor a soldier, nor yet a statesman. He was first, last, and always a tradesman, and his measure of the value of any project was his estimate of the financial profit in it. The capture of the fleet from the West Indies he approved and the capture of the Baltic fleet he approved, for there was money in both; but he saw no sense at all in shooting up Liverpool and Leith, for there was no money in either and each involved a heavy risk. That such raids would shorten the war was an argument of doubtful validity, as far as he was concerned. Did he want the war shortened? He would have said that he did, of course, because that was the proper thing to say; but as a matter of fact he was making money out of the war in very considerable sums and without much trouble, and it is not often that a tradesman sincerely wishes to end any situation that is profitable to him.

As for the captains of the *Monsieur* and the *Granville*, they were perfectly frank about their own attitude. The last thing they wished was to shorten the war, for the end of the war would mean the end of privateering. To attach them to the squadron, therefore, was to attach an element frankly opposed to the main purpose of the cruise, as well as to give it the look of a privateering expedition.

The decision was out of Jones's hands, however, for Franklin had already consented to the presence of these two ships. Franklin, on his part, consented because he was aware that the *Monsieur*, at least, had been fitted out in part with the money of a group of great ladies of the capital, headed by the Duchess of Chartres. This was a reason that Jones could understand— indeed, it was a reason that stopped him dead. He was far too deeply obligated to Madame la Duchesse to oppose her wishes in anything that did not involve absolute destruction.

Indeed, she was indirectly responsible for his having a ship at all, for it was she who had taken him to the King, and it was that hour spent with Louis XVI that had established the Captain in the monarch's estimation. More than that, she had certainly assisted financially in converting the *Duc de Duras* into a warship; Buell says that she gave ten thousand louis d'or, that is to say, fifty thousand dollars, when money was worth much more than it is today. This may be a fable, but Jones himself says she helped; and her last act just before the squadron sailed was to present him with a watch as a token of personal good will.

Then if Madame la Duchesse and her friends wanted to send along a privateer of their own, Jones could see why Franklin had consented. There was nothing for him to do but to choke down his distaste and consent too.

So they put to sea, and if the British, fully informed of the whole situation by their spies, regarded it as resembling the cruise of the Three Wise Men of Gotham rather than a serious naval operation, who is to blame them? It was fantastic. There is no other word to describe it, and the odds against its accomplishing anything at all would have been overwhelming except for one fact that the British knew, all right, but that they did not assess at its true value. This was the fact that John Paul Jones was in command.

They made the south coast of Ireland and picked up a prize

or two; but Jones insisted that whatever ship took them, they all belonged to the fleet and must be sent to the agents appointed by Chaumont in order that the money received from their sale might be equally divided among all the crews. This was too much for the *Monsieur* and it sulkily slipped away and was seen no more. Shortly thereafter the *Granville*, having taken a prize, sneaked away with it and was not heard from again.

In the meantime Jones proceeded slowly along the Irish coast, standing in as close as possible with the intention of deliberately alarming the country. From the standpoint of a corsair this was idiotic, and Landais protested loudly, but it was Jones's purpose by concentrating attention upon his own squadron to distract it from the main French fleet under Orvilliers, which was preparing a descent upon the south English ports of Southampton and Plymouth. In other words, he was making war, not making money.

But he very nearly overdid it. On one occasion he got in too close and the *Bon Homme Richard*, always sluggish, did not respond to the helm against the current; so he put the captain's barge overside with a towline to swing her head around. Unfortunately, the boat's crew were British, who, seeing themselves close to land, cut the towline and made for the beach. Without orders Cutting Lunt, third lieutenant, took another boat and with twenty men went in pursuit. A fog came up and Lunt lost sight of the barge. He tried to make his way back in response to the *Bon Homme Richard*'s signal guns. Suddenly a ship loomed up out of the fog and fired on him. Certain that he had run into a British man-o'-war, he made all speed in the opposite direction, ran up on the beach, and was captured.

The ship that had fired on him, and caused his capture, was the *Cerf*. Doubtless this was a blunder, but two days later it was no blunder when she deserted and went back to France.

These events brought Peter Landais, boiling with rage, to the *Bon Homme Richard* to denounce his commander on his own quarterdeck. There Jones made the mistake of his life. Instead of instantly clapping the mutinous officer in irons and turning the *Alliance* over to a competent and trustworthy man, the squadron commander let him get away with it; indeed, he tried to pacify him.

Yet if he had arrested Landais at this time, he would have been furiously denounced by Chaumont, Arthur Lee, John Adams, and the whole American Congress. Even today it is not unknown for an admiral to be hampered by politics in maintaining discipline, and things were far worse in the eighteenth century. There was some excuse for Jones in this instance; but it was nevertheless a mistake that was to cost him dear.

All the captains were worried. Hanging about so close to the Irish coast was dangerous. The alarm ashore was certain to bring down upon them a powerful force of cruisers. Jones knew it, but he also knew that eight West Indiamen were due from Jamaica any day, making for the mouth of the Shannon; and he hoped that a prize of such enormous value would keep the crews contented while he carried out the more important part of his mission.

But not even the hope of gain could soothe the alarm of Landais, a poltroon at heart. He was seeing a British frigate in every white cap. He announced flatly that he was leaving, and he left. That tore it. The Indiamen would certainly be escorted, and with the *Pallas* and *Vengeance* only, the *Bon Homme Richard* could not hope to take care of the escort and capture the fleet, too. So, reluctantly, Paul Jones steered north—and three days later the eight Indiamen sailed in, serene and untroubled.

Jones saw no more of the *Alliance* until he reached the rendezvous off Cape Wrath, at the northwest tip of Scotland, where he found her with a prize. Jones instructed Landais to put a prize crew aboard and send her to one of the ports indicated by Chaumont, but of course the Frenchman did nothing of the kind. Instead he sent her, and another prize he picked up later, to Bergen, in Norway, which then belonged to Denmark. From the start of the war the Danes had been distinctly unfriendly to the Americans, and now, in defiance of international law, they promptly seized both prizes and gave them back to the British. Such was Landais's contribution to the success of the cruise.

Landais's conduct had now defeated two of the four objects Jones had had in mind, the capture of the West Indiamen and the raid on Liverpool. There remained the raid on Leith and the capture of the Baltic fleet.

Leith is the port of Edinburgh, lying on the south side of the Firth of Forth, and Jones's information was that at the moment it was practically undefended. There was a considerable garrison in Edinburgh itself and other troops fairly close; but it seemed entirely practical, by making a sudden descent, to seize the town itself and hold it to ransom. If the garrison from Edinburgh attacked it could not be held, but it could be burned. It was Jones's purpose to give the burghers the choice of putting up £200,000 in cash or seeing the place laid in ashes. It was a rich city, and he believed they would pay; but he did not greatly care what they did, for if Leith were laid in ashes by an American force, the British would think twice before burning another American town.

He therefore made for the Firth of Forth, but everything was against him, including the weather, until he actually arrived in sight of the place. Then for once he had a perfect day, but once more the human element failed. Landais was gone, heaven only knew where. During the stormy passage down the east coast of Scotland the *Alliance* had simply vanished, and it was useless to go hunting for her. And now Cottineau, of the *Pallas,* and Ricot, of the *Vengeance,* who had hitherto done pretty well, both failed. An attack on Leith was more than they had stomach for.

In all fairness, a certain allowance must be made for the two Frenchmen. Leith looked vastly more formidable than it really was. Indeed, from where the vessels were tossing out in the Firth, it looked like a fortress all but impregnable to anything less than a tremendous battle fleet. Edinburgh Castle loomed above it with grinning tiers of twenty-four-pounders, and to

Cottineau and Ricot it seemed that they must pass within easy range of that monstrous ordnance. To assail such a place with three ships mustering a total of eighty-two guns among them must have seemed suicidal to them.

Furthermore, and perhaps more important, throughout the cruise they had been subjected to the disintegrating influence of Landais. They were serving under a foreign flag, a circumstance that invariably arouses distrust in either sailors or soldiers. Their compatriot Landais had been telling them constantly that the squadron commander was an incompetent fool, and while they had their own opinion of Landais, it is highly probable that his words had had more effect upon them than they themselves realized. At any rate, to attack Leith without even the doubtful assistance of the *Alliance* was too much. They balked.

The concordat made it impossible for Jones to order them. He had to persuade them. It took him until eleven o'clock at night to do it, but he did. The fact is, Cottineau and Ricot were basically good men. They hesitated because they were not quite up to Jones's standard as officers, but who was? By comparison with most with whom he had to deal, these two shine.

However, the delay was fatal. It was morning before all preparations were complete, and by morning the wind had changed. It was necessary for the ships to beat their way against a head wind, which was painfully slow work. Yet they did it. Little by little every obstacle was overcome, and eventually they drew into position. Chamillard—whose record, by the way, was excellent throughout—got 140 of his French marines into small boats and took his place with them, equipped with a letter from Jones to the town authorities demanding £100,000 within thirty minutes, or good-by Leith! Dale, the first officer, was just going over the side to take his place in the lead boat when a squall struck the *Bon Homme Richard* and held things up.

They waited for the wind to go down, but it didn't go down. On the contrary, it increased. They had to take in the marines from the small boats. Then they had to work their way farther offshore. Then the wind developed into a regular gale, and there was nothing for it but to get out of there. The chance had passed and the third objective of the cruise had been lost.

As a matter of fact, it had not been altogether lost, by any means. The shock to Scotland vastly exceeded that administered by the seizure of Lord Selkirk's teapot. Everyone realized with painful clarity that Leith had escaped, not by British prowess, but by the chance of that summer storm—or, if you choose to believe the people of Kircaldy, a village ten miles across the Firth, by the extraordinary influence on heaven of the Reverend Mr. Shirra, a local divine who assembled his congregation on the beach at the critical moment and prayed so powerfully that he raised the wind.

In any event, it was borne in upon all Scotland that John Paul Jones was perfectly capable of taking Leith and would have taken it had not the elements stopped him. Obviously, they could not always rely on a storm, and where else was any protection against this terror? Scotland could see none, and denunciation of the government and its silly war against the Americans rose to new heights.

But Paul Jones could not know this. All that he knew was that he was foiled again, and he retreated from the Firth of Forth raging; but all the more determined that the fourth and last chance should not be missed.

IX.

The arrival of the Baltic fleet was unusually important this year because Rodney, the British admiral, lying in the estuary of the Thames with the main battle fleet, was short of all the supplies it was bringing and especially of masts and spars. His condition was so bad, indeed, thanks to Jemmy Twitcher's inefficiency, that he was in no condition to put to sea, and if Orvilliers had descended upon Plymouth and Southampton during the summer the British would have been in a very tight place indeed. Rodney had no intention of moving until the Baltic fleet arrived; but it was working its way south and he expected to see it soon.

Paul Jones found it, coming down upon Flamborough Head, on the east coast of England—a fleet of forty-one sail, convoyed by the *Serapis*, a fine, brand-new frigate carrying fifty guns, although rated as a forty, and the *Countess of Scarborough*, a converted yacht of twenty guns.

For reasons of his own, still unknown to the rest of the world, Landais had chosen to return to the squadron, so Paul Jones, lurking south of the cape, had technically under his command the *Bon Homme Richard*, forty guns, the *Alliance*, thirty, the *Pallas*, thirty, and the *Vengeance*, twelve. In mere weight of metal he had thus a distinct superiority, 112 guns against 70; but this advantage was apparent only, not real, even disregarding the quality of his captains; for the battery of the *Bon Homme Richard* was old and unreliable, while all the American ships were slow and hard to handle. Either of the British ships was capable of sailing rings around the American squadron. Had every captain in Jones's squadron been well disciplined, bold, and skillful, still the odds, on form, would have been pretty nearly even.

That the advantage was, in fact, in favor of the British was indicated when Jones made his first signal, for the formation of line of battle. The *Alliance* paid not the slightest attention. By this time the British were swinging around the cape and Richard Pearson, captain of the *Serapis,* discovered what he was running into. Instantly he signaled the convoy to come about and make for the coast, while the two warships threw themselves between the Americans and their prey.

When he had seen that all the merchantmen were scuttling for shelter, Pearson himself began to edge toward the coast. It was the correct move, for the British captain knew his business. It left the American only the choice of attacking the warships, or of retiring, baffled. Since the *Alliance*, disregarding all signals, had withdrawn and was now far out of reach, and since the

Bon Homme Richard was not a match for the *Serapis,* let alone both warships, Cottineau not unnaturally assumed that Jones would have to withdraw. So when he saw the *Bon Homme Richard* make a dash to get between the *Serapis* and the shore line, only one explanation occurred to him. He thought the crew had mutinied, captured the ship, and was now going in to surrender. Under this impression the *Pallas* lit out for the open sea with all the speed she could make.

So, except for the little *Vengeance,* which maintained a discreet distance, the *Bon Homme Richard,* with her forty worn-out guns, went forward alone to encounter a first-class frigate of fifty, and an excellent auxiliary of twenty guns.

The action that followed is one of the most voluminously written-up battles in the history of naval warfare. To begin with, we have the detailed report of Captain Jones himself. Then First Lieutenant Richard Dale wrote a narrative that historians have discounted somewhat because of his strong partiality for his captain. Midshipman Nathaniel Fanning wrote a narrative discounted somewhat because of his strong partiality for Nathaniel. Pierre Girard, the Frenchman who was acting as interpreter for the Captain, wrote a narrative discounted somewhat on account of his uncertainty with the language. Dr. Ballantyne, surgeon of the *Serapis,* wrote a narrative from the British side discounted somewhat because the doctor himself saw nothing, being busy with the wounded throughout the battle, but which nevertheless has stood up pretty well under critical examination. Half a dozen other participants wrote partial accounts, and half a hundred people who were nowhere about wrote extended descriptions frequently exhibiting extraordinary imaginative powers.

Naturally, there are discrepancies and even flat contradictions in these stories. It is what would be expected by anyone whose business has familiarized him with the analysis of evidence—a lawyer, a historian, a biographer, or a psychiatrist. Discrepancies in the accounts of many eyewitnesses of one event indicate not that someone is consciously lying, but rather that no one is, for no two people see the same event in exactly the same way, and they will not report it in the same way unless they have agreed on their stories in advance.

It may be assumed, therefore, that we have as exact an idea of what went on off Flamborough Head on the evening of September 23, 1779, between the hours of six and half past ten o'clock as we have of any historical event. The differences refer to details; as to the more important movements all the witnesses are in substantial agreement, so there is no doubt about what happened on the spot.

Yet not a man of them, least of all John Paul Jones himself, reported that battle adequately. Not a man of them knew, or suspected, what was really happening, and for the best of reasons, namely, that not a man of them was still alive when the effect of what they did there began to be revealed; indeed, more than a century and a half later it is doubtful that we can measure the full effect.

It was a fine, late-summer evening when the *Serapis* accepted the challenge of the *Bon Homme Richard* and bore down upon her.

"It is probably Paul Jones," said Captain Pearson, lowering the glass through which, in the gathering twilight, he had been studying the approaching ship. "If so, there's work ahead."

On the gun decks of the *Bon Homme Richard* the tension was terrific as the gun crews stood by, guns shotted, matches lighted, while the gentle breeze brought the two ships slowly and silently closer and closer together. On the quarterdeck they had identified the Briton and like lightning the news flew through the ship. Suddenly the silence was broken by a shout from a ribald gunner.

"Look out for yourselves, boys," he bawled, "here comes the Sea-raper!"

A whoop of laughter and a volley of Rabelaisian comment suddenly loosened taut nerves, and the enemy's first broadside a moment later shook nobody.

At seven-fifteen Pearson opened and got an instant return.

Thereafter for a while it was a straight slugging match, devoid of science or craft, each ship battering the other with everything it could bring to bear.

This was ruinous for the *Bon Homme Richard.* The old eighteen-pounders on the lower gun deck had borne out Jones's worst fears. Two of them burst at the first fire, killing the entire crews except Red Cherry, whose duty was to touch off No. 2 gun, wounding Acting Lieutenant Mayrant, in command, and completely wrecking the deck. First Lieutenant Dale, commanding the main battery on the deck above, thereupon ordered Mayrant to abandon his useless battery and join him on the main deck.

The *Bon Homme Richard*'s heaviest armament was thus out of action almost from the beginning, and the enemy's broadsides were doing fearful execution on her hull. Dale, applying the Jones formula, was working manfully on the *Serapis'* masts and rigging, and with considerable effect. But the question was, how much longer would the old East Indiaman stand up under the blows she was taking?

In came the *Countess of Scarborough,* running past the port side of the *Bon Homme Richard* and pouring in a broadside, then back again with another.

Miles away, the *Alliance* lay to and stared. Entreaties of officers and crew could not arouse Landais from the stupefaction that seemed to have seized him.

But Cottineau, equally stupefied when the outburst of cannonading told him that the American ship had run in to fight, not surrender, was not paralyzed. He brought the *Pallas* about and rushed back, coming within range just about the time the *Countess of Scarborough* delivered her second broadside. He went for her, hammer and tongs, and thereafter she was too busy to give Jones further trouble.

Meanwhile, on the top of the two-hundred-foot chalk cliff of Flamborough Head, six miles away, a fascinated audience looked on. The sea was calm and there was still plenty of light when the action began. It was estimated that fifteen hundred people climbed to that lofty gallery; nor did they lose track of the drama as the dusk deepened, for the moon rose and flooded the scene with light so that the people could see almost as clearly as they had at the beginning.

They looked on with awe and incredulity as British warships fought for their lives within plain sight of the coast of England. Presently the sea was lighted with a red glare that did not come from the flashes of cannon. The ships were afire. Now they were locked together in a death grapple, and the smoke of the cannonade mingled with the smoke of burning timbers to shroud them both from the straining eyes of the watchers on the cliff.

Impressed they certainly were. Many who were boys and girls on Flamborough Head that night, as old men and women told the story to their grandchildren, remembering it after half a century and more as vividly as if it had happened yesterday.

They were impressed, yet their awe and incredulity would have been far greater had they had any idea of what they were really witnessing. For vastly more than the fate of two ships and a few hundred men was being decided on that calm, moonlit stretch of water. A new power was coming into being there, a new force was entering the world. John Paul Jones was proving on the sea what on land had first been suggested at Bunker Hill and then confirmed at Saratoga. At Bunker Hill American soldiers found that they could withstand the shock of an assault by British regulars. At Saratoga they found that they could themselves carry an assault against a British army.

American ships had fought British ships before, and when they fought on equal terms had sometimes won; but they usually fought of necessity and they never challenged with inferior forces. This night they were doing just that. They were taking a leaf out of the British book, doing what Drake and Nottingham had done on the other side of this same water nearly two hundred years before, when they did not wait for the Spanish Armada, but sent their fireships driving into Calais Harbor.

Since then the British had been beaten at sea, not once, but repeatedly. Nearly always, though, when they lost they lost through recklessness, through being caught in ambush, through false information of the enemy's strength, or sometimes through the desperate valor of men who had to win or die. For two hundred years the British had chosen the time and place to fight, and usually they won. Once only had they been sternly challenged in their own waters. A hundred and twenty-five years before old Maarten Tromp had sailed through the Channel with a broom at his masthead, symbol of his having swept the British from the narrow seas; but a year later Tromp had died under British guns.

The Dutchman had no successors. Frenchman and Spaniard, Russian and Dane and Swede were content, at most, to fight defensively against the aggressive British. On land they might attack without hesitation; but on the sea no one carried the war to Britain.

No one, that is, until this night; but the guns of the *Bon Homme Richard* were smashing more than the rigging of the *Serapis;* they were blowing the old tradition to pieces, they were announcing the arrival of a sea power that in the course of time would not hesitate to attack anything afloat and that eventually would carry the war, not merely to Britain, but to the continent of Europe, to Africa, to Asia, and to the uttermost isles of the sea.

Nor was tradition all that they were blasting down. They were shattering the very system of government that prevailed not in England only, but throughout the world. Absolutism, too, was crumbling under the impact of their shot—the system that put Jemmy Twitchers in control of the navy and Germains in control of colonial affairs. Lord North, that imitation statesman, was being heavily battered off Flamborough Head, and the flames that crackled through the ships were burning up the pasteboard reputations of sawdust men as well as the oaken timbers.

It was a tremendous drama that was enacted before the fifteen hundred on the cliff, far more tremendous than any of them suspected; more tremendous, perhaps, than we know today, for the echoes of that cannonade are still reverberating. What John Paul Jones started that night is still in progress, and it will end no man knows where.

But it was not done easily. Lieutenant Richard Dale, stained with sweat, grimy with powder smoke, spattered with blood, found the Captain beside him in the inferno that was the gun deck.

"Dick, his metal is too heavy for us!" he exclaimed. "He is hammering us to pieces. We must close with him. Bring your men on the spar deck and give them the small arms."

It was true. Dale had the proof before his eyes. Following the British custom of going for the hull, the *Serapis* had staved in the sides of her opponent, dismounted most of the guns, and killed the crews. The *Bon Homme Richard* had caught fire half a dozen times, and once the flames had crept within inches of the magazine before they were smothered. Most of the gun ports were by now simply gaping, jagged holes, and British shot was sweeping straight across the gun deck and out the other side.

But the *Serapis* had not escaped unscathed. Thanks to Dale's excellent gunnery, her rigging was a tangled mess and the once smart ship was responding as sluggishly to her tiller as the old *Bon Homme Richard* herself. The Briton's speed had been killed and there was now a chance to come to grips with her.

That was what Jones had been trying to accomplish from the start, but without success. Only a sailor and an experienced one can understand the intricate maneuvering of the two ships, for if Jones was a great seaman, Pearson was a good one and had the better ship. Every effort to come to close quarters the Briton skillfully eluded. Time and again Jones thought the two were bound to touch, but always at the last moment the Briton slipped away, to stand off and give the *Bon Homme Richard* another smashing broadside.

But little by little the *Serapis* was being worn down. Steadily, doggedly Dale was cutting the rigging to pieces. After each broadside his guns were fewer, but still the shot went whistling over the *Serapis'* deck, cutting a few more ropes, splinter-

ing another yard, slamming into another mast to weaken it
still further.

Unable quite to close, Jones still managed to stay within
musket shot, and Chamillard's French marines and the fighting tops, especially the main top, where Stack commanded,
beat a steady and deadly tattoo on the British deck with musket
balls. Pearson couldn't keep enough men on that exposed deck
to handle the sails properly.

After more than an hour of this the American seemed to have
succeeded; by a quick turn when the ships were alongside he
actually rammed the *Serapis;* but Pearson, with all his hand-
icaps, made nearly as quick a turn, and it was merely a touch.
The swiftly hurled grappling irons slipped and scratched along
the *Serapis'* rail, but failed to hold; she triumphantly slid clear,
and the American took another staggering broadside.

It is interesting to note the variations in the different accounts of this part of the battle. Most of them were written some
time later, some several years later, and the Americans, without
exception, seem to have considered it their duty to put into the
mouth of the Captain lofty sentiments and resounding periods.
But one did not. This was Pierre Girard, unquestionably the
most active Frenchman on the ship. He had to be, for it was his
duty, as interpreter, to stick within arm's length of the Captain,
and the Captain was everywhere. Girard panted and perspired,
but he kept up; he heard everything and he saw everything, and
it is his testimony that, flying from one threatened point to another, commanding, adjuring, pleading, encouraging, Captain
John Paul Jones put on the finest exhibition of plain and fancy
endurance swearing it was ever his privilege to listen to in a
long experience in armies and navies. Nor did he make a single
orotund remark.

But the *Serapis* was losing more and more of her speed and
precision of movement. Pearson knew what to do, but he was
less and less able to do it with the swiftness necessary when
timing was a matter of split seconds. Presently Jones saw a
chance to throw his ship across the bow of the British vessel;

that would have been perfect, for in that position he would have been clear of those terrible broadsides, while with his deck guns he could rake the *Serapis* at his leisure. He tried it, and Pearson instantly countered by swinging away; but this time he was not quite fast enough. He ran his bowsprit straight across the *Bon Homme Richard*'s deck and rammed her. Jones himself snatched up a line and leaped forward with a yell to lash the ships together.

Everyone on the quarterdeck heard him, including, of course, Pierre Girard. The Americans decorously edited his remark after the battle. They reported that as he leaped he cried, "Well done, my brave lads, we have got her now!" which is, of course, correct and proper stuff for grammar-school textbooks. But the shameless Frenchman set down his remark verbatim; according to him, what Jones said in this critical moment was hardly a copybook maxim. To be exact, it was, "I've got the son of a whore!" Somehow, though, that sounds more like what an American captain would say at a moment of high excitement.

Pearson instantly perceived his peril if the lashing held, and men ran forward to cut the line; but the French marines shot them as fast as they came. Tradition has it that Jones snatched a musket from the nearest marine and knocked over the first one himself. The British did not lack courage; it is said that no less than fourteen tried it, and fourteen were killed or crippled before they could touch the rope, which by this time was passed around and around the bowsprit of the *Serapis* and the mizzenmast of the *Bon Homme Richard*. Then Stacey, the acting master, brought up a hawser, which was substituted for the ropes first used.

Pearson then let go an anchor, hoping that the wrench plus the leverage of the *Bon Homme Richard*'s own length would tear the ships apart. But they didn't. All that happened was that the two ships were brought together full length, bow to stern, starboard to starboard, so close that the guns touched and the gunners of the *Serapis,* to swab out their pieces, had to run the rammers actually into the *Bon Homme Richard*. But the

American ship's gun deck was now occupied only by the dead, and the terrible broadsides served merely to tear her sides.

Dale and his men were now on the poop deck, where the nine-pounders were the only guns left working. A blast of small-arms fire from the *Serapis* decimated the marines. Chamillard fell and the men wavered.

"Frenchmen, will you give way before the eyes of the Americans and the British?" stormed Jones. They cheered and rallied to sweep the Briton's deck again.

The nine-pounders were dragged into position to bear on the *Serapis'* mainmast, the Captain himself pointing one of them, because Mr. Mease, the admirable seagoing merchant of Philadelphia, had taken a shot in the head and was out of action. Shot after shot hit the mast and it began to wobble.

Then over the moonlit sea, from the far horizon came the swift and powerful *Alliance,* swooping down upon the deadlock. Landais had emerged from his stupor at last and apparently it was all up with Pearson; she had only to come down on his other side and he was done for beyond all hope. But instead she swept past the stern of the *Bon Homme Richard* and poured a terrific broadside into her own consort!

They screamed and yelled at her as she went past within pistol shot, they signaled frantically, they prayed to Jones to be permitted to fire on her as she drove by, firing as she went. But he restrained them, and would do no more than put up a string of emergency signals. Half a mile away the *Alliance* turned and came back. It is impossible to believe that she couldn't see the signals. It is impossible to believe that in the bright moonlight she could not distinguish between the jet-black hull of the *Bon Homme Richard* and the bright yellow hull with a black stripe of the *Serapis.* Nevertheless, again her broadside crashed into the American ship. This time Landais was using grape and chain shot because they would scatter. He killed the last officer left on the forecastle. He killed six or eight men crowded into the waist of the ship; then he sailed by and disappeared to be seen no more during the battle.

The starboard side of the *Bon Homme Richard* was torn wide open from the rail almost to the water line. She had taken several eighteen-pound shot between wind and water and was leaking like a sieve. She was afire in half a dozen places. There were many feet of water in the hold. But Stack and the now leaderless French marines were still bouncing musket balls as thick as hailstones on the deck of the *Serapis,* and no Englishman could stick his head above the hatch combings without getting it shot off. Jones was still hammering at the masts with his nine-pounders and Mayrant was gathering a party of boarders in the waist.

At this moment Burbank, the master-at-arms, seems to have gone stark mad. At any rate, he released two hundred British prisoners who had been confined below and they came swarming upon the deck, Burbank at their head, scattering confusion among the crew and threatening dire peril to the ship.

Jones tried to shoot Burbank, but his pistol missed fire. Then he made a valiant effort to bend it over the head of the master-at-arms, who went down like a log and took no further interest in the proceedings for hours. One prisoner took a swing at the Captain, and the interpreter, Girard, shot him dead. With two prostrate bodies blocking the way, the stampede stopped; and with the help of Dale and some sailors the prisoners were herded back and put to manning the pumps.

But Burbank was not the only wild man. The Captain, sweat pouring from him and utterly exhausted, sat for a moment on a shattered timber to catch his breath. An officer whom he never named, but who was, he said, a good man and a courageous one, spoke up.

"For God's sake, strike, sir!"

"I will sink, but I will not strike," returned the Captain shortly, and darted away to another threatened point.

Away up under the forecastle, though, a gunner and the carpenter, both wounded, lost their heads and cried to the English for quarter. The gunner rushed aft to tear down the flag with his own hands, but he couldn't, because it had been carried away by a cannon shot long before.

Still, the Englishman was uncertain. He heard the shouts and he could no longer see the ensign, so he clapped his speaking trumpet to his lips as there came a momentary lull in the din and shouted, "Have you struck, sir?" The crews of both ships heard him clearly, and all strained their ears for the reply.

It was the most theatrical moment in the history of the American navy, it was the moment that is fixed forever as the glittering center of all the glamour, all the romance, all the gallantry, the chivalry, the purple and gold of service traditions. The ship was afire and sinking, the guns were all out of action, a third of the crew was dead or wounded, the prisoners were loose, the *Alliance* had turned traitor, there was neither help nor hope by land or sea.

"I," said Jones in his official report, "answered him in the most determined negative."

But Pierre Girard, who was standing at his elbow, and Richard Dale, who was a few feet away, declared that what he said was: "Struck, sir? No, I have just begun to fight!"

What Pearson heard is a matter of no moment. What Dale and Girard reported is what the American people heard, what they have continued to hear for five generations, and what they will continue to hear as long as American naval tradition lasts. It was the first great shout of all those that have come ringing down the centuries and we have heard its echo in all the others. Long years afterward and thousands of miles away we heard it again in Mobile Bay: "Damn the torpedoes! Full speed ahead!" A generation after that we heard it again on the other side of the world, not a shout this time, but a voice in a quiet conversational tone: "You may fire when you are ready, Gridley." Then after forty years more in a pitch-black midnight in the Slot off Savo, of dreadful and glorious memory, not in the air this time, but in the ether waves full of the sibilant whispering of unseen enemies: "This is Ching Chong Lee. Get out of the way, I'm coming through."

The words were different, but the voice was the same. It was the battle cry of the Indomitable Man, the challenge of the human spirit to a material world it disdains.

But Pearson merely said, "Then let them have it," and the terrible broadsides roared again, and the shot tore the entrails of the old *Bon Homme Richard,* and the prisoners pumped like mad, but the water crept up in the hold and the flames crackled among the timbers.

Yet the musketeers drummed madly upon the decks of the *Serapis* and no Englishman stuck his head above the hatches. It was stalemate.

Then upon the scene came Phaëthon, like an old Greek *deus ex machina,* to supply a solution. Nate Fanning claimed that it was he, which is possible, but John Paul Jones thought not. He said it was a Scotch sailor named William Hamilton, and he probably knew. In any event, it is better drama, for we know nothing else about Hamilton—"Wullie" he would have been, back in Galloway—other than this one act. Like Phaëthon erratically driving his father's chariot, Wullie comes into history swinging dizzily between sky and sea, hangs poised for a moment, and then goes out of history with a roar.

In the main top Stack and his men—including, it must be admitted, Nathaniel Fanning—found themselves out of a job. So hot had been their fire that no Englishman now stuck his head up, and there was nothing left to shoot at. So Wullie and some others crept out along the yards to see if they could fling grenades into sheltered spots that the muskets could not reach. Wullie followed the main yard, which was projecting directly over the *Serapis'* deck. She, too, was afire now—in ten or twelve places, said Pearson—and in the light cast by the flames he spied a hatch with its cover half off.

It was a small target, hardly two square feet, at a range of sixty feet, but Wullie tried for it. His first grenade hit the deck and spat venomously, but did no material damage to the stout oak planks. His second, also, was a miss, but his third curved in a graceful trajectory over the hatch, closer, closer, and disappeared into the opening. A bull's eye!

Wullie did not know it then, but on the gun deck below the powder monkeys had been serving the guns too well. They had been bringing up cartridges, that is to say, large bags of gunpowder used for charging the guns, faster than the gunners could use them and had laid a row of the deadly things down the full length of the deck. Straight into this row plunged Wullie's grenade, detonating the whole business. Instantly the gun deck was converted into an inferno. Hideous remnants of twenty men were hurled in all directions; many who were not killed outright had the last shred of their clothing blown off and were shockingly burned. Stanhope, the first lieutenant in command, with his uniform all aflame, plunged overboard to extinguish the fire.

That did it. Amid the fearful din Wullie Hamilton crawled back along the main yard into the total obscurity whence he had emerged, but he had done his work. With his main battery out of commission, Pearson could no longer inflict any damage on his antagonist. He was a good man, but not fool enough to continue the fight when he could hope to accomplish nothing but the slaughter of his remaining men. So when John Mayrant and his boarding party came swarming over the side, the British captain with his own hands hauled down the flag.

At Jones's nod Richard Dale followed. One British seaman gave Mayrant a thrust in the thigh with a pike, but that was all. Dale found Pearson standing on the lee side of the quarterdeck and said to him, "Sir, I have orders to send you on board the ship alongside."

At that moment an officer—Dale says the first lieutenant, which would indicate that Stanhope had climbed aboard again —came up and asked if the Americans had struck.

"No, sir, the contrary," said Dale. "He has struck to us."

"Have you struck, sir?" said the officer to Pearson.

"Yes, I have," he replied.

Both officers went then to the rail and stepped across to the *Bon Homme Richard,* so close were the ships together. Pearson handed his sword to Jones without a word. The latter said, "You have fought gallantly, sir, and I hope your sovereign will reward you," at which Pearson bowed, but made no reply, and followed a junior officer to the Captain's cabin.*

Hardly had Captain Pearson stepped upon the *Bon Homme Richard* than the mainmast and mizzenmast of the *Serapis* crashed down and fell over the side. Jones thereupon ordered Dale to take command of her, cut loose the lashings, and follow the *Bon Homme Richard.* Dale thereupon issued the necessary orders, and the lashings were cut loose, but nothing else happened. He was sitting on the binnacle, according to Lorenz, when a British sailor informed him that the ship was anchored. Intending to go forward and see about it, he jumped up—and promptly crashed to the deck. Then, and not until then, he discovered that sometime during the fight he had taken a shell splinter in the leg. However, he was able to order the cable cut and to see that the *Serapis* was following her captor before he was taken off in a small boat to receive the attentions of the surgeon.

When Jones had time to look around he found that Cottineau, at least, had done his duty. The *Pallas* had had an extremely lively sixty minutes with the *Countess of Scarborough,* but Cottineau's thirty guns were too much for the Englishman's twenty and in the end the *Countess* had struck. Cottineau, however, had been pretty well beaten up himself, and what with clearing away wreckage, making his prize secure, and taking due care of his wounded and prisoners, his hands were full and he had

---

* Later fantastic stories were told about this incident. They portrayed Pearson as an arrogant boor who handed his sword to Jones with the insulting comment that he hated to give it up to a man with a rope around his neck. If anything like this had happened, Jones being as touchy as he was on all questions of honor, Pearson would have found himself in irons, not in the Captain's cabin; but more conclusive is the fact that the Englishman is known to have been a well-bred gentleman, conversant with naval courtesies and scrupulous in their observance. No man of breeding could possibly have been guilty of so gross a breach of manners. The story undoubtedly was fabricated by landsmen, British or American, who knew nothing of good usage in the navy.

no time to go chasing after prizes. As for the *Vengeance,* Ricot prudently decided that that terrific arena was no place for a twelve-gun sloop and had busied himself in keeping out of the way.

Somewhere in the neighborhood were forty-one magnificent prizes, the whole Baltic fleet. Jones's one hope was that the *Alliance,* since it had taken no part in the battle except to do harm, had at least played havoc among the merchant ships. He could do nothing himself. His own ship was a wreck and the *Serapis* was little better. He couldn't run down a mud scow, much less a fast-sailing merchant ship. His one idea at the moment was to get out of sight of Flamborough Head as soon as possible, for he knew couriers were riding madly to spread the alarm and it was a matter of hours until half the British navy would be tearing furiously to the spot, burning to wipe out the insult.

Crippled as they were—for one item, the *Bon Homme Richard*'s rudder was completely shot away—he got the ships moving and over the horizon before morning dawned. But by morning it was plain that the old *Richard* was finished. The carpenter, whose duty it was, came to the Captain and made his formal report that he couldn't save her. It was a pure formality, for Jones could see for himself that the ship was doomed. Yet he had not the heart to condemn her himself. He sent for Ricot and Cottineau to come on board with their carpenters and make a survey. In the meantime the wounded and the prisoners were transferred to the *Serapis*. The French captains came over, made their independent inspection, declared that the ship could not be saved, and formally recommended that she be abandoned.

Jones then went on board the *Serapis* himself, leaving only a prize crew on the *Richard* with a boat waiting to take them off at the last minute. The first lieutenant of the *Pallas* was in command and he kept the pumps going all day; but during the night the wind rose and by the morning of the twenty-fifth it was evident that it was all over. At nine o'clock Jones ordered the prize crew off, the water being then up to the lower deck, "and a little after ten I saw, with inexpressible grief, the last glimpse of the *Bon Homme Richard.*" Pearson wrote that she went down by the head, the stern and the mizzenmast being the last to disappear.

X.

After the shooting was over the *Alliance* had come up jauntily enough, but with never a prize in her possession. Neither Landais nor the *Vengeance* had made the slightest effort to interfere with the Baltic fleet, which escaped intact in a convenient fog.

Jones's next move is interesting for its audacity and simplicity. He knew that he had stirred up the hornets' nest indeed. The whole British navy was now intent on his destruction—big ships, little ships, middle-sized ships, anything and everything that could sail and shoot was bent upon expunging the insult to British naval power. Not to mention frigates, it was said that no less than thirteen line-of-battle ships were detailed to the search. The natural assumption was that he would make for some port, preferably a French one, to refit. So the British scattered in every direction to cover every possible bolt hole. They promptly blocked the Channel, of course. They had swarms of frigates around the Orkneys and Shetlands to stop the northern exit, if possible. They patrolled the Dutch and Danish coasts vigilantly, hoping to catch him no matter which way he turned.

So he turned no way at all. He simply retired to the middle of the North Sea, and there he stayed for ten days while his carpenters were getting the *Serapis* into some sort of shape. He couldn't do much with her, but he could at least rig jury masts and get her into such condition that she couldn't be run down by an old lady in a rowboat.

The loss of time did not matter. On the contrary, it was to his advantage, for every day he was invisible meant that the searchers would grow more frantic, and the more frantic they were the more likely it was that some loophole through which he could slip would be presented.

As for his final destination, Chaumont had ordered him to proceed to the Texel, but he now had four or five hundred prisoners whom he preferred to land on French soil. There they would certainly be available for exchange, while if he landed them in neutral territory they were likely to be released. He wished, therefore, to try for Dunkirk.

Now the wretched concordat got in its evil effect again. The other captains maintained that they had been ordered to the Texel, and to the Texel they would go. Captain Jones could do as he pleased, but they considered themselves under Chaumont's orders, not his. They stuck with him until the *Serapis* was fairly seaworthy again; but at the end of ten days they headed for the Texel, leaving him to follow or not, as he chose.

Unwilling to start another political row, he followed. Not a single British ship appeared, and October 3, 1779, the squadron dropped anchor in the Dutch port.

So Captain John Paul Jones had won another victory, this time the most brilliant in American naval annals up to that time. He had administered another and a tenfold more violent shock to the British Empire. With an inferior ship he had fought a British man-o'-war within sight of the British coast and had captured it. Although he had not seized the Baltic fleet, he had scattered it far and wide, thereby delaying Rodney in the Thames for nearly two months. He had sent marine insurance rates soaring again, to the great distress of British business. He had still further undermined confidence in the government of George III and Lord North. He had materially shortened the war.

Above all, he had given the United States Navy a great tradition. He had inspired in it a self-confidence it had never had before, but which it was not to lose for at least a hundred and seventy years. He had given to its officers an ideal of a naval officer worthy of a great service. He had given to the flag he served mighty gifts of honor and pride. Obviously, the Americans must do something for such a captain.

They did. They relieved him of his command.

CHAPTER VII.

I.

THERE WAS no sense whatever in running into the Texel.
The squadron should have made for Dunkirk. Paul Jones
knew it and, to the extent that they were capable of rational concepts, the others knew it, too.

But they were also aware that the French navy department
was not governed by rational concepts. They were mere captains,
and if a captain swerves by a hairbreadth from his written orders, nothing is easier than for some swivel-chair admiral, or
some civilian department official, to make him the scapegoat
for whatever goes wrong.

The original instructions to end the cruise at the Texel had
a reasonable foundation. When they were issued it was hoped
that by the end of the cruise the squadron would be loaded
down with prizes. If it had taken the Baltic fleet, for instance,
it would have been sheer idiocy to try to run a convoy of forty
sail through the Channel, and it would have been highly im-
prudent to go as far south even as Dunkirk.

Furthermore, as international law stood then, belligerents
had a right to run prizes into neutral ports. The Dutch government would have had no legal basis for a protest. But prisoners
were different. Prisoners landed on neutral soil were automat-
ically freed. Therefore since the squadron had only two prizes,
both warships, and several hundred prisoners, the original
reason for the order no longer existed and the order itself became insensate.

But the French captains knew better than to give Chaumont
the least excuse to blame the results of his own inefficiency on

their disobedience of orders. He had said the Texel, and the Texel it was. It was the old, familiar error of making general orders too detailed to allow the officer on the spot to use the brains God had given him.

The results Jones had foreseen followed rapidly. Sir Joseph Yorke, British ambassador at the Hague, was instantly on the doorstep of Their High Mightinesses the States-General with a whole sheaf of demands, supported by documents, pleadings, precedents, citations, protests, and injunctions, calling for immediate action against "a certain Paul Jones, a subject of the King, who according to treaties and the laws of war can only be considered a rebel and a pirate." Yorke coolly demanded not merely the instant return of the ships to His Majesty, but also that their captor be handed over in irons to be dealt with by British Admiralty courts.

However, "a certain Paul Jones" was no bad legal skirmisher himself. He too showed up with a fistful of treaties, agreements, precedents, quotations from Grotius, the great Dutch authority on international law, affidavits, and depositions showing that as a captain in the United States Navy he was entitled to the status of a belligerent, and demanding that the Dutch supply him at once with his immediate necessities, including especially medicines and medical care for his wounded and the right to purchase such stores and materials as were necessary to make his ships seaworthy again. He was supported by the French ambassador with voluminous extracts from the special arrangements existing between Holland and France touching such matters as the right of asylum and the assistance owed French mariners in distress both according to the laws of war and according to the special treaties in such case made and provided.

It was all a terrific headache for the Dutch, and it was not simplified when Jones put Landais under arrest and forwarded charges against him to Franklin at Paris. But the two ambassadors, Yorke and the Duc de la Vauguyon, representing France, had a gorgeous time, sneering at each other's arguments, denying each other's allegations, capping each other's writs with other writs drawn from older and more obscure recesses of international law.

Nor is it to be denied that for a while Jones wasn't having too bad a time himself. The States-General and the Prince of Orange might be worrying over what to do, but there was no doubt about where the Dutch people stood. They were frankly and joyously for the American. Any man who could go out and snatch two British warships from the very shadow of Flamborough Head had their hearty approval, and they didn't care who knew it. The Captain visited Amsterdam while the legal battle raged, and on the floor of the Exchange there the brokers nearly mobbed him in their efforts to shake his hand and congratulate him. The street crowds whooped for him, and eventually it became difficult for him to get about at all, so certain was a crowd to collect wherever he appeared.

Nor was officialdom altogether unfriendly, in spite of the trouble he was causing. They put no obstacles in the way of his procuring necessary supplies, and even in the matter of the prisoners they were not adamant. Jones was flatly not going to release them, for they were his only hope of securing the exchange of an equal number of Americans, now languishing in British jails. Yet their condition on the terribly overcrowded ships was pitiable, especially that of the wounded. Couldn't the Dutch stretch a point for humanity's sake?

They could. They pointed out to Captain Jones that near where his squadron lay was an old fort, no longer used as part of the coast defenses, and therefore without a garrison. It was habitable, however, and it was roomy. If he sent a landing party ashore and seized it, there would be nobody there to oppose him, and they would take their time in making up their minds what to do about it. The hint was sufficient. The fort was seized and the wounded transferred to more comfortable quarters. Sir Joseph Yorke stormed, but the Dutch blandly denied that they had given Captain Jones permission to land prisoners, and said they would certainly compel him to remove them from Dutch soil—when they got around to it. They didn't get around to it until the need for use of the fort was past.

Jones's ardent desire, of course, was to get the *Serapis* refitted to replace the *Bon Homme Richard* as soon as possible, so that he might get to sea again. In Dunkirk this would have been easy; but as the Texel was a neutral port, all sorts of legal difficulties were in the way. For one thing, in a neutral port the *Serapis* would have to be formally sold as a prize and the United States would have to purchase it. Yorke, of course, threw an enormous tangle of court orders in the way of this, and Franklin was handicapped by having no money with which to buy prizes or authority from Congress to go into any such business.

So the battle of writs and injunctions raged for weeks that ran into months, while the smartest fighting captain and the toughest fighting crew in the service of the United States sat around twiddling their thumbs and the war dragged on without their participation. Rodney, the British admiral, couldn't catch the *Bon Homme Richard*, and Pearson, the British captain, wished he hadn't; but what these first-class fighting men couldn't achieve, Chaumont and Yorke between them accomplished neatly—they put John Paul Jones out of action. In another generation another American in another connection stated the case exactly—

> The harpies of the shore shall pluck
> The eagle of the sea!

Students of international law and of diplomatic history may find some interest in unraveling the tangled skein of the negotiations among the various parties, but the only point of much interest to the average reader is the fact that by sending the squadron into the Texel, instead of allowing the commander to run for whatever friendly port he could make, Chaumont prevented it from doing any further damage to the English. In recognition of his gallant fight Pearson was given a knighthood; but if George of England wished to reward real service, he should have knighted Chaumont, for it was the Frenchman who eliminated the menace that hung over Britain.

Even to the general reader, though, it is of some interest to note that one way in which they prevented Jones from doing anything violent during this lawyers' squabble was by holding out promises that he might even yet acquire the *Indienne*, which was still at Amsterdam although she was now the property of Luxemburg.

Of course, he never got her. The *Indienne* was a really good ship and it was flatly contrary to American naval practice to give a good ship to a good captain. The *Hancock* went to Manley, the *Raleigh* to Carpenter Thompson, the *Alliance* to Landais. These were all thirty-twos. John Barry got the *Effingham*, a twenty-eight, Lambert Wickes the *Reprisal*, a sixteen, John Paul Jones the *Providence*, a twelve. Most remarkable of all, though, was the final disposal of the *Indienne*, a fifty, and undoubtedly the best of them all.

She was not entrusted to any captain of the United States Navy. She went, instead, to a preposterous mountebank named Gillon, who sailed, not under the Stars and Stripes, but under the flag of South Carolina. Even thus early that politically stupidest of all the states was developing the peculiar function that she was to exercise for the next hundred years, the function of starting what she could not finish. In this case it was a navy of her own. She dispatched this Gillon to France with a commission in the rank of commodore, a higher rank than any in the United States Navy, and a demand upon Franklin to assist him in securing ships.

Being an utter fraud, he was, of course, clasped to the bosom of Arthur Lee, who moved heaven and earth to get hold of all the money Franklin could borrow to turn it over to this fellow. He did get enough to enable Gillon not to buy the *Indienne*, but to acquire her from Luxemburg under a charter arrangement. Gillon took her to sea, neglecting the formality of paying the agreed price, ran her across the Atlantic, seizing a few prizes —a fifty-gun frigate used for nothing better than to run down merchantmen!—and made Philadelphia, where he found that her owners were instituting legal proceedings to get their money. So he ran her out to sea again, where she was promptly captured by the British.

Thus the Americans made sure that the *Indienne* should never strengthen the squadron of Paul Jones. Instead, she went to strengthen the fleet of Rodney, the British admiral! How did we ever win that war?

In Holland, in the meantime, the embattled attorneys-at-law had succeeded in entangling things beyond hope of any reasonable settlement. Vauguyon developed the curious notion that the case would be assisted if Paul Jones could be induced to haul down the American flag and hoist French colors, but there he ran into a brick wall. Paul Jones was no expert on diplomatic protocol, but he knew what striking his colors meant, and he wasn't doing it for any man, not even a duke. The *Serapis,* which had never been an American ship, he might give up, but not the *Alliance.*

The final decision was that he must leave the *Serapis* under the French flag for sale as a prize; but he might put his men aboard the *Alliance* and run for a French port if he thought he could elude the British cruisers waiting for him outside.

This was a trifle to a seaman of Paul Jones's capacity. He simply waited for the first easterly gale that forced the cruisers back a little, and out he went. Much more serious was the problem of keeping the peace on his own ship when he loaded the survivors of the *Bon Homme Richard*'s crew on the *Alliance.* Those broadsides were very definitely still in the minds of the *Richard's* men, and what they thought of the crew of the *Alliance* they did not hesitate to proclaim. The result was that riot impended every foot of the way from the Texel to Lorient, and the Captain's authority, as well as his tact, was strained to the limit. It was with vast relief that Jones dropped anchor in the French port—not relief at having escaped the British, but at arriving without having half his ship's company murdered by the other half.

But he made it, and when he went up to Paris to report to Franklin he had reason for some complacency. Once more, insubordination and cowardice had defeated the main objects of his cruise. The British had sunk his flagship, and the French and Dutch had taken from him the better one he had captured to replace it. Landais, despite the charges hanging over him, was making plenty of trouble, and at one time had even drawn Cottineau and Ricot into opposition to Jones. The *Indienne* had been turned over to the egregious Gillon and had escaped him forever. He had no command except the *Alliance,* and Landais was claiming that.

But he had shattered the tradition of British invincibility at sea that had lasted for two hundred years. He had compelled every maritime nation to recognize the existence of a new sea power, and, what was to prove of vastly greater worth, he had established in the hearts of American seamen confidence in their own ability. Then, as affecting the immediate situation, he had won a brilliant victory against the traditional enemy of France, so he was the lion of Paris.

Things might have been better, but they weren't too bad.

II.

At this point, the reader who is interested in John Paul Jones solely as a potent figure in American history may close the book, saying, with Browning's serving man, "When the liquor's out, why clink the cannikin?"

He had twelve years yet to live and some of his gaudiest exploits were still ahead; but what he did to affect the destiny of the United States was already done. We tied his hands and permitted him to do no more. Henceforth his history is the story of an individual, an extraordinary one, to be sure, fascinating as a psychological study, peopled with figures as amazing as Jones himself, including the Empress of all the Russias and her bizarre entourage, and the smoke-shrouded apparitions of the first days of the French Revolution. But as an influence on American history Jones was now finished. Except for one short cruise, never again was he able to overcome the weight of dull inertia that opposed him. The man of fire and power was beaten, crushed, and stifled under the dull weight of the men of lead.

So here seems to be the appropriate place to examine this opposition. Jones never understood it. He regarded himself as the victim of active enemies, animated by envy, jealousy, and personal hatred. He thought that if a few villains could have been removed, his path would have been clear.

This is to be doubted. Villains were the proximate cause of his troubles, to be sure; yet if Arthur Lee, Esek Hopkins, Sam Purviance, and Peter Landais had all been hanged on the same gallows in 1776, still John Paul Jones would have run into trouble.

His real difficulty was not hatred, but misunderstanding. Nobody knew what he was driving at, so it was impossible for people to support him heartily and intelligently. He was a man who was proposing to take a step forward, and such men are always in trouble. He wanted a strong professional navy and no such thing existed anywhere in the world. The British service came nearest it, but even in the British service the corps of officers was selected on a fantastically nonprofessional basis, and promotion went by anything and everything except demonstrated efficiency. Jones wanted to change all that. He realized that it must be changed if the navy were to be made an instrument fit for the purposes of a democratic republic.

But he had no model, no standard of comparison to which he could refer inquirers. The Founding Fathers ran into the same difficulty. It is estimated that of the three million people in America in 1776, not over twelve hundred thousand supported the Revolution at any time, yet an even smaller number actively supported the King. The rest constituted, not opposition, but mere dead weight.

For lack of any precedent the first effort of the Founding Fathers was hopelessly bad. The Articles of Confederation, as we see plainly now, could not serve as the organic law of a nation composed of rational men. The miracle of the Constitution was not the document itself, for that was the resultant of contending forces, but the explanation of it that was offered in the *Federalist*. Hamilton, Madison, and Jay performed the astounding intellectual feat of constructing a hypothesis so perfect that it served the purpose of a precedent and enabled the people to understand a new thing, at least far enough to approve it.

Paul Jones had no such press agents of genius as Hamilton, Madison, and Jay, therefore his argument never was clearly understood. Indeed, he had been dead a hundred years before it was really understood; and a superficial examination of the debates in the *Congressional Record* is enough to prove that there are those in the councils of the nation who do not understand it to this day.

All of which would seem to work out to the conclusion that we are a pretty hopeless nation, which in fact doesn't follow at all. In this we were merely an average nation, acting as humanity generally acts in distrusting and denouncing the man who gets out in front. But a leader cannot lead unless he does get out in front. Shrewd fellows can seem to lead when they are doing nothing of the sort—James Nicholson and, for a time, Esek Hopkins are examples. Because they are not really separated from the crowd, everyone agrees with them and they are pelted with bouquets with never a dead cat among them. But the man who starts something really new compels people to think, which is always resented. In all ages and all nations the prophets have been stoned, while the soothsayers and Chaldeans have lived as prosperous gentlemen—that is, until the real crisis comes and they collapse.

Paul Jones had plenty of evidence of this before his eyes. Horatio Gates seemed to be a leader, but Washington was one. Who got the kicks? Arthur Lee was mistaken for a leader, but there was no mistake about Franklin; nor is there any doubt about who took the battering. So it has been ever since. Thaddeus Stevens did very well for himself in the Civil War period, but Lincoln was shot. Lodge flourished after the First World War, but Wilson was repudiated and broken.

In being frustrated at every turn, in being denied justice and subjected to contumely, Paul Jones was not, as he imagined, suffering a unique and unprecedented fate due entirely to the evil machinations of scoundrels. He was merely meeting the usual fate of the man who has the genius to perceive what is the logical next step and the courage to insist on taking it.

Yet if there is nothing surprising in the fact that he was treated shabbily, this quite ordinary procedure is, for the modern generation, the most important fact in his career. It would be better for us to forget the *Drake,* to forget White-haven, to forget the *Serapis,* perhaps to forget even "I have just begun to fight," than to forget the fact that John Paul Jones was denounced, reviled, and beaten down for no reason except that he insisted on organizing the Navy according to common sense instead of according to outworn customs and traditions that had always prevailed.

Lincoln wanted to do the same thing after the Civil War, except in his case it was the South that he wished to reorganize according to the dictates of common sense. He was killed, and his successor, trying to carry out his policy, was repudiated and impeached; with the result that after eighty years the South is still a sore spot—politically gagged and bound, economically backward, socially distracted, the spawning ground of such incredible things as antievolution laws, national prohibition, the Huey Long regime, the Ku Klux Klan, and, recently, the Columbians.

Wilson wanted to do the same thing after the First World War, except that in his case it was the world that he wished to reorganize according to the dictates of common sense. He fought a war to clear the way at a cost of fifty thousand dead and a debt of forty billions. He was laughed to scorn and repudiated. So, within a quarter of a century, we had to fight another war, this time at a cost of three hundred thousand dead and a debt of two hundred and sixty billions, in order to get back to the point to which he had brought us in 1918.

John Paul Jones who, like them, argued for common sense,

the most radical program that can be presented to the human mind, was, like them, contemptuously cast aside. Among the results were the War of 1812 and a naval impotence that made it impossible, in 1861, for the national government to throttle insurrection before it got a fair start.

This would hardly be worth emphasizing if it were an inevitable part of the trend of human events, or at least of American events. But it is not inevitable. We have not always acted with such utter folly. We did support Washington—rather less than halfheartedly, but we did support him, and so we have a nation. We did support Hamilton, Madison, and Jay—moved thereto by the advice of Washington, Jefferson, Franklin, and the rest—and so we have a constitution under which the nation prospered miraculously. We did support Lincoln to the extent of agreeing that the union is worth fighting for, and so it survived and incidentally got rid of slavery.

At the time of John Paul Jones's two hundredth anniversary it was apparent that this time we might support those leaders who are trying to carry out at last the program that Wilson urged; and if we do, it may be that we shall still be counting the benefits at the four hundredth anniversary.

A man or a nation that is a fool by nature can hardly profit by studying folly; but one that has occasionally risen to wisdom can always hope to do so again, and may be assisted in realizing that hope by scrutinizing the errors of the past.

So much for the didactic element in the story of our first great sailor, which was substantially ended when the *Alliance* dropped anchor in Lorient Harbor. What comes after is entertaining, but not particularly relevant to the lives or business of Americans two hundred years later.

III.

In Paris Jones ran into the usual difficulties in the usual forms —conspiracies, penny pinching, sneers, and slander—but he also tasted his moment of glory.

By this time romanticism was more than the fashion in

France. It was a pathological condition. It was raging like the Black Death in the Middle Ages and producing as many extravagancies. Jean Jacques Rousseau had been erected into a veritable demigod and anything was possible provided it had a touch of glamour.

Anywhere and at all times a sea fighter has been a glamorous figure. A sea fighter who has whipped the traditional enemy is twice as glamorous. At this time a sea fighter who had whipped the traditional enemy in the name of liberty and the rights of man was ten times as glamorous. Such was Paul Jones and all Paris was at his feet. The King conferred upon him the rank of chevalier—equivalent to an English knighthood—and presented him with a gold-hilted sword of honor. The Duke and Duchess of Orléans banqueted him and presented him to the world as their particular protégé. Even the Queen, having no occasion to be jealous of him, was pleased to be gracious, and Jones promptly became the captive of her beauty.

As he was a Mason, the famous Lodge of the Nine Sisters, which counted among its membership Voltaire, Helvetius the philosopher, and Houdon the sculptor, invited him to attend to be eulogized. What is of more interest to this generation, the lodge also commissioned Houdon to make a portrait bust, which turned out to be one of the artist's most successful works. Jean Antoine Houdon was affected by the romantic frenzy of the times, and he has perhaps put into the bust a little more of the noble Roman—of Cato and Brutus, be it understood, not of Nero and Caligula—than seems likely to have characterized a man from Kirkcudbright; but it is generally agreed that this bust is probably the best likeness of John Paul Jones in existence.

The subject, at least, was pleased. He immediately ordered a number of plaster casts of the original made and presented them to his friends. Franklin got one, of course, one went to Washington, another to Lafayette. Before Washington received his, Houdon had visited America and had carved a similar bust of the General; Washington wrote Jones that when the replica arrived he had placed the two together, which the sailor never ceased to regard as one of the greatest compliments he ever received.

Some time after this distribution he received a request from a former member of Congress for another replica for the state of North Carolina. Jones at once ordered it in memory of his friend Joseph Hewes, who had died in 1779; except the original, made for the lodge, this seems to have been the only official presentation, the others all having been personal. It was appropriate, for after all he was still officially Captain Jones of North Carolina.*

Even in America there was, for the moment, nothing but praise for the brilliant commander. The capture of the *Serapis* made such a tremendous impression that Robert Morris and John Hancock were able to introduce into the marine committee a resolution that the Captain should be promoted to the rank of rear admiral; but the paper in the archives of the committee bears the notation "Not to be acted upon." It was agreed, however, that Congress should have a gold medal struck to commemorate the event; but as there was nobody in America capable of executing such a commission, action on that too was held up until after the war. Still, Congress had agreed that it should be done, which was, as far as the honor was concerned, the important thing.†

Nor was it officers and statesmen and lodge brothers alone who delighted to honor John Paul Jones. The ladies were equally enthusiastic. The sailor was the lion of all the *salons* and the hostess who could capture him for an evening had scored a triumph of no small proportions.

John Adams returned to Europe in 1780 as minister to Holland, bringing with him this time his brilliant and formidable wife, Abigail, who met Jones in Paris somewhat later. Abigail

* It is one of these plaster casts that may be seen in one of the niches that surround the tomb of John Paul Jones in the crypt of the chapel of the United States Naval Academy at Annapolis.

† In 1947 Congress awarded the Congressional Medal of Honor posthumously to John Paul Jones.

Adams cherished almost as low an opinion of the human race in general as her husband, and she was particularly censorious of men who were more interested in achieving their aims than in always abiding by the rules of decorum. Regarding this one she had written her husband years earlier, "Will a foreigner . . . act with the same zeal, or expose himself to equal dangers with the same resolution for a republic of which he is not a member, as he would have done for his own native country?" Abigail obviously thought he would not.

But time had proved her wrong and, like Honest John, she admitted it—somewhat wryly, but she admitted it. She learned of the man's exploits and eventually met him and his personality astonished her as much as his career. Some time later—in 1784— she summed up her impressions in a letter to a female relative.

> Chevalier Jones you have heard much of [she wrote]; I dare say you would be as much disappointed in him as I was. From the intrepid character he justly supported in the American Navy, I expected to have seen a rough, stout, war-like Roman—instead of that I should sooner think of wrapping him up in cotton wool, and putting him in my pocket, than sending him to contend with cannon balls. He is small of stature, well proportioned, soft in his speech, easy in his address, polite in his manners, vastly civil, understands the etiquette of a lady's toilette as perfectly as he does the masts, sails and rigging of his ship. Under all this appearance of softness he is bold, enterprising, ambitious and active. . . . We do not often see the warrior and the abigail thus united.

To a stern and rock-bound New England woman it may have been as displeasing as it was to Gloster to note that

> Grim-visag'd war hath smooth'd his wrinkled front;
> And now . . .
> He capers nimbly in a lady's chamber
> To the lascivious pleasing of a lute,

but to the ladies of Paris it was enchanting and they lost no opportunity to make the most of it.

Some of them made a great deal of it indeed, and one in particular ran wild. She was the Comtesse de Nicolson, whose husband derived his decidedly un-French name from a Scottish ancestor who had immigrated to France generations earlier. She fell in love with Jones at first sight, and it was no amourette, but a devouring passion. Jones kept many of her letters, although he had the grace to remove any identifying marks, and for a long time she was known to historians only by her signature of "Delia." Subsequently, though, their authorship was thoroughly established.

Today it is fairly evident that the man was more flattered than deeply involved emotionally. It does not necessarily follow that he was insincere. At the time he probably believed that he was deeply in love, and the affair, at least on Delia's side, moved with torrential force.

"No, never, I feel, never did I love until the moment at once so dear and fatal to my peace when fate revealed you to my ravished sight," she wrote to him. "That moment fixed my destiny forever." Then, later, when he was about to sail again, "Six posts, and still no tidings from you. My heart sinks at the thought of so cruel a neglect. Are you ill or have you ceased to love me? Heavens, the idea chills my heart." Again, "I have just received, my most dear lover, your letter of the 18th. How tender it is and expressive of the most touching and delicate feelings. Every line paints a sentiment. Oh, my dearest Jones, what will be the joy, the transport of your Delia when she beholds again the author of those adorable letters."

Oh, yes, Delia was smitten by Cupid's arrow and it struck deeply. She was foolish, of course, and she was appallingly sentimental. She left herself open to ridicule for generations, and yet there is something in her letters that commands respect. She was neither a mercenary nor a snob. She may have been dazzled by the hero's fame, but she did not wish to capitalize that fame either to advance her worldly interests or to flatter her vanity. She was a woman genuinely in love and her every impulse was to give, not take. More than anything else she wished to abandon everything and go with him when he left for America. It was an impossible project, but it wasn't a mercenary one. With all her folly, she was so much more decent than most of the men with whom Jones had to deal that they are not worthy to be mentioned in the same breath.

It would please the romantic were one able to record that the object of her affection was equally moved, but it just didn't happen that way. The depressing truth seems to be that although he was momentarily bewitched, no long time passed before Jones began to be a little bored by Delia. He was gallant enough never to admit it, but he was an extremely ambitious man, his head full of vast projects and his mind occupied with ways and means of putting them into effect.

In France in 1780 every worldly wise man knew that the influence of women, skillfully used, could smooth the path of ambition marvelously. Paul Jones knew it well, and he did not scruple to make use of his knowledge. The great object of his ambition was still unattained—a squadron of fast and powerful warships with which really to play havoc in British waters. The *Indienne* was gone, but there were other ships, and the man felt in his bones that with a real fleet under his command he could set such a record as would make his name immortal forever. He was the peer of Drake and Frobisher. With ship for ship and gun for gun he would not have feared, he would have rejoiced to meet Black Dick Howe or Rodney on the open sea.

It wasn't braggadocio. He knew what he could do, but he detested swashbuckling. It was about this time that some wit concocted that story that when Paul Jones was told that Pearson, captain of the *Serapis,* had been knighted, he remarked, "Well, if I ever meet him at sea again I'll make a lord of him." It exasperated Jones intensely, for from his point of view it was cheap deprecation of an able and honorable opponent. He had no humor, so to that side of the story he was completely blind.

But a squadron he had to have, if he were ever to achieve

what he knew he could do. Therefore neither for love nor for money would he omit any effort that might assist him toward securing that squadron. This was Delia's misfortune, as it is likely to be the misfortune of any woman who commits the indiscretion of falling in love with a first-rate man. They simply won't be absorbed.

Indeed, at the very moment when the affair was flaming half Paris was convinced that Jones was desperately in love with another woman, and he was furnishing plenty of evidence to support the belief. This was the Comtesse de la Vendahl, to whom his protestations were violent enough.* For one thing, he desired her to keep for him, while he was at sea, the sword of honor that the King had given him, which is a proposal he would never have made to a mere light-o'-love.

Nor did the lady fail to encourage him. She painted his portrait in miniature—being a pupil of Van der Huydt, the Dutch artist—and gave it to him, with other evidences of esteem, not to say affection. But in the end it proved that what she really desired was a promotion for her husband, which she hoped to secure through Jones's influence, and when that was not forthcoming she dismissed him tartly. Madame de Chaumont was avenged.

* An Englishwoman, a Miss Edes, whose stepfather was engaged in arranging an exchange of prisoners and therefore in close contact with Jones, has left in her correspondence a lively account of Jones's pursuit of the Countess, including a copy of some impromptu verses he composed for Mademoiselle Genêt, which are of interest as illustrating the sailor's quality as a poet.

*Verses addressed to the ladies who have done me
the honor of their polite attention.*

Presented by Paul Jones to Mademoiselle G——.

Insulted Freedom bled—I felt her cause,
And drew my sword to vindicate her laws,
From principle, and not from vain applause.
I've done my best; self-interest far apart,
And self-reproach a stranger to my heart;
My zeal still prompts, ambitious to pursue
The foe, ye fair, of liberty and you;
Grateful for praise, spontaneous and unbought,
A generous people's love not meanly sought;
To merit this, and bend the knee to beauty,
Shall be my earliest and my latest duty.

He was not exclusively the philanderer, however. He had many genuine friends among women, first and firmest among them being the Duchess of Orléans—formerly Chartres—but including Mesdames Genêt, de Saint Julien, Thilorie, de Bonneuil, and Hunolstein among others. He was no Turk, he was capable of appreciating intellectual qualities, as well as beauty, in a woman. But this only made it the harder for any one to hold him long in subjection. The flat truth is that his first love was the sea and he was incapable of a blinding, overmastering passion for any woman. He was but an indifferent subject for romance.

A question that is bound to interest the practical, but which history cannot answer authoritatively, is on what did John Paul Jones live all this time? He had not yet drawn a cent of his pay from the United States; he never was paid until the war was over, if then. On the contrary, before the *Ranger* was equipped he had advanced £1,500 out of his own pocket to help equip her. He had obtained little, if any, of his prize money. Yet he had now been living in France for the better part of two years and not in any hole-and-corner way. He was a courtier and a successful one; and the expenses of a successful courtier were by no means light.

It is possible that he had some personal assistance from the King. It is probable that the Duke of Orléans, who is known to have helped generously in equipping his ships, also advanced something toward the Captain's personal expenses.

In any event he lived, and lived well. He was always impressively turned out. Indeed, his spick-and-span appearance provoked snorts from Honest John when that misanthrope first encountered him at Lorient. Adams was especially indignant because Jones was wearing two gold epaulets, whereas sober and decorous New England officers were accustomed to confine themselves to one. A dozen other witnesses have testified that the Captain was habitually smart as far as his uniform and accouterments were concerned.

It may be that this mystery is simply more evidence that Jones was a child of his century. We know that early in life he had shown evidence of unusual talents as a businessman, and there is no reason to suppose that his capacity in this line had deteriorated. A born businessman doesn't lose his talent any more than a born musician. We also know that throughout the war he was in touch with able businessmen—Robert Morris and Langdon, for instance, in this country, Beaumarchais and Chaumont in France—which at least suggests that many business opportunities may have come his way. We also know that he usually had money when need for it arose, as witness the £1,500 he put up for the *Ranger*. It is then a natural, if not quite inevitable, inference that during his many long periods ashore he did some brisk and shrewd trading.

But he never admitted it. He could admit entanglements with women and fight whoever chose to make anything of them. He could admit killing that sailor at Tobago. He could admit that circumstances forced him to be a fugitive from the law. He readily admitted, not without pride, that if he fell into the hands of the British he would probably be hanged as a pirate. But he would not, could not, and did not admit that he ever engaged in legitimate and profitable business deals, other than the collection of prize money.

There was a reason for this—doubtless a very bad reason, but a strong one. It is the fact that Paul Jones's social position was too precarious for him to admit the stain that trading would have laid upon him. For Beaumarchais, the writer of farces, it was all right. For Chaumont, born and bred to it, it was all right; but for an officer of His Most Christian Majesty's Navy to admit that he had made a penny in honest trade would have been a deeper disgrace than to have eloped with the admiral's wife, or to have killed a dozen men in duels. French officers looked upon Jones with jealousy and suspicion enough; it would have been foolish to give them an excuse for contempt as well.

Therefore the business ability that would be highly creditable to him today he ignored, and removed from his papers all documentary proof of it as carefully as he would have removed evidence of an infamous crime. The result is that to this day we do not know exactly where and how he got his money. All we know is that he had it, not in any great amounts, but sufficient for his not inconsiderable needs.

IV.

Yet although his life during these months was notably pleasurable, it was far from being a continuous round of gaiety. Along with the honorifics of the great and the adulation of the fair, he was being showered with troubles, and of the most exasperating kind. His victories at sea had not at all facilitated his progress on land except socially. Professionally, he was on the same old treadmill. It could not be otherwise, for while his operations at sea could put heart into the American navy and stir the enthusiasm of the French people, they could not restore life to a dying political system. Absolutism was so feeble in France that it could no longer compel its own servants to serve it. Instead, they served themselves.

Chaumont, for example, was only mildly interested in getting a squadron to sea. His first endeavor was to make sure that every penny of the prize money came into his hands, and his next was to make sure that all contracts were favorable to him.

Jones, observing this, became convinced that Chaumont was a scoundrel, and it infuriated him to have to deal with a scoundrel. Perhaps he was right as regards Chaumont, but he was wrong in permitting it to ruffle him. When a governmental system reaches a certain stage of decay nobody but a scoundrel can function under it. France itself had proved this a few years earlier when it put Turgot, an honest man, in charge of finances, only to have him prove more impotent even than such persons as Chaumont.

Poor old Franklin, caught between the two, was driven to distraction. His opinion of Chaumont was probably about that held by Jones, but he was philosopher enough to accept the inevitable. He knew that Jones's charges and Chaumont's countercharges were both wasted energy, but as American minister he had to keep the peace as well as he could. He was not a sailor and the intricacies of the business of equipping ships, paying seamen, arranging the sale of prizes, looking after promotions, and all the rest were completely beyond him. He had to take the advice of others, and that advice was contradictory. In the end he turned furiously on Jones, ordering him in blistering terms to quit bothering the ministry with his incessant demands.

This was grossly unfair, and from any other man living—Joseph Hewes being dead—it would have driven the Captain into blind fury. But he knew that Benjamin Franklin was a great man and at bottom a fair one; he knew also that the minister was overwhelmed with demands, not a tenth of which he could satisfy; he knew that the physical and mental strain on him was inordinately great. Therefore he accepted the rebuke meekly and promised to do better.

Nothing in the man's whole career shows him in a more admirable light than this incident. His refusal to be offended by the momentary irritation, unjust though it was, of a harried, harassed, and terribly overworked official is evidence of a largeness of spirit that is a sounder patent of nobility than his title of chevalier. His refusal to permit a petty incident to blind him to Franklin's real size is proof of his own size.

But Peter Landais was a horse of another color. This ineffable specimen now entered into a firm compact with Arthur Lee, who was still hanging around, to make trouble for everybody. Here Franklin's consciousness of his own ignorance of naval affairs had disastrous consequences. Instead of moving promptly and vigorously to have the mutinous officer court-martialed and hanged for treason, compounded by the deliberate murder of loyal officers and seamen of the *Bon Homme Richard*, he didn't know what to do. He hesitated and, hesitating, was lost. For Landais's impudence was infinite, and his talent for lying, impressive in itself, was raised to a terrific power by being multiplied by that of Arthur Lee. Together they confused the situation to such an extent that Franklin was completely befogged, and in the end he determined that the *Alliance* should return to America and dump the problem into the lap of home authorities. Lee decided to go back in her, and as long as she was making the trip anyhow Jones was ordered to load her with a cargo of badly needed military supplies.

This was done, but while the cargo was being assembled Jones remained in Paris making a last effort to get out of Chaumont part, at least, of the prize money due him and his men. Lee proceeded to Lorient, carrying with him quantities of personal possessions he had acquired during his long stay in Europe. One item was a pair of magnificent carriages that by their bulk, not their weight, took up as much room as several tons of gunpowder or cases of arms.

Arriving at Lorient and finding Jones absent, Lee, in his quality of American commissioner—he still was one, although assigned to Spain, not to France—authorized Landais to assume command of the *Alliance*. Then he ordered that enough military supplies be thrown out and left on the dock to make room for the Lee personal baggage, including the carriages. This, though, was too much, even for Landais; he made Lee put the carriages on another ship, but he did take the rest of his luggage. Finally Lee instructed Landais to sail.

News of this came to Paris, and Jones set out for Lorient posthaste to stop it, but before he arrived the ship had already been warped away from the wharf and was lying out in the stream. Landais refused to permit Jones to set foot on board and announced his determination to depart immediately. At the narrow mouth of the harbor where she would have to pass was a French fort, and Thevenard, the French commander, cheerfully pointed out to Jones that it had enough heavy guns to blow the *Alliance* out of the water if she attempted to pass. He assured the American that he would be happy to do it, if Jones gave the word.

But for once John Paul Jones faltered. As the *Alliance* bore stubbornly down on the passage, he realized that to fire on an American ship was one thing he could not do. No matter if she had been seized by a mutineer. No matter if she did carry Arthur Lee, his deadly enemy and a curse to the country. All the same, she was a United States ship and Paul Jones was an officer of the United States Navy. He couldn't fire on her. He told Thevenard to let her go, and plodded wearily back to Paris.

That cruise of the *Alliance*, by the way, was one of the marvels of naval history. In the beginning, Landais had summoned all the officers and told those who would not accept him as captain to get ashore. Richard Dale and the others of the *Richard* promptly did so. But no such alternative was offered the forty seamen of the old *Richard*. They were compelled to go, whether they liked it or not. They didn't like it. They disliked it so heartily that they refused duty, and Landais's answer to that was to arm his own men, round them up, and put them in irons in the hold.

A few days out Lee, Landais, and Degge, the first lieutenant, began to quarrel. Strife increased steadily and Landais's actions became more and more eccentric. Halfway across the Atlantic he shut himself in his cabin and refused to appear on deck. So Lee, reverting to his quality as a physician, formally pronounced him insane and instructed Degge to take command, putting Landais under restraint. In this shape she came home.

She was the one survivor of the squadron that had made naval history, shaken the British Empire, startled the world. The results of that feat were truly remarkable. The captain who beat the *Serapis* had been kicked off his ship and replaced by a lunatic. The officers who beat the *Serapis* had been tossed onto the beach in a foreign land. The seamen who beat the *Serapis* were brought back to their grateful country chained in the hold. This was hardly the event that presently moved David T. Shaw to burst into song:

> With her garlands of vict'ry around her,
> When so proudly she bore her brave crew,
> With her flag proudly floating before her,
> The boast of the red, white and blue!

V.

So five years' active service in time of war worked out to bring Jones exactly to the point where he had been in 1776—a sailor ashore in a foreign country pleading for a chance to serve. After the most brilliant career achieved by any American naval officer up to that time he was, in fact, a little worse off than he had been in the beginning, for he was now in France and his chief backer, Benjamin Franklin, was by no means as influential with the French navy as Joseph Hewes had been with the American.

Yet he was still the indomitable man who regarded utter defeat as only the beginning of the fight. He knew that a squadron could play havoc with England. He knew that one fast, powerful ship might produce such an effect as to shorten the war materially. All he asked was a chance; but he might as well have asked for the moon. The French government was no longer capable of intelligent, energetic action. The American government had not yet become capable of it. It was an interregnum between two eras, when no real authority existed; and at such times able and sincere men are driven mad.

Paul Jones came close to that fate. The *Indienne* was lost forever, but he hoped to get the reconditioned *Serapis;* he was not flatly refused, but nothing was done. Then for a time he had hopes of the fine *Terpsichore*, of the French fleet; but nothing was done. Meanwhile, the war in America was going from bad to worse. The government was disintegrating. The dollar had fallen to two and a half cents—that is to say, one silver dollar would buy forty paper ones. Arnold had sold out, and Pennsylvania, New Jersey, and Connecticut troops had mutinied because they had not been paid. The British had stumbled upon a general who knew his business in Charles Cornwallis and, contrary to custom, were actually giving him some small support, with the result that he was tearing the southern part of the country to pieces. It was the time of all times for a diversion of some sort, and nothing could have been better than a shattering blow at England's naval supremacy. But nothing was done.

The French had assisted Franklin in assembling a cargo of munitions for Washington's hard-pressed troops and eventually someone found a small ship, the *Ariel*, to transport them. At last, in the autumn of 1780, Jones was given the command of this vessel and ordered to sail for America—the best naval fighter afloat turned into a blockade runner!

He accepted, but how close frustration and exasperation had come to driving him crazy is revealed by his collision with Thomas Truxtun, then a merchant captain, but later to make a distinguished career in the Navy. Truxtun, coming into Lorient Harbor, paid no attention to the *Ariel*, a naval vessel of his own country, and when his attention was called to the discourtesy, sent back an insolent message to Captain Jones. The latter, in fury, filed charges against Truxtun as having insulted the United States and demanded that he never be permitted again to command an American ship. Truxtun, appalled, then conformed to the usages of the sea and perhaps gathered from the incident some of that respect for naval discipline which later he became famous for enforcing rigorously on his own ships.

The *Ariel* first sailed in October, but three days out ran into a storm so terrific that it was remembered for decades all along the coast of Europe. The *Ariel* was caught in a very nasty spot, to windward of the Penmarque Rocks, off the southwest tip of Brittany. The storm struck with such suddenness and such fury that the vessel was all but on the rocks before anything could be done. The ship was dismasted. Jones tried to anchor and all the lines parted but one. For the better part of three days it seemed to be all up with the ship and her company, and the Captain's feat of seamanship in finally clawing off made his reputation as a sailor forever.

The *Ariel*, however, was no longer seaworthy. Jones rigged jury masts and limped back into Lorient, where the carpenters were busy two months making repairs. On December 18, however, she got to sea again. Since he was carrying important dispatches, as well as an invaluable load of military stores, the Captain evaded British warships instead of seeking them out.

He did, however, encounter the twenty-gun *Triumph* and battered her into calling for quarter; but when the *Ariel's* men abandoned their guns to cheer the victory, the *Triumph* suddenly filled her sails and, being much the faster ship, escaped.

"A knave!" snorted Jones, referring to the British captain, and ignoring that fact that it was just the sort of trick he delighted in playing.

This was to be the last time he ever fired upon a British ship, for he encountered nothing more all the way to Philadelphia, and Congress saw to it that Captain Jones was not permitted to go to sea again in time to do the enemy any more damage.

The *Ariel* arrived at Philadelphia February 18, 1781, three years and three months after the *Ranger* had departed from Portsmouth. In those three years Paul Jones had risen from obscurity to become the most celebrated naval officer afloat. Although he had never commanded anything better than a fifth-rate warship, he had invaded English soil, he had captured two British men-o'-war and beaten a third even if she escaped, he had taken thousands of prisoners, he had forced exchanges thereby delivering hundreds of Americans languishing in British jails, he had disrupted British commerce and driven marine insurance rates to appalling figures, he had established the existence of the United States as a maritime power.

So Congress deemed it proper to investigate him.

The principal charge was that he and Franklin by their neglect and incompetence, if nothing worse, had held up the delivery of military supplies to Washington's army. The charge was supported by fifty-seven questions that the Captain was required to answer in writing.

Many of them were the "Have you stopped beating your wife?" type of questions. That is, they were traps so carefully laid that either yes or no would convict the answerer of some dereliction perhaps not mentioned in the list at all. He had but to read these questions once, said Jones, to know that Arthur Lee had reached America before him.

Lee was the mainspring of the whole project, without doubt,

but Samuel Adams helped, and Gillon, the incredible South Carolinian who had lost the *Indienne*, had a hand in it. So did some of the officers of the regular navy who wanted to see this Scotchman put in his place, or at least prevented from taking rank ahead of them. Some Congressmen who cared little about either Jones or the Navy took a hand because they hated Franklin and hoped to get at him through Jones.

All this, be it remembered, took place at the moment when the fortunes of the country seemed to be at their lowest ebb. The Rhode Island blacksmith Greene, the best soldier Washington had, was being slowly forced up into Virginia; he had just fought Cornwallis at Guilford Courthouse and had lost the field. Nobody, not even Greene at this moment, realized that in losing the battle he had won the campaign, since Cornwallis could not recoup his terrible losses. It seemed merely another chapter in the dismal story of defeat.

It was against this background that "a little group of willful men" undertook to break John Paul Jones and Benjamin Franklin. It was an exhibition of American politics at its worst; but unpleasant as is the picture, it cannot be ignored. For it is the sort of thing that has destroyed every democratic government that has gone down in the past and the thing most likely to destroy this republic in the end. From the time of the Athenians who succeeded Pericles, through the Carthaginians to the Roman republic, no people's government fell to assault from without until it had grown so dim-witted within that it prefered its Lee and Gillon to its Jones and Franklin. Howe and Cornwallis were never such dangers to the republic as were the petty-minded grafters who, for their own profit, tried to sacrifice Washington and did drive Arnold to treason; and who, from that day to this, have opposed and vituperated every able and patriotic man who has tried to get something done.

But in 1781, low as were its military fortunes, the republic was not utterly corrupt. Paul Jones wrote his answers to the fifty-seven questions carefully and skillfully. He demolished every lie embodied in them, he dragged into the light every

evil-smelling insinuation, and challenged sharply every aspersion on his own character or that of the minister to France. He
wrecked the scheme so completely that Congress, in a revul-
sion of feeling, swept the whole thing aside with contempt and
reaffirmed its faith in the officer by resolving that he should be
given command of the largest and finest warship ever built in
the United States, the *America*, a ship of the line of seventy-four
guns, then under construction at Portsmouth.

Robert Morris and John Hancock had, however, accomplished another thing for Jones. They put through Congress a
resolution approving his acceptance of a decoration and title
from Louis XVI. This was done two days before the Articles
of Confederation at last went into effect; and since the Articles
specifically forbade any American officer thereafter to accept
any gift or emolument from a foreign prince, Jones's title of
chevalier remained unique in the American service.

But rank, the only recognition of real value to an officer, he
could not have. James Nicholson, ranking captain, whose chief
claim to fame is his loss of two frigates successively entrusted to
him, saw to that. A committee appointed to look into the matter
recommended that Captain Jones be promoted to the rank of
rear admiral; but Nicholson organized the other captains to
oppose it, and with the help of Lee and Sam Adams blocked the
promotion.

Jones never received any advancement except by seniority in
the service after his commission as captain. The committee
declared that even by seniority he should rank no lower than
fifth and, if his commission as lieutenant be considered, as
second; but the bitter hostility of the other officers frightened
the committee into doing nothing, and Jones's name remained
where it was on the roster. He was now ninth captain, and it is
interesting to see how he had advanced that far. Of the seventeen originally above him, one—Biddle—had been killed in
action, one lost at sea, one had died of natural causes, and one
had resigned; but five had been kicked out of the service for
good and sufficient reasons.

Incidentally, a board of inquiry broke Landais and dismissed him before Jones's arrival. Ironically, Landais paid the price, not for his perfidious conduct in actual battle, but for behaving badly in the presence of the ineffable Arthur Lee. In the absence of Jones the board did not have before it Landais's record in the battle with the *Serapis;* it considered only his conduct during the voyage of the *Alliance* from Lorient to Boston, and booted him out on that alone.

Optimistically, Jones decided that rank would eventually take care of itself. "It was more agreeable to Captain Jones," he wrote in his Journal, "to be so honorably elected captain of the line than to have been, as was proposed by the committee, raised at once to the rank of rear admiral, because Congress had not then the means of giving a command suitable to that rank." With the ancient, waterlogged *Bon Homme Richard*, a forty, he had won great fame; with a line-of-battle ship, a spanking, brand-new seventy-four, he felt that there was nothing he couldn't accomplish. Let him once get among the British with a ship of that sort, and he would be a rear admiral fast enough.

This is the one occasion on which Paul Jones's business ability seems to have failed him, for with no pay and no prize money available, he was so short of cash that Robert Morris had to lend him enough to pay his fare to Portsmouth; and when he arrived what he got was not another ship, but John Langdon on his hands again. The *America*'s planking was not even finished. Only twenty-four carpenters were at work on her, and there was not enough metal on hand for her ironwork. Funds sent by Congress were expended and Langdon was advancing none of his own.

If the reader, like a moviegoer, says, "This is where we came in," he will be justified, for it was the *Ranger* business all over again. Shipbuilder and ship captain promptly started squabbling. Jones ordered alterations and Langdon fought him at every step. Jones denounced Langdon for dilatoriness and Langdon denounced him for arrogance. Nobody had any money and the uproar was terrific, yet somehow the work slowly forged ahead. The ship was so far advanced that Jones began to assemble his crew—she called for a complement of 626 officers and men—when Congress took a hand.

A French fleet under Vaudreuil had reached the United States expecting to join D'Estaing and a Spanish fleet in the West Indies for a smashing blow against the British. A storm struck it and one of its seventy-fours, the *Magnifique,* was wrecked in Boston Harbor. At first Jones, although deploring the accident, thought it might be a stroke of luck, since a good deal of equipment could be salvaged from the wreck to be used on the *America.*

But Congress had a great spasm of generosity, at the climax of which it presented the *America* to the King of France to replace the loss of his ship, and ordered Jones to surrender command of the incomplete vessel to a French captain.

It was the tenth time that a vessel had been promised him only to be snatched away at the last moment, yet he rallied and took the blow beautifully. His letter to Robert Morris, accepting the decision of Congress, was so temperate and good-humored that Morris transmitted a copy to Congress, commending it as a model of subordination and good sportsmanship. Indeed, all that grated upon Jones was the fact that in the rather fulsome resolution in which Congress made the gift, not a word was said about the American captain whose hopes were disappointed. Jones felt that they might at least have mentioned his name, but he made no point of it.

The truth is that Congress was more generous in appearance than in reality. Morris admitted later that he consented to the gift mainly because he had given up all hope of raising enough money to complete the ship in any case. The French captain to whom Jones turned it over profited little. He couldn't hurry John Langdon any more than Jones could. The war was over before the ship was finished. The only satisfaction John Paul Jones derived from this deal was sentimental. When the ship at last was completed and joined the French fleet her name was changed; in honor of the American minister and Jones's friend, she sailed under the name of the *Franklin*.

Once more a sailor without a ship, Jones begged at least permission to join the French in their expedition against the English. To this Congress was agreeable, so in 1782 he sailed with Vaudreuil for the West Indies. But the great moment had passed. Smitten by the Rhode Island blacksmith, Cornwallis had reeled down toward the Virginia coast. Greene, after watching him for a while, had left him to Washington and had moved toward South Carolina. Washington, realizing that at the moment when, as he himself had confessed, he was at the end of his tether, contrary to all expectation the time had come. Summoning Rochambeau and Grasse with part of the French fleet, he pounced. Germain, of course, had not supported Cornwallis after the first month or two, and the only first-rate general the British had sent to America was crowded into the Yorktown peninsula and battered into surrender.

If this had been followed up by a tremendous naval blow in the West Indies, Britain might have been reduced at once to the level of Denmark or Sweden; but as a matter of fact the absolutism of Charles III in Spain was, if anything, more decrepit than that of Louis XVI in France. That of George III in England was far gone, but not so far as either of the others. The fleets of France and Spain faltered and fumbled. They were incapable of concerted, intelligent, and resolute action; so nothing of real importance had been accomplished before a message came flying across the Atlantic that peace had been signed.

Captain John Paul Jones cheered with the rest and promptly hurried back to the United States to advance his pet project, which now seemed possible of realization—the development of a professional navy.

As a matter of fact, it was farther removed from possibility now than ever. A few of the wiser leaders understood what he had in mind and agreed with him; but the bulk of the people, including the bulk of the politicians, regarded the Navy strictly as a combat force, and now that the fighting was over they could perceive no good reason for maintaining such a force.

This view was by no means as irrational as it seems to us now. In this generation we understand professionalism because we have seen it in operation over a period of many years, and it is clear to us that a navy may be professional without being political.

But even in the closing years of the eighteenth century the truth seemed to most people to lie in the opposite direction. If officers were maintained on regular duty in time of peace it was assumed as a matter of course that they would interfere in politics; and if their number were considerable they would be a formidable power. All experience supported that view. Naval officers had been among the most persistent and effective lobbyists throughout the war, and their political activity had hampered both Congress and the service.

When Paul Jones talked of the desirability of maintaining a body of men to devote their whole time to studying the art of war at sea, the average American was not impressed. He simply didn't believe that any officer corps would do that. None ever had. Political intrigue was rife in the French and British services and had pretty well ruined Spanish sea power. The navy, indeed, was not an end in itself, but an avenue to political power. Why become a sailor except in the hope of gaining such power?

Therefore when Paul Jones urged the appointment of an admiral to command the American fleet in time of peace, what he brought to the minds of most of his countrymen was not the picture of such a man as King or Cunningham, that is to say, a specialist in a particular type of warfare, but such a man as Coligny or Medina-Sidonia, that is to say, a powerful official at court whose influence was contended for by all parties. Even as fine a seaman as Black Dick Howe was a member of parliament before he became a peer, and relied upon politics to assist his career.

For that sort of thing Americans had no taste at all, and their assumption that he was trying to introduce it accounts for part of their indifference to Jones's urging. In any event, the rickety confederation had no money for a navy, or for anything else— not even for Paul Jones's back pay—and now that the emergency was over what small authority it had possessed was rapidly dissolving. Washington and John Adams were among those who could see the value of a small but efficient establishment in time of peace; but there were not enough such farsighted men to get the idea accepted.

So Jones turned to a more practical matter, the collection of the prize money due him and the men of the *Bon Homme Richard*, which Chaumont had held now for a matter of three years. Franklin could not get any money out of the slippery Frenchman; the minister, in fact, had too much else on his hands to press the matter vigorously. So Jones applied to Congress for a commission as special agent to collect the money. This Congress was willing to grant, although Arthur Lee insisted that he be made to give bond for $200,000, something over five times the sum he eventually collected, for the faithful performance of his duty. He spent the summer of 1783 at Bethlehem, Pennsylvania, trying to get rid of a tropical fever he had picked up on his cruise with the French, and sailed on November 10, 1783. A fellow passenger on his ship, the *George Washington*, was the famous Major L'Enfant, who planned Washington city, and the captain was the gay and redoubtable Joshua Barney, almost as colorful a figure as Jones himself.

Right at the end of the voyage the ship ran into baffling head winds, so Jones, who was carrying dispatches for John Adams in London, asked to be set ashore at Plymouth, believing that he could make better time overland to London and thence across the Channel to Paris. Barney was appalled. He knew the bitterness of British feeling toward Jones, even though the war was over, and urged him not to set foot on British soil. But the courier was insistent, so reluctantly the captain put him ashore. Nothing happened. Jones made a swift journey to London, delivered his dispatches, and went on immediately to France, without being molested in any way.

Lorenz thinks that the speed of his journey is accounted for by his anxiety to see the Comtesse de Nicolson again, but since he had not written her since 1781 this is open to some doubt. More than that, after his arrival in Paris it was ten days before he called on her. Undoubtedly, the affair with Delia was cooling rapidly.

There is little reason to doubt that, as far as the man was concerned, it was pretty much all over before he left America. But the finality of it was soon made clear by the appearance of a third party in the picture. This was the woman known to history only as Madame T. We know that she was an illegitimate daughter of Louis XV, but, owing to the amorous proclivities of that monarch, the knowledge is hardly an identification. France was full of illegitimate children of Louis XV. She was long identified with a certain Madame Tellisson, but Lorenz has cast serious doubts upon that theory; some have held that she was a Madame Thilorie, but that, too, is open to question.

All that we know with certainty is that she seems to have held John Paul Jones's interest longer than any other woman, and that he felt a sense of responsibility for her that he exhibited for no other. There is a passage in one letter that has convinced some biographers, notably Mrs. De Koven, of the existence of a child born to the pair. But nothing is certain except that for some years Jones was very much concerned about the welfare of Madame T. He bought a house for her, but there was still a mortgage resting upon it when he left for Russia and it became necessary to arrange for its payment by correspondence; which gave rise to the odd circumstance that the American minister to France, at that time Thomas Jefferson, busied himself preventing the eviction of a sailor's mistress.

But this came later. First of all, Jones applied himself to the formidable task of prying money out of Chaumont. It was so difficult that from the strictly business standpoint it was hardly worth while; but this had come to be much more than a business proposition to Jones. His men had won that money at the price of blood and peril, and no swab of a ship chandler was going to have it, if it took Jones all the rest of his life to recover it.

At times it seemed likely that it would do just that. Chaumont was in serious financial difficulties, if not insolvent. His accounts were in a frightful tangle. The French treasury was not in much better case. Every official Jones approached was far more anxious to evade responsibility by passing it on to someone else than to get anything done. Weeks passed into months and months dragged into years while he hounded and harassed officialdom. Franklin went home and was succeeded by Jefferson. Still the money was not paid.

But the Captain was as grimly determined to obtain payment as the French were to avoid it—more so, for at last he succeeded. True, he obtained only a fraction of the sum actually due; but in the end he was able to present Jefferson with a draft for the equivalent of about $36,000. He had spent two years and five months and $11,000 getting it, but he got it. He had at least the satisfaction of making Chaumont disgorge to that extent.

Jefferson permitted him to deduct his expenses and his captain's share, about $3,000, then on orders from America impounded the rest and used it for the expenses of the embassy —not, however, including his own salary, not a dollar of which he collected until after his return to this country. The sailors were referred to the United States Treasury for payment of their share, but Congress did not see fit to appropriate the money, preferring to let them wait. After a hundred and sixty years they are still waiting.

It is hardly necessary to explain that this was due in part, if not entirely, to the malevolence of Arthur Lee. His first amiable assumption was that Jones and Jefferson had probably stolen a lot of the money, and he attempted to make trouble for Jones's bondsmen. When Jefferson blocked that, Lee, as a member of the committee having power in the case, went into a leisurely investigation, which produced no evidence of wrongdoing, but did serve as an excuse for delaying the appropriation and, in the long run, of effectively preventing it. Jones had to make a flying trip back to America to avoid serious trouble. Lee never succeeded in blackening the Captain's character, but he did prevent the sailors from getting their money.

Brought home in chains and swindled of the money they had earned with their blood—the men who fought under John Paul Jones on the *Bon Homme Richard* were indeed singularly rewarded by the country they defended!

Chaumont settled, the next job was Denmark, in which country also there were prize-money accounts outstanding. Jones moved to Copenhagen.

But before he left he achieved a feat that is worth more attention than historians customarily give it—he had made, momentarily, a strong-navy man of Thomas Jefferson. Since Jefferson is usually charged with reducing the United States Navy to relative impotence, it is interesting to note that under the influence of Jones he was at this time advocating the opposite policy. He should have been made a rear admiral from the date of the taking of the *Serapis*, said Jefferson, adding, "I look to this officer as our great future dependence on the sea, where alone we should think of ever having a force. He is young enough to see the day when we shall be more populous than the whole British dominions and able to fight them ship to ship. We should procure him then every possible opportunity of acquiring experience."

This is a restatement of Jones's argument for a professional navy. Had he been at its head fourteen years later, when Jefferson became President, our naval history might have been very different indeed.

But he was not head of the Navy. He was merely a glorified bill collector, and to Jefferson this seemed as incongruous as it did to Jones himself; and this led them jointly into a great mistake.

Catherine II, empress of Russia, was at war with the Turks in the Black Sea, and threatened by Sweden with war in the Baltic. The Russian naval service was notoriously hopeless, so Catherine had employed to defend the Baltic a Scottish admiral named Grieg, and now Baron Grimm, her confidential representative in Paris, suggested that she employ John Paul Jones to defend the Black Sea. The business was first broached to him in Paris, and he consulted Jefferson as to whether his commitments to the United States would interfere with his acceptance.

Jefferson thought not. Our relations with Russia were entirely friendly, and it seemed to be an excellent opportunity for a young naval officer to obtain needed experience in actual service. He therefore advised Jones to accept.

The definite offer came while he was in Copenhagen trying vainly to collect prize money from Denmark. Satisfied that his standing in the American service would be in no way impaired, he accepted, and instantly posted away to Russia and to ruin.

CHAPTER VIII.

I.

S T. PETERSBURG, now Leningrad, the capital of Russia, was rather less accessible in those days than Lhasa, capital of Tibet, is now. The story of Paul Jones's journey to Russia is a minor epic in itself. One of its episodes was crossing the ice-choked Gulf of Finland in an open boat, sailed by two terrified boatmen held to their posts at point of the Captain's pistols. Incidentally, there is some reason to suppose that the rigors of this terrible journey may have undermined the man's health permanently.

However, he arrived with a promptness admirable in its way, but injudicious. The sailor had no suspicion as yet that the way to deal with Cathcrine of Russia was never to treat her decently, but to smash down her arrogance with greater arrogance, to cheat her before she cheated you, and to quit her dominions between dusk and dawn just before she gave orders to throw you out. Probably if he had known it, the knowledge would have done him no good, for he was too civilized a man to follow that course; but if he had known the true character of the Russian court he might have stayed away from it altogether.

The court of the empress Catherine the Great can be adequately described only by the old-fashioned word "stews." For the stews of an eighteenth-century city were not merely brothels; they were the scene of every imaginable kind of swinery, up to and including throat-slitting. If the life of the German duchy of Courland can be called civilization, Catherine, coming from Courland, had laid a thin veneer of civilization over a barbarism almost unchanged since the Mongols had been ejected. But it was exceedingly thin and it was a pretty low form of civilization anyhow.

The Empress did have energy, however, and it is this that has caused her to be known in history as "the Great." She had the physical endurance of a sturdy German peasant and the craft of the peasant sharpened by some acquaintance with the outside world. The utter vapidity of the lives led by most of her royal contemporaries filled her with contempt; and because she had a moderate desire to know what was going on, she had gained the reputation of being a wonderful patroness of arts and letters. She corresponded with Voltaire and purchased the library of Diderot; and in those days a monarch with the energy and intelligence to write a letter or read a book not absolutely required of him seemed glamorous. Paul Jones, always too willing to believe romantic stories about the highborn, accepted this creature as a woman of civilized tastes, a very Aspasia, in whom any man of intelligence was sure to find understanding sympathy.

It was a silly idea, of course, for the one man who did find understanding sympathy in Catherine of Russia was hardly a man at all, but rather a troglodyte, squat, hairy, one-eyed, and misshapen, but with the strength as well as the savagery of an orangutan, and an animal passion to match and master the Empress's own. This was Grigori Potemkin, master of everything in Russia except Catherine herself, and master of her, too, on occasion.

Prince Potemkin was an animal so utterly disgusting to sight, hearing, touch, and smell that it is a temptation to dismiss the fellow as a man of no worth. But it would be fatuous to do so. Potemkin was an able administrator who extended the boundaries of Russia vastly. Perhaps it took just such qualities as his to hold that country, considering how barbarous was its state at the time. But he was not the sort of employer into whose service a self-respecting gentleman should enter.

However, John Paul Jones did it, and not without warning. He admits that one "high councilor" in Paris advised him to go at once to Constantinople and seek a commission under the

Sultan rather than enter the service of Russia, but he rejected that advice.

Nor was he disillusioned at once. His reception at St. Petersburg was all that he could have desired. He was something new, and Catherine found him interesting and amusing. When she wished the Empress could be gracious, and she wished, in this case. She promoted the Captain to rear admiral and promised him a chance to win glory against the Turks. Jones was convinced that here was a sovereign he could serve with delight. He burned to reach the scene of action at once.

There were hints of trouble, even before he started. He had been distinctly promised command of all Russian naval forces in the Black Sea. Now he was informed that he would have to share that command with the Prince of Nassau-Siegen, and that both of them would be subject to Prince Potemkin, who commanded both the army under Suvorov and an additional fleet. This did not look promising, but he was in for it now, so he went ahead.

The scene of action at the moment was the estuary of the Dnieper and Bug Rivers, known locally as the Liman. There the Turkish fleet was hampering the advance of Suvorov toward Odessa, and the so-called Russian naval officers had proved utterly incapable of dealing with this annoyance. Since the only practical route for the advance of an army lay along the coast of the Black Sea, Suvorov was stuck at the Liman. To proceed farther would have been to lay his communications open to raids by the enemy fleet and to invite disaster. Even Potemkin, commander in chief, was soldier enough to see that, and with the motley array of Greeks, Germans, Italians, Englishmen, and even Turks that he had for naval officers he had tried to clear away the Turkish squadrons.

The Turkish fleet was far from being first-class, by Western standards, but at that it was better than Potemkin's nondescript outfit, and the more or less desultory encounters that had taken place were uniformly unfortunate for the Russians. By the time Jones arrived on the scene half Potemkin's fleet was bottled up in Sebastopol and the other half in the Liman, where a Turkish squadron not only held it but threatened momentarily to come in and destroy it as it lay at anchor.

While this threat continued Suvorov's army lay for the most part on the east bank of the Dnieper. His logical course was to cross that river and the Bug and attack the strong Turkish fortress of Otchakov, at the mouth of the Liman; but he dared not cross while at any moment the Turkish fleet might burst into the Liman, move up the rivers, and cut him off from his base of supplies. Until that fleet had been dealt with adequately the entire campaign was stalled. While the campaign was stalled the reputation of the commander in chief suffered, but that was Prince Potemkin's affair. Suvorov lay quietly east of the Dnieper and waited for someone to clear the way. The someone chosen for that job was John Paul Jones.

To do it, he had a fleet of seventeen sail, headed by the *Vladimir,* of forty-eight guns. It was a force sufficient to the task if the ships had been what they were supposed to be. But they were ill found, worse armed, and still worse manned. There was hardly a semblance of discipline anywhere in the fleet, and as for staff work, they had not even established a uniform system of signaling. Jones's first task was to instruct the officers in Pavillon's system, which he preferred to any other, thereby arousing the opposition of the Englishmen in his cosmopolitan group.

Aside from his seventeen vessels there were about sixty galleys, lightly armed but of great potential value in the Liman, which, except for some rather narrow channels, was too shallow for large ships. But these were under command of the Prince of Nassau-Siegen and Jones now learned that this officer was not under him, but had orders to report directly to Prince Potemkin. If Nassau-Siegen chose not to co-operate, there was nothing Jones could do about it.

The one man involved in the campaign who unquestionably knew his business was the general commanding the Russian land forces. Aleksandr Vasilievich Suvorov was a military genius who whipped everything that came against him, from Turks to French; but he was also a veteran of long experience with Russian courts, and therefore a thoroughgoing cynic. Paul Jones's first inquiry of him was why he had not fortified Kinburn Spit, a sandbank thrusting out opposite Otchakov, and Suvorov's reply should have enlightened the American about many things. It was obviously the thing to do, Suvorov agreed, but he had learned long ago that in this service the only safe course was to obey orders, not generate ideas. If the order came from Prince Potemkin, he would be happy to fortify the spit, but he valued his head too much to act on an idea of his own.

Jones understood at least far enough to do some skillful work in planting the idea in Potemkin's mind. Suvorov got his orders and the spit was fortified.

This made the rest of the sailor's strategy practicable. To take the open sea against the Turks with the sort of fleet he had would have been suicidal; therefore he proposed to entice them into the Liman by a false retreat, then, by turning on them suddenly, force them back, hoping to throw them on Suvorov's guns on the spit.

To make a long story short, it worked. But it was a very long story, and not only long but complicated, repetitious, dull, and dismal. It has been handled to the length of a volume by F. A. Golder, more succinctly but still comprehensively by Lorenz, and rather fully by others. The reader who is interested will find it yet another instructive illustration of the way John Paul Jones battled successfully against forces vastly more formidable than the enemy before he could come at the enemy—forces of inertia, prejudice, ignorance, suspicion, insubordination, and incompetence. The Russian example differs from the others only in that it was nastier than any of the others. Venality was more impudent, treason more blatant, envy more spiteful, stupidity more astounding here than it had been during the American Revolution, but essentially the story is the same.

It took three trials to achieve the objective, because the first two efforts were wrecked and the whole fleet brought into imminent danger of destruction by the cowardice and imbecility of the Prince of Nassau-Siegen. The third time Jones relied on him not at all, but by a sudden reckless countermaneuver threw the advancing Turks into confusion, and in their effort to withdraw far enough to re-form their dispositions they ran under Suvorov's guns. The storm of shot with which that highly competent artilleryman lashed them completed their disorganization. They recoiled blindly in the other direction and the sand bars got them.

Then Nassau-Siegen, who had kept prudently out of harm's way, swept down with his small boats, and instead of capturing the stranded Turkish vessels for the Russian fleet, as Jones had ordered, proceeded to burn them all and massacre the crews.

This is in brief the story of the campaign of the Liman, as neat a bit of work as John Paul Jones ever did, regarded purely as a naval operation, but wasted work as far as the man himself was concerned and of no significance whatever in American history.

It is interesting to observe, however, that if he survived long enough to do it, the credit probably belongs to Suvorov. The old cynic advised him constantly in his relations with Potemkin. The Prince must get all the credit, he insisted, and the Prince's creature, the egregious Nassau-Siegen, must also be anointed with goose grease lavishly. Following this advice, Jones did not spare the flattery. By doing so, he probably kept his command long enough to win the battle, but he also supplied the ape man and the stuffed man with documentary evidence to use against him. Were not the praises of Nassau-Siegen and Potemkin written in his own hand? How, then, could he later bring accusations against them?

He had now served his purpose. The Turkish fleet was effectively abolished as a threat. Suvorov crossed the rivers and began what was to be one of the most brilliant campaigns of his career. Potemkin had no more need of John Paul Jones, so his destruction was ordered. A word to the Empress resulted in his summary recall from the Black Sea, ostensibly to take command

in northern waters, but in reality to be disposed of as contemptuously as Potemkin would have tossed aside a broken pot.

II.

Had the sailor but known it, it was his own fault. The practical lessons Suvorov gave him had come too late, for at his first
encounter with the Empress, before he had ever seen the General, he set himself to be as charming as he could; and we remember Franklin's testimony that when the man really tried
to be charming there were few who could resist him. Catherine
could. That battle-scarred veteran of countless amorous campaigns was capable of resisting any human being, and probably
Orpheus himself, whose charm could move rocks and trees. That
is to say, she could resist when she chose, but she did not always
choose, and there is ample evidence that at their first meeting
she found Captain Jones amusing and pleasant company.

This was enough for Potemkin. He had long since ceased to
be Catherine's lover, but he jealously reserved the right to se-
lect or at least to pass approval on her favorites. This one had
not been selected by him, therefore he must not be allowed
to advance far in the royal favor. If she must have a pet
sailor around the court, Potemkin had one for her in Nassau-
Siegen. There was a specimen that the Russian prince understood thoroughly and whom he could control with little effort.
This Scot was bold, stubborn, and able, therefore dangerous.
He must be eradicated. The appropriate orders went out.

It was simple to the point of absurdity, yet it was an impene-
trable mystery to John Paul Jones. Potemkin addressed him in
words that he understood. Potemkin had ideas about military
strategy that were sometimes comprehensible and on a few occasions sound. Potemkin could rattle off professions of friendship as readily as the supplest courtier around Louis XVI. Potemkin was the *de facto* ruler of a mighty empire. Therefore
Jones fell into the delusion that Potemkin was at least an ap-
proximation of a civilized man.

It never occurred to him that if one proceeded from the level of such a man as, say, George Washington, to reach Potemkin one must go more than half the distance to the level of the anthropoid apes. Potemkin knew no more of the concepts of honor and decency than he did of the numerical value of Planck's constant, which was not to be discovered for more than a hundred years. To call the Russian dishonorable and indecent is inexact; those terms describe a man who has renounced virtues whose existence, at least, he knows. A man must once have been loyal before he can be a renegade. He must perceive the existence of righteousness before he can be immoral. It is doubtful that this one had ever reached that low eminence. He had a brain, and an exceptionally good one, but no sort of ethical development had ever ruffled his existence.

His brain instructed him how to poison the mind of the Empress. He reported that Jones had proved a disappointment, no more, indeed, than a strutting braggart who would certainly have lost the fleet had he not been rescued by the brilliant work of the Prince of Nassau-Siegen. Then a little later he asserted that he had grave doubts of the man's loyalty; he was suspected of being secretly in touch with both the Turks and the Swedes. Therefore Potemkin urged his removal from the southern theater of war, though he should by no means be allowed to go to the Baltic, where the Swedes were threatening. Let him cool his heels a while at a safe distance from any front until Potemkin could collect the evidence.

So John Paul Jones found himself kicking his heels in St. Petersburg, unable to communicate with the Empress, unable to secure a command, unable even to discover what was the matter. It was the old story—the Arthur Lees and the Chaumonts were still able to hobble and hog-tie a man whose only desire was to render honest service. As for the ideal of the professional naval officer, perhaps in all the Russias the only man who understood it was old Suvorov, and he was past caring.

But even Arthur Lee and Chaumont had been somewhat

disciplined by civilization as this crew never had. Once a troublesome man was out of their way, the Westerners were content; but Potemkin was filled with the Oriental vindictiveness that pursues its victim beyond the tomb. To have had Paul Jones murdered would have been the simplest solution, but unfortunately the fellow was famous and his murder would have caused a great deal of inconvenient talk. It seemed better to befoul him.

This they undertook, Nassau-Siegen apparently having the leading part, although others among Potemkin's sycophants were involved, by means of what is known to later generations as "the badger game." They sent a young strumpet to his room, posing as an innocent girl seeking mending for her old mother to do, a notorious bawd being posted in the street to act as the mother. As soon as the door closed behind the servant who had showed her up, the girl tore her clothes and began screaming, whereupon various conspirators, placed there for the purpose, rushed in and claimed barely to have saved her from being raped by the lecherous rear admiral.

Jones, utterly bewildered, sent for his lawyer, who at first reassured him, saying he knew all about that kind of thing and how to deal with it. The Admiral could leave it to him in all confidence. But the next day he sent a note saying that on further consideration he found that he could not take the case. Furthermore, he was informed and believed that no other lawyer in St. Petersburg would touch it.

Incredible as it seems, Jones did not yet realize the truth. There was only one man powerful enough to frighten off all the lawyers in Russia, so when they fled in a body there could be no doubt who was behind them; but for a long time to come Jones clung to the fiction that his troubles had been engineered by jealous underlings and that if he could reach Prince Potemkin he would be rescued.

The man who did rescue him was that hardheaded realist Louis Philippe Comte de Ségur, ambassador of Louis XVI at the court of Russia, but before that one of Rochambeau's officers in America and therefore cherishing a fraternal interest in all veterans of the American Revolution.

As was the amiable custom of the time in St. Petersburg, Ségur maintained his own force of secret police in the Russian capital. He had no difficulty at all in ferreting out the plot and identifying its principal instigators. He permitted the usual legal procedure to go ahead while he gathered plenty of evidence; but just before the case actually was brought into court he demanded audience of the Empress, which she could hardly refuse to the French ambassador, and when he was admitted Ségur dropped a verbal bombshell at the royal feet.

It was all done in meticulously correct diplomatic language, of course, and it was so heavily wrapped up in the verbiage of the time that a modern reader has difficulty in discovering that it has any meaning at all. But stripped of its wrappings it was very simple.

This man, said Ségur in effect, might be guilty of every crime in Newgate calendar. Ségur thought not, but he didn't care. This man was not to be tried. Ségur's master, the King of France, had himself warranted Jones's character in sending him to Russia; therefore any attack on that character was an attempt to make the King of France a liar, and he, the ambassador of that King, knew how to resent it.

Furthermore, he had the honor to inform the Empress that he had collected the evidence, and if the case ever came into court that evidence would be presented to the last jot and tittle; for if it were not, the French government would publish it throughout the wide world. That evidence, circumstantial to the last detail, involved persons of the highest rank, and many of them in infamies that, if exposed, would make the court of Russia stink in the nostrils of mankind.

He suggested, therefore, that the case be dropped and Rear Admiral Jones be permitted to withdraw from Russia honorably.

That was the sort of dealing that Catherine could understand

and appreciate. She had no great personal animosity against Jones, nothing against him, in fact, save that he seemed to have become something of a nuisance to her dear Potemkin. Not for a dozen such would she have this crazy Frenchman raising a stench all over Europe and bringing Russia and its empress into contempt. By all means let the rascal go and make it good, so good that Ségur would subside.

The court proceedings were instantly dropped, and presently it was announced that Rear Admiral Jones had been granted two years' leave with pay, partly to recover from the fatigues of his late campaign and partly that he might pursue abroad his studies of the art of war to the end of rendering Her Majesty yet more valuable services in the future.

The Comte de Ségur did subside, but not until he had seen that the Rear Admiral's travel orders were issued promptly and in absolutely correct form and that the officer took advantage of them to get across the border without a moment's delay. Ségur explained grimly that while his services might be valuable in getting Jones out from under a criminal charge, they would be quite useless if the sailor were fished out of the Neva some morning with a bullet in his back.

III.

Yet Potemkin had reason to be satisfied. He killed his man. It took two years for the poison injected by the Russian to do its work, and there is a grim satisfaction in the reflection that Potemkin himself did not live to hear of the end, for his debaucheries finished him in 1791. But Nassau-Siegen, the other wallower in this mire, had a long and elegant career. He stole the credit for one more victory, but then he had the bad luck to run into the Swedes when they were in a fighting mood and lost a fleet for Catherine. But the Empress, instead of hanging him, consoled him, and he continued to infest Europe in fraudulent splendor until 1808.

But John Paul Jones was a broken man when he left Russia. His slow odyssey across Europe—Warsaw, Strasbourg, Vienna,

Amsterdam, London—is as melancholy a spectacle as the wandering of a rudderless ship at the mercy of tides and currents. It is the more pathetic in that the man did not realize what had happened to him. He was still deluding himself with hopes of obtaining justice from Russia, still concocting great schemes for campaigns in the service of France, of the United States, of Austria. The one opportunity that might have been open to him he would not consider—the service of Sweden. He was still technically in the service of Catherine, and although she had betrayed him it was unthinkable that he should betray her.

It was probably during this period that he obtained assurance of what he had been suspecting for some time—that Madame T. also was false. We have no certainty of what happened, but there is evidence that the lady had always been more interested in money than in the man and that Jones now realized it. That mortgage about which he wrote Jefferson may have furnished the conclusive proof, for apparently Jones had already given Madame T. the money to pay it and she had not done so. But he left no evidence against her in his papers. She simply disappears from his life with no explanation.

The brightest spot in this shadowy journeying was, curiously enough, London. Some of the die-hards among the retired admirals perhaps were still bloodthirsty, but the city as a whole had decided that the war was over in theory as well as in fact, and not a few among its illustrious received the famous sea fighter not merely courteously, but cordially. Horace Walpole and Fox, for instance, were gracious, as were the Earl of Wemyss, Lady Ossory, and others. In addition to social honors the London business world dealt justly with him. Harries, a business partner, paid him money due from trading operations that relieved his immediate necessities. Here too he encountered his old friend the Duke of Chartres, now Orléans, whose mission in London may have been an effort to seize the French throne, as his enemies charged, but more probably was an effort to save it.

While he was in London Jones was strongly advised to stay

out of France. This counsel came from the new American minister there, for Jefferson had gone home and had been replaced
by Gouverneur Morris, perhaps the most unfortunate choice in
our long history of diplomatic blundering. Morris was frankly
contemptuous of the whole revolutionary movement, and his
great desire was to have as little to do with any of it as possible.
Every additional American in Paris meant more work for him
and a famous American would probably mean a great deal more
work, so he did all he could to keep John Paul Jones away.

But there was nowhere else for the sailor to go. His health
was irretrievably shattered, but he did not realize it. Nephritis
was probably already well advanced. Even today its causes are
not too well understood. Its onset is not always easy to detect,
and two hundred years ago it was even more mysterious. There
is some reason to believe that Jones never fully recovered from
the exposure incident to his wild dash to St. Petersburg, for
he complained of being more or less ailing throughout the Russian adventure. But he thought it a minor indisposition; it probably never occurred to him that his kidneys were hopelessly
damaged. He cherished the delusion that he was still fit for
active sea duty, and the French navy seemed to offer his only
chance of that; so to Paris he went, despite Morris.

It was not the old Paris that he found, however, and at first
he was inexpressibly shocked. The two years he had spent in
Russia were so fateful that he came back a good ten years out
of date in all his political ideas. Then, too, he had been in in-
timate contact with a despotism so savage that by comparison
the despotism of Louis XVI seemed positively benevolent,
which made it difficult for him to understand the fury of the
revolutionists.

The king who had been so gracious to him and the queen
who had dazzled him by her beauty were under guard, in effect
if not in name prisoners of the Revolution. Paul Jones was vastly
indignant and all for using then and there that "whiff of grape-
shot" with which Napoleon Bonaparte did end the Revolution
three years later. Yet some excellent people were mixed up in

this business, even his friend Lafayette, even, to some extent, the Duke of Orléans. Paul Jones could not understand it, and he cried out against it, much to the satisfaction of Gouverneur Morris, who noted, "Paul Jones called on me this morning. He is much vexed at the democracy of this country."

He remained vexed, but he did not long cling to the foolish notion that a salvo of artillery could settle the troubles of France. If he had been there from the start, perhaps he would never have entertained it; but he had been out of the contemporary world, he had been visiting the Middle Ages, therefore he was ill prepared to judge the complex situation then existing in Paris.

It was this departure from his own times and from his proper place in the scheme of things that had ruined John Paul Jones. Without in the least extenuating the vermin that attacked him, we must admit that he brought his destruction upon himself.

He had a great ideal, but it was not quite great enough. He strove to establish the honor of the naval officer as a professional man, which was a concept too new and perhaps too lofty for the contemporary world to accept; and yet it was not enough to safeguard the integrity of the individual himself. Professionalism in its highest sense is the devotion of a man to his art, rather than to the emoluments, whether in money, in power, or in fame, that may attach to successful practice of that art. It is a splendid ideal and few are they who attain it, either in the navy or anywhere else—in law, in medicine, in painting or music or sculpture, in science or in philosophy.

Yet professionalism alone is not enough. Unless a man's art is bigger than the man it is a petty craft indeed. Yet if the man is to remain whole there must be something beyond, something bigger than the art, something to which the art is dedicated. It may be any one of a number of things, beauty, truth, faith, mercy, or even as small an entity as patriotism, but there must be something to which both the man and his art are devoted if his professionalism is to be justified and if he is to keep his bearings in a chaotic and bewildering world.

Old Suvorov could be a professional soldier in the service of Catherine the Great and survive, but John Paul Jones could not. In the case of Suvorov, he could view with cynical detachment the degradation of his imperial mistress because beyond and above her there was another mistress who was not, in his eyes, degraded. Suvorov fought incidentally for Catherine and Potemkin but above and beyond that he fought for his country, and Holy Russia could not be degraded by any human agency. He remained a whole man—brutal undoubtedly, evil perhaps, but not divided against himself.

In the service of the United States John Paul Jones fought for a country not his own, but that was incidental. Above and beyond that, he fought for freedom and recognition of the dignity of the individual; and that is every man's country. As long as he remained in the service of freedom it would have mattered little under how many different flags he fought, for the service would have been essentially the same, and the more austerely he adhered to his professional ideal, the greater he would have been.

But the moment he drew his sword in the service of despotism, the situation was reversed. At that moment his professionalism, instead of being his great virtue, became the chief of his vices. He then became like the mad scientist beloved of manufacturers of thrillers; the greater the scientist who has turned against mankind, the greater the villainy he may perpetrate, and the more urgent the need to destroy him as a measure of social sanitation.

This was the calamity that befell John Paul Jones. What the bawds and the titled pimps of St. Petersburg did to him was but an episode in the working out of the tragedy that began when he failed to realize that destiny had called him to fight always in the cause of freedom and he would desert that cause at his peril.

IV.

So it happened that in the convulsion rocking Paris in 1791 he was confused and uncertain, no longer sure on which side he stood. How could he be? He was, in essence, a renegade. His record as a true man had been irreparably flawed, not by evil intent, but by a certain cloudiness of spiritual vision, by a failure in perception, by too great a preoccupation with the smaller ideal of professionalism to be true to the greater one that professionalism acquires merit by serving.

He hesitated, he turned this way and that, he evolved grandiose projects utterly divorced from reality, and he accomplished nothing. He was not the old Paul Jones. He was a changeling, a traveler returned from beyond the bounds that man is permitted to cross, hence somehow unreal, a sort of apparition. Thomas Carlyle understood it, and, understanding, drew that immortal picture in *The French Revolution:*

In faded naval uniform Paul Jones lingers visible here; like a wineskin from which the wine is all drawn. Like the ghost of himself! Low is his once loud bruit; scarce audible, save, with extreme tedium, in ministerial ante-chambers, in this or the other charitable dining-room, mindful of the past. What changes; culminatings and declinings! . . . For in far lands, with scarlet Nassau-Siegens, with sinful Imperial Catherines, is not the heart broken, even as at home with the mean? Poor Paul! hunger and dispiritment track thy sinking footsteps; once or at most twice, in this Revolution-tumult the figure of thee emerges; mute, ghost-like, as "with stars dim-twinkling through." And then, when the light is gone quite out, a National Legislature grants "ceremonial funeral"! As good had been the natural Presbyterian Kirk-bell, and six feet of Scottish earth, among the dust of thy loved ones.

So it seemed to the Honorable Gouverneur Morris at the time. So it seemed to Mr. Carlyle fifty years after the event. Pretty much so, but not quite, it seemed to President Theodore Roosevelt a hundred and fourteen years later. So, in part, it seems today. But certain other considerations, one of them being the United States Navy, force us to perceive the importance of details that escaped the earlier observers.

For one thing, Carlyle wrote "hunger and dispiritment track thy sinking footsteps." Not hunger—at least not physical hunger. Paul Jones lived in modest but decent quarters in Paris and had enough to eat. Harries, in London, had settled his accounts honestly; and, to grant her the scant justice that is her due, "sinful Imperial Catherine" seems to have paid up through her ambassador in Paris. The United States had not paid him a cent since 1781, not even the money he had put up to equip various United States ships, and did not pay until 1848, when Jones had been dead fifty-six years. But Catherine, although she sought to rob him of his good name, at least did not snatch his purse.

For another thing, we know now that the man's disabilities were not all psychological. The physical body was breaking down, too. The kidneys were suffering progressive deterioration, which eventually became manifest in swelling of the legs that gradually crept up, accompanied by increasing lassitude.

On July 11, 1792, he made his last public appearance, at a session of the National Assembly, and that night he attended a dinner at the Café Timon.

Exactly a week later two visitors dropped in to see him, one an American, Colonel Samuel Blackden of North Carolina—he was somehow associated with that state to the very end—the other a French army officer, Major Beaupoil, who had served at Yorktown. They were so alarmed by his haggard appearance that they insisted on his making his will, which, to be legal, must be attested by an American official. On the spot they dispatched a messenger for Gouverneur Morris.

Mr. Morris was annoyed. Mr. Morris was a great gentleman, in his own estimation, who ought not to be dragged away from the company of the charming ladies whom he was entertaining at lunch to attend to the affairs of a woebegone derelict who, having no money, was hardly to be considered a full-fledged member of the human race. Such was the Honorable Mr. Morris, the most incredible ass that ever brayed his way to a dubious immortality in American history.

However, he came, bringing notaries, took down the will at Jones's dictation, and had it duly attested by the notaries. In fact, when he found that the property devised might run, if the debts were collectible, to the respectable total of something like fifty thousand dollars, Mr. Morris even condescended to be helpful. Jones had named Robert Morris of Philadelphia as one executor, and the minister advised a change because Robert Morris was known to be in pretty bad financial shape. Jones asked the minister himself to act, but that was out of the question. Mr. Morris was rather shocked by the impudence of the suggestion. So Jones stuck to Robert Morris.

When it was done the notaries left and Morris returned to his charming friends, no doubt admiring his own stern devotion to public duty that led him constantly into contact with such nobodies as this sailor.

In the deepening dusk Jones remained alone, sitting in an armchair. At some time in the evening he seems to have picked up a book, said to be a volume of Voltaire, and apparently tried to read. Then he laid it aside, perhaps feeling some premonitory twinges, and attempted to go to bed. He could not make it. He reached the bed, but fell across it, face down, with his feet touching the floor. He was found there, dead, the next morning, July 19, 1792.

Someone approached Morris, suggesting a public funeral, but Morris curtly refused. Jones, he said, was too poor for him to authorize any but the simplest of ceremonies. Difficulties then arose because Jones was a Protestant and legal burial for a Protestant in Paris at that time meant unwinding endless red tape. But the King's commissary in charge of such matters, Pierre-François Simonneau, was not a gentleman of the stripe of Mr. Morris. When he was approached for the necessary permission the idea of hustling John Paul Jones underground at the least possible expense and in a furtive sort of way shocked him. This man, he said, was a great hero of two nations, a Chev-

alier of the Order of Ste. Anne, honored by Congress and the
King. To bury him like a nameless pauper would be a public
scandal. He immediately ordered that the body should be decently prepared for burial and interred in the Protestant cemetery in a dignified way, the bill to be sent to him.

Then Blackden went to the National Assembly with formal
notice of the death, and the Assembly, swept by a sentimental
nostalgia for the great old days, decreed that, Protestant or not,
this man should be given a state funeral attended by twelve
members of the Assembly, as an expression of the gratitude of
France.

It was done accordingly. A group of Americans also attended,
including Joel Barlow, the poet, Blackden and another man
from North Carolina, and one from Maryland, the state in which
the body eventually was to rest.

Naturally, the American minister was formally invited, but,
naturally, he could not accept "as he had persons to dine with
him that day." In his diary he has left an explicit account of how
he spent the evening of July 20, 1792 (the funeral was held at
eight o'clock). "I have a large company to dinner. After dinner
go to visit Madame de Narbonne, who is my neighbor, thence
to the British Ambassador's; Madame is abroad. Thence to visit
Madame de Guibert, sit with her a little while and go afterwards to Madame Le Coutleux's. Chat with her and to my
surprise she declares for gallantry without the least scruple so
that I conjecture rather the reverse. Return home early. The
weather is pleasant this evening, but we had a storm in which
the lightning struck very near me about seven o'clock."

After reading this one no longer wonders that this donkey
left Tom Paine to rot in jail without lifting a finger to save him
from the guillotine—nay, worse, giving Paine the impression
that Morris was acting under Washington's orders!

V.

Well, John Paul Jones was dead and done for and the nation
that he had served cheerfully forgot him. After fifty-six years—

in 1848—it did get around to paying his heirs $5,040, being his pay from June 1781 to May 1788, and $2,598.42, which he had advanced out of his own pocket to help equip its ships. It did more—it added $21,202.44 as Jones's share of the prize money due from Denmark, although Denmark had never paid the claim—nor has yet.

With that the United States considered that it had done pretty well by John Paul Jones, and even its historians reduced him from the rank of captain in the United States Navy to the questionable status of a corsair.

It is an embarrassing record, yet, in a manner of speaking, the account was not as much out of balance as it seems because the basic truth is that Jones, dead and buried in a long-forgotten grave, had not yet accomplished his greatest work for the United States of America.

That work was the slow infiltration into the United States Navy of a true appreciation of what the man stood for. Decade after decade passed with the Navy still a pretty nondescript service, shot through with politics, inefficient, and only sporadically respected by either Congress or the public. Through all those decades Paul Jones was remembered, when he was remembered at all, only as a bold and hard-hitting fighter.

But little by little the service began to acquire a new significance. One incident after another, not always connected with war, went to strengthen the impression that a naval officer was, or might be, not merely a combat leader, but a technician of a special, highly developed type, useful for many things besides gunnery. Matthew Fontaine Maury, for example, gained a great reputation without either fighting a battle or organizing a lobby in Washington, but simply as a naval officer pursuing the scientific development of his profession. Matthew Calbraith Perry opened up Japan relying much more upon skillful diplomacy than upon his main battery. The Civil War doubled, redoubled, and multiplied again the importance of an officer's ability as a mathematician.

Gradually it dawned upon men who really thought about

naval problems that whenever they urged the adoption of some new idea as imperative, it nearly always proved to be basically in accord with something that John Paul Jones had advised generations earlier. The recommendations that he had written out for Robert Morris, and which the Naval Academy still calls to the attention of every entering midshipman, were, are, and always will be the structural plan of an officer who is as certainly a professional man as any doctor of law or medicine or theology, as any physicist or chemist, as any sociologist or economist. The naval officer's Hippocratic oath is that declaration of John Paul Jones, and although he does not formally swear to it, it is just as binding. If he seeks four stripes not to be a captain, but only that the rank may help him as a candidate for Congress, he is a caitiff to be bracketed with the doctor who keeps a patient ill to get more money out of him, or with the ambulance-chasing lawyer. Quackery and shysterism are possible in this as in any other profession; the naval quack and shyster is the man who seeks to use the service; the officer is the man who strives to be useful to it.

But his contribution was not confined to the realm of ideas alone, else Jones might rank as a sage but not as a hero. He also made an emotional contribution of enormous value in establishing the legend of the Indomitable Man. That has persisted from the beginning even through those periods when the service was at its lowest ebb. The man on the sinking ship who had just begun to fight needs no explanation, no argument, no philosophical analysis. He is his own explanation, his own argument. The greenest landsman just enlisted can see him plainly, but Mahan himself cannot explain him. Admiral and raw recruit alike can only wonder and admire.

Nor will any prudent biographer undertake to do more. John Paul Jones was the captain in the United States Navy who said, "I have just begun to fight" when all the world was certain that he was already whipped. When all is said and done, that is the story, and all the rest is mere elaboration of the great central fact.

He gave us a soundly reasoned foundation on which to build a great officer corps, and through the years that corps has been built on that basis. This is one of the main reasons why the Navy has grown mighty in the years since his death.

But he also gave us a lift of the spirit that night off Flamborough Head, he gave us a demonstration that we could be great; and it is this emotional gift that has enshrined him in our hearts.

VI.

Without doubt it was not the naval philosopher, it was the defiant man on the sinking, burning ship that Horace Porter had in mind when he found himself ambassador of the United States to France at the turn of the century and learned that a slum-clearance project in Paris was about to uncover the long overbuilt Protestant cemetery where the body of John Paul Jones was supposed to be buried.

For Horace Porter was a fighting man himself. A West Pointer, he had won the Congressional Medal of Honor when thousands all around him broke and fled on the dreadful field of Chickamauga; and he knew the value to a fighting man of the knowledge that he has a proud tradition behind him. Therefore he set himself to long, arduous, and expensive toil to recover the body, not of the first professional naval officer, but of the captain of the *Bon Homme Richard*.

The search is a long and fascinating story in itself—a story of tireless energy, inexhaustible patience, extraordinary resourcefulness on the part of a public servant intent on doing something far beyond the line of duty. Incidentally, it is another story of scurvy treatment of a public servant by the Congress of the United States, for Porter was never compensated for his outlay in the search, although it involved him in lawsuits that seriously impaired his fortune.

But it was successful. The site of the grave was located within a few feet. There is no argument as to that. Within those few feet five bodies were found, only one of which could possibly be that of John Paul Jones; but that one conformed to what was known in so many particulars that the best pathologists and anatomists in France were satisfied.

Then the President of the United States, Theodore Roosevelt, who was urging a big-navy program, saw the dramatic possibilities of the find. He ordered an American naval squadron, under command of Rear Admiral Charles D. Sigsbee, hero of the *Maine,* to proceed to France to bring the body to America. The French government responded finely; it sent a squadron as an escort of honor to accompany Sigsbee's ships across the Atlantic. The combined fleet brought the body to Annapolis, where it was deposited temporarily in a brick vault on the United States Naval Academy grounds.

There, on April 24, 1906, a great public ceremony was held. The President of the United States, the French ambassador, the American ambassador to France—Porter—and the governor of Maryland made speeches, while four rear admirals, three American, one French, stood by. It was one of the most terrific outbursts of oratory Annapolis had ever heard, everyone was tremendously impressed, and the big-navy program was notably assisted. So, John Paul Jones having served his turn, the body was placed on a couple of sawhorses behind the stairs in Bancroft Hall. There it remained for seven years.

But the American people had been reminded of the man, and this treatment of him grated on them. The thing became such a crying scandal that at length even the Congress of the United States was prodded into action. In 1910 it appropriated funds to complete the Naval Academy chapel, including the crypt for the remains; in 1913 they were finally deposited there.

It must be admitted that when Congress did act, it acted handsomely. The body rests in a sarcophagus resembling that of Napoleon in the Invalides, except that it is of black and white instead of red porphyry. The sarcophagus is supported by four bronze dolphins and in the marble floor around it are incised the names of the ships that he commanded—*Providence, Alfred,*

Ranger, Bon Homme Richard, Serapis, Ariel. Before it in letters of bronze appear the words "He gave our navy its earliest traditions of heroism and victory."

He gave it form and dignity as well, but that story is still unfolding. It is the world's greatest naval service today, but it is in the hearts of its people to believe that its true greatness has only begun, seeing that there is ground for hope that it has completed its task of conquest and has now entered upon its greater task of keeping the sea lanes peaceful and safe for honest men of all nations.

The tradition he established has had much to do with this; therefore it is true to say that when he fell across the bed that night his great service to the United States of America had only begun. Not defeated only, but killed, dead, and buried for a century and a half, he still miraculously cries out to armored wrong, "I have just begun to fight!"